PHILOSTRATUS

THE LIFE OF APOLLONIUS OF TYANA

THE EPISTLES OF APOLLONIUS AND THE TREATISE OF EUSEBIUS

WITH AN ENGLISH TRANSLATION

BY F.C. CONYBEARE, M.A.

LATE FELLOW AND PRELECTOR OF UNIVERSITY COLLEGE, OXFORD

IN TWO VOLUMES

I

I

APOLLONIUS OF TYANA. (?)
BUST IN THE CAPITOLINE MUSEUM, ROME.

INTRODUCTION

THE Life of Apollonius of Tyana has only been once translated in its entirety into English, as long ago as the year 1811, by an Irish clergyman of the name of E. Berwick. It is to be hoped therefore that the present translation will be acceptable to the English reading public; for there is in it much that is very good reading, and it is lightly written. Of its author, Philostratus, we do not know much apart from his own works, from which we may gather that he was born in the island of Lemnos about the year 172 of our era, that he went to Athens as a young man to study rhetoric, and later on to Rome. Here he acquired a reputation as a sophist, and was drawn into what we may call the salon of the literary and philosophic Empress Julia Domna, the wife of Septimius Severus. She put into his hands certain memoirs of Apollonius, the sage of Tyana, who had died in extreme old age nearly 100 years before during the reign of the Emperor Nerva, and she begged him to use them for the composition of a literary life of the sage in question. These memoirs had been composed by a disciple and companion of Apollonius named Damis, a native of the city of Nineveh, whose style, Philostratus says, like that of most Syrian Greeks, was heavy and wanting in polish. Besides these memoirs Philostratus used for his work a history of the career of Apollonius at Aegae, written by an admirer of the name of Maximus. He also used the many letters of Apollonius which were in circulation. His collection of these agreed partly, but not wholly, with those which are preserved to us and translated below. He tells us further that the Emperor Hadrian had a collection of these letters in his villa at Antium. Philostratus also possessed various treatises of Apollonius which have not come down to us. Beside making use of the written sources here enumerated Philostratus had travelled about, not only to Tyana, where there was a temple specially dedicated to the cult of Apollonius, but to other cities where the sage's memory was held in honour, in order to collect such traditions of the sage as he found still current. From these sources then the work before us was drawn, for although Philostratus also knew the four books of a certain Moeragenes upon Apollonius, he tells us he paid no attention to them, because they displayed an ignorance of many things which concerned the sage. The learned Empress seems never to have lived to read the work of Philostratus, for it is not dedicated to her and cannot have been published before the year 217.

It has been argued that the work of Damis never really existed, and that he was a mere man of straw invented by Philostratus. This view was adopted as recently as the year 1910 by Professor Bigg, in his history of the origins of Christianity. But it seems unnecessarily sceptical. It is quite true that Philostratus puts into the mouth of the sage, on the authority of Damis, conversations and ideas which, as they recur in the Lives of the Sophists of Philostratus, can hardly have been reported by Damis. But because he resorted to this literary trick, it by no means follows that all the episodes which he reports on the authority of Damis are fictitious, for many of them possess great verisimilitude and can hardly have been invented as late as the year 217, when the life was completed and given to the literary world. It is rather to be supposed that Damis himself was not altogether a credible writer, but one who, like the so-called *aretalogi* of that age, set himself to embellish the life of his master, to exaggerate his wisdom and his supernatural powers; if so, more than one of the striking stories told by Philostratus may have already stood in the pages of Damis.

However this be, the evident aim of Philostratus is to rehabilitate the reputation of Apollonius, and defend him from the charge of having been a charlatan or wizard addicted to evil magical practices. This accusation had been levelled against the sage during his life-time by a rival sophist Euphrates, and not long after his death by the author already mentioned, Moeragenes. Unfortunately the orations of Euphrates have perished, and we know little of the work of Moeragenes. Origen, the Christian father, in his work against Celsus, written about the year 240, informs us that he had read it, and that it attacked Apollonius as a magician addicted to sinister practices. It is certain also that the accusations of Euphrates were of similar tendency, and we only need to read a very few pages of this work of Philostratus to see that his chief interest is to prove to the world that these accusations were ill-founded, and that Apollonius was a divinely-inspired sage and prophet, and a reformer along Pythagorean lines of the Pagan religion. It is possible that some of the stories told by Byzantine writers of Apollonius, notably by John Tzetzes, derive from Moeragenes.

The story of the life of Apollonius as narrated by Philostratus is briefly as follows. He was born towards the beginning of the Christian era at Tyana, in Cappadocia, and his birth was attended according to popular tradition with miracles and portents. At the age of sixteen he set himself to observe in the most rigid fashion the almost monastic rule ascribed to Pythagoras, renouncing wine, rejecting the married estate, refusing to eat any sort of flesh, and in particular condemning the sacrifice of animals to the gods, which in the ancient world furnished the occasion, at any rate for the poor people, of eating meat. For we must not forget that in antiquity hardly any meat was eaten which had not previously been consecrated by sacrifice to a god, and that consequently the priest was the butcher of a village and the butcher the priest. Like other votaries of the Neo-Pythagorean philosophy or discipline, Apollonius went without shoes or only wore shoes of bark, he allowed his hair to grow long, and never let a razor touch his chin, and he took care to wear on his person nothing but linen, for it was accounted by him, as by Brahmans, an impurity to allow any dress made of the skin of dead animals to touch the person. Before long he set himself up as a reformer, and betaking himself to the town of Aegae, he took up his abode in the temple of Aesculapius, where he rapidly acquired such a reputation for sanctity that sick people flocked to him asking him to heal them. On attaining his majority, at the death of his father and mother, he gave up the greater part of his patrimony to his elder brother, and what was left to his poor relations. He then set himself to spend five years in complete silence, traversing, it would seem, Asia Minor, in all directions, but never opening his lips. The more than Trappist vow of silence which he thus enforced upon himself seems to have further enhanced his reputation for holiness, and his mere appearance on the scene was enough to hush the noise of warring factions in the cities of Cilicia and Pamphylia. If we may believe his biographer he professed to know all languages without ever having learned them, to know the inmost thoughts of men, to understand the language of birds and animals, and to have the power of predicting the future. He also remembered his former incarnation, for he shared the Pythagorean belief of the migrations of human souls from body to body, both of animals and of human beings. He preached a rigid asceticism, and condemned all dancing and other diversions of the kind; he would carry no money on his person and recommended others to spend their money in the relief of the poorer classes. He visited Persia and India, where he consorted with the Brahmans; he subsequently visited Egypt, and went up the Nile in order to acquaint himself with those precursors of the monks of the Thebaid called in those days the Gymnosophists or naked philosophers. He visited the cataracts of the Nile, and returning to Alexandria held long conversations with Vespasian and Titus soon after the siege and capture of Jerusalem by the latter. He had a few years before, in the course of a visit to Rome, incurred the wrath of Nero, whose minister Tigellinus however was so intimidated by him as to set him at liberty. After the death of Titus he was again arrested, this time by the Emperor Domitian, as a fomenter of sedition, but was apparently acquitted. He died at an advanced age in the reign of Nerva, who befriended him; and according to popular tradition he ascended bodily to heaven, appearing after death to certain persons who entertained doubts about a future life.

Towards the end of the third century when the struggle between Christianity and decadent Paganism had reached its last and bitterest stage, it occurred to some of the enemies of the new religion to set up Apollonius, to whom temples and shrines had been erected in various parts of Asia Minor, as a rival to the founder of Christianity. The many miracles which were recorded of Apollonius, and in particular his eminent power over evil spirits or demons, made him a formidable rival in the minds of Pagans to Jesus Christ. And a certain Hierocles, who was a provincial governor under the Emperor Diocletian, wrote a book to show that Apollonius had been as great a sage, as remarkable a worker of miracles, and as potent an exorcist as Jesus Christ. His work gave great offence to the missionaries of the Christian religion, and Eusebius the Christian historian wrote a treatise in answer, in which he alleges that Apollonius was a mere charlatan, and if a magician at all, then one of very inferior powers; he also argues that if he did achieve any remarkable results, it was thanks to the evil spirits with whom he was in league. Eusebius is careful, however, to point out that before Hierocles, no anti-Christian writer had thought of putting forward Apollonius as the rival and equal of Jesus of Nazareth. It is possible of course that Hierocles took his cue from the Emperor Alexander Severus (A.D. 205-235), who instead of setting up images of the gods in his private shrine, established therein, as objects of his veneration, statues of Alexander the Great, Orpheus, Apollonius of Tyana, Abraham, and Christ. This story however in no way contradicts the statement of Eusebius, and it is a pity that this significant caution of the latter has been disregarded by Christian writers of the last three centuries, who have almost unanimously adopted a view that is utterly unwarrantable, namely, that Philostratus intended his life of Apollonius as a counterblast to that of the Christian gospel. The best scholars of the present generation are opposed to this view, for they realise that demoniac possession was a common feature in the ancient landscape, and that the exorcist driving demons out of afflicted human beings by use of threats and invocations of mysterious names was as familiar a figure in old Pagan society as he was in the early church.

We read that wherever Apollonius travelled, he visited the temples, and undertook to reform the cults which he there found in vogue. His reform seems to have consisted in this, that he denounced as derogatory to the gods the practice of sacrificing to them animal victims and tried to persuade the priests to abandon it. In this respect he prepared the ground for Christianity and was working along the same lines as many of the Christian missionaries. In the third century Porphyry the philosopher and enemy of Christianity was as zealous in his condemnation of blood-offerings, as Apollonius had been in the first. Unquestionably the neo-Pythagorean propaganda did much to discredit ancient paganism, and Apollonius and its other missionaries were all unwittingly working for that ideal of bloodless sacrifice which, after the destruction of the Jewish Temple, by an inexorable logic imposed itself on the Christian Church.

It is well to conclude this all too brief notice of Apollonius with a passage cited by Eusebius[1] from his lost work concerning sacrifice. There is no good reason for doubting its authenticity, and it is an apt summary of his religious belief:—

"In no other manner, I believe, can one exhibit a fitting respect for the divine being, beyond any other men make sure of being singled out as an object of his favour and good-will, than by refusing to offer to God whom we termed First, who is One and separate from all, as subordinate to whom we must recognise all the rest, any victim at all; to Him we must not kindle fire or make promise unto him of any sensible object whatsoever. For He needs nothing even from beings higher than ourselves. Nor is there any plant or animal which earth sends up or nourishes, to which some pollution is not incident. We should make use in relation to him solely of the higher speech, I mean of that which issues not by the lips; and from the noblest of beings we must ask for blessings by the noblest faculty we possess, and that faculty is intelligence, which needs no organ. On these principles then we ought not on any account to sacrifice victims to the mighty and supreme God."

The text followed by the translator is that of C. L. Kayser, issued by B. G. Teubner, at Leipzic in 1870.

---

[1] Eusebius, *On the Preparation for the Gospel*, Bk. iv. Ch. 13.

PHILOSTRATUS

BOOK I

CHAPTER I

THE votaries of Pythagoras of Samos have this story to tell of him, that he was not an Ionian at all, but that, once on a time in Troy, he had been Euphorbus, and that he had come to life after death, but had died as the songs of Homer relate. And they say that he declined to wear apparel made from dead animal products and, to guard his purity, abstained from all flesh diet, and from the offering of animals in sacrifice. For that he would not stain the altars with blood; nay, rather the honey-cake and frankincense and the hymn of praise, these they say were the offerings made to the Gods by this man, who realized that they welcome such tribute more than they do the hecatombs and the knife laid upon the sacrificial basket. For they say that he had of a certainty social intercourse with the gods, and learnt from them the conditions under which they take pleasure in men or are disgusted, and on this intercourse he based his account of nature. For he said that, whereas other men only make conjectures about divinity and make guesses that contradict one another concerning it,—in his own case he said that Apollo had come to him acknowledging that he was the god in person; and that Athena and the Muses and other gods, whose forms and names men did not yet know, had also consorted with him though without making such acknowledgment. And the followers of Pythagoras accepted as law any decisions communicated by him, and honored him as an emissary from Zeus, but imposed, out of respect for their divine character, a ritual silence on themselves. For many were the divine and ineffable secrets which they had heard, but which it was difficult for any to keep who had not previously learnt that silence also is a mode of speech.

Moreover they declare that Empedocles of Acragas had trodden this way of wisdom when he wrote the line

"Rejoice ye, for I am unto you an immortal God, and no more mortal."

And this also:

"For erewhile, I already became both girl and boy."

And the story that he made at Olympia a bull of pastry and sacrificed it to the god also shows that he approved of the sentiments of

Pythagoras. And there is much else that they tell of those sages who observe the rule of Pythagoras; but I must not now enter upon such points, but hurry on to the work which I have set myself to complete.

CHAPTER II

FOR quite akin to theirs was the ideal which Apollonius pursued, and more divinely than Pythagoras he wooed wisdom and soared above tyrants; and he lived in times not long gone by nor quite of our own day, yet men know him not because of the true wisdom, which he practiced as sage and sanely; but one man singles out one feature for praise in him and another another; while some, because he had interviews with the wizards of Babylon and with the Brahmans of India, and with the nude ascetics of Egypt, put him down as a wizard, and spread the calumny that he was a sage of an illegitimate kind, judging of him ill. For Empedocles and Pythagoras himself and Democritus consorted with wizards and uttered many supernatural truths, yet never stooped to the black art; and Plato went to Egypt and mingled with his own discourses much of what he heard from the prophets and priests there; and though, like a painter, he laid his own colors on to their rough sketches, yet he never passed for a wizard, although envied above all mankind for his wisdom. For the circumstance that Apollonius foresaw and foreknew so many things does not in the least justify us in imputing to him this kind of wisdom; we might as well accuse Socrates of the same, because, thanks to his familiar spirit, he knew things beforehand, and we might also accuse Anaxagoras because of the many things which he foretold. And indeed who does not know the story of how Anaxagoras at Olympia in a season when least rain falls came forward wearing a fleece into the stadium, by way of predicting rain, and of how he foretold the fall of the house,—and truly, for it did fall; and of how he said that day would be turned into night, and stones would be discharged from heaven round Aegospotami, and of how his predictions were fulfilled? Now these feats are set down to the wisdom of Anaxagoras by the same people who would rob Apollonius of the credit of having predicted things by dint of wisdom, and say that he achieved these results by art of wizardry.

It seems to me then that I ought not to condone or acquiesce in the general ignorance, but write a true account of the man, detailing the exact times at which he said or did this or that, as also the habits and temper of wisdom by means of which he succeeded in being considered a supernatural and divine being.

And I have gathered my information partly from the many cities where he was loved, and partly from the temples whose long-neglected and decayed rites he restored, and partly from the accounts left of him by others and partly from his own letters. For he addressed these to kings, sophists, philosophers, to men of Elis, of Delphi, to Indians, and Ethiopians; and in his letters he dealt with the subjects of the gods, of customs, of moral principles, of laws, and in all these departments he corrected the errors into which men had fallen. But the more precise details which I have collected are as follows.

CHAPTER III

THERE was a man, Damis, by no means stupid, who formerly dwelt in the ancient city of Nineveh. He resorted to Apollonius in order to study wisdom, and having shared, by his own account, his wanderings abroad, wrote an account of them. And he records his opinions and discourses and all his prophecies. And a certain kinsmen of Damis drew the attention of the empress Julia to the documents containing these documents hitherto unknown. Now I belonged to the circle of the empress, for she was a devoted admirer of all rhetorical exercises; and she commanded me to recast and edit these essays, at the same time paying more attention to the style and diction of them; for the man of Nineveh had told his story clearly enough, yet somewhat awkwardly. And I also read the book of Maximus of Aegae, which comprised all the life of Apollonius in Aegae; and furthermore a will was composed by Apollonius, from which one can learn how rapturous and inspired a sage he really was. For we must not pay attention anyhow to Moeragenes, who composed four books about Apollonius, and yet was ignorant of many circumstances of his life. That then I combined these scattered sources together and took trouble over my composition, I have said; but let my work, I pray, redound to the honor of the man who is the subject of my compilation, and also be of use to those who love learning. For assuredly, they will here learn things of which as yet they were ignorant.

CHAPTER IV

APOLLONIUS' home, then, was Tyana, a Greek city amidst a population of Cappadocians. His father was of the same name, and the family descended from the first settlers. It excelled in wealth the surrounding families, though the district is a rich one. To his mother, just before he was born, there came an apparition of Proteus, who changes his form so much in Homer, in the guise of an Egyptian demon. She was in no way frightened, but asked him what sort of child she would bear. And he answered: "Myself." "And who are you?" she asked. "Proteus," answered he, "the god of Egypt." Well, I need hardly explain to readers of the poets the quality of Proteus and his reputation as regards wisdom; how versatile he was, and for ever changing his form, and defying capture, and how he had a reputation of knowing both past and future. And we must bear Proteus in mind all the more, when my advancing story shows its hero to have been more of a prophet than Proteus, and to have triumphed over many difficulties and dangers in the moment when they beset him most closely.

CHAPTER V

NOW he is said to have been born in a meadow, hard by which there has been now erected a sumptuous temple to him; and let us not pass by the manner of his birth. For just as the hour of his birth was approaching, his mother was warned in a dream to walk out into the meadow and pluck the flowers; and in due course she came there and her maids attended to the flowers, scattering themselves over the meadow, while she fell asleep lying on the grass. Thereupon the swans who fed in the meadow set up a dance around her as she slept, and lifting their wings, as they are wont to do, cried out aloud all at once, for there was somewhat of a breeze blowing in the meadow. She then leaped up at the sound of their song and bore her child, for any sudden fright is apt to bring on a premature delivery. But the people of the country say that just at the moment of the birth, a thunderbolt seemed about to fall to earth and then rose up into the air and disappeared aloft; and the gods thereby indicated, I think, the great distinction to which the sage was to attain, and hinted in advance how he should transcend all things upon earth and approach the gods, and signified all the things that he would achieve.

CHAPTER VI

NOW there is near Tyana a well sacred to Zeus, the god of paths, so they say, and they call it the well of Asbama. Here a spring rises cold, but bubbles up like a boiling cauldron. This water is favorable and sweet to those who keep their paths, but to perjurers it brings hot-footed justice; for it attacks their eyes and hands and feet, and they fall the prey of dropsy and wasting disease; and they are not even able to go away, but are held on the spot and bemoan themselves at the edge of the spring, acknowledging their perjuries. The people of the country, then, say that Apollonius was the son of this Zeus, but the sage called himself the son of Apollonius.

CHAPTER VII

ON reaching the age when children are taught their letters, he showed great strength of memory and power of application; and his tongue affected the Attic dialect, nor was his accent corrupted by the race he lived among. All eyes were turned upon him, for he was, moreover, conspicuous for his beauty. When he reached his fourteenth year, his father brought him to Tarsus, to Euthydemus the teacher from Phoenicia. Now Euthydemus was a good rhetor, and began his education; but, though he was attached to his teacher, he found the atmosphere of the city harsh and strange and little conducive to the philosophic life, for nowhere are men more addicted than here to luxury; jesters and full of insolence are they all; and they attend more to their fine linen than the Athenians did to wisdom; and a stream called the Cydnus runs through their city, along the banks of which they sit like so many water-fowl. Hence the words which Apollonius addresses to them in his letter: "Be done with getting drunk upon your water." He therefore transferred his teacher, with his father's consent, to the town of Aegae, which was close by, where he found a peace congenial to one who would be a philosopher, and a more serious school of study and a temple of Asclepius, where that god reveals himself in person to men. There he had as his companions in philosophy followers of Plato and Chrysippus and peripatetic philosophers. And he diligently attended also to the discourses of Epicurus, for he did not despise these either, although it was to those of Pythagoras that he applied himself with unspeakable wisdom and ardor. However, his teacher of the Pythagorean system was not a very serious person, nor one who practiced in his conduct the philosophy he taught; for he was the slave of his belly and appetites, and modeled himself upon Epicurus. And this man was Euxenus from the town of Heraclea in Pontus, and he knew the principles of Pythagoras just as birds know what they learn from men; for the birds will wish you "farewell," and say "Good day" or "Zeus help you," and such like, without understanding what they say and without any real sympathy for mankind, merely because they have been trained to move their tongue in a certain manner. Apollonius, however, was like the young eagles who, as long as they are not fully fledged, fly alongside of their parents and are trained by them in flight, but who, as soon as they are able to rise in the air, outsoar the parent birds, especially when they perceive the latter to be greedy and to be flying along the ground in order to snuff the quarry; like them Apollonius attended Euxenus as long as he was a child and was guided by him in the path of argument, but when he reached his sixteenth year he indulged his impulse towards the life of Pythagoras, being fledged and winged thereto by some higher power. Notwithstanding he did not cease to love Euxenus, nay, he persuaded his father to present him with a villa outside the town, where there were tender groves and fountains, and he said to him: "Now you live there your own life, but I will live that of Pythagoras."

CHAPTER VIII

NOW Euxenus realized that he was attached to a lofty ideal, and asked him at what point he would begin it. Apollonius answered: "At the point at which physicians begin, for they, by purging the bowels of their patients prevent some from being ill at all, and heal others." And having said this he declined to live upon a flesh diet, on the ground that it was unclean, and also that it made the mind gross; so he partook only of dried fruits and vegetables, for he said that all the fruits of the earth are clean. And of wine he said that it was a clean drink because it is yielded to men by so well-domesticated a plant as the vine; but he declared that it endangered the mental balance and system and darkened, as with mud, the ether which is in the soul. After then having thus purged his interior, he took to walking without shoes by way of adornment and clad himself in linen raiment, declining to wear any animal product; and he let his hair grow long and lived in the Temple. And the people round about the Temple were struck with admiration for him, and the god Asclepius one day said to the priest that he was delighted to have Apollonius as witness of his cures of the sick; and such was his reputation that the Cilicians themselves and the people all around flocked to Aegae to visit him. Hence the Cilician proverb: "Whither runnest thou? Is it to see the stripling?" Such was the saying that arose about him, and it gained the distinction of becoming a proverb.

CHAPTER IX

NOW it is well that I should not pass over what happened in the Temple, while relating the life of a man who was held in esteem even by the gods. For an Assyrian stripling came to Asclepius, and though he was sick, yet he lived the life of luxury, and being continually drunk, I will not say he lived, rather he was ever dying. He suffered then from dropsy, and finding his pleasure in drunkenness took no care to dry up his malady. On this account then Asclepius took no care of him, and did not visit him even in a dream. The youth grumbled at this, and thereupon the god, standing over him, said, "If you were to consult Apollonius you would be easier." He therefore went to Apollonius, and said: "What is there in your wisdom that I can profit by? for Asclepius bids me consult you." And he replied: "I can advise you of what, under the circumstances, will be most valuable to you; for I suppose you want to get well." "Yes, by Zeus," answered the other, "I want the health which Asclepius promises, but never gives." "Hush," said the other, "for he gives to those who desire it, but you do things that irritate and aggravate your disease, for you give yourself up to luxury, and you accumulate delicate viands upon your water-logged and worn-out stomach, and as it were, choke water with a flood of mud." This was a clearer response, in my opinion, than Heraclitus, in his wisdom, gave. For he said when he was visited by this affection that what he needed was someone to substitute a drought for a rainy weather, a very unintelligible remark, it appears to me, and by no means clear; but the sage restored the youth to health by a clear interpretation of the wise saw.

CHAPTER X

ONE day he saw a flood of blood upon the altar, and there were victims laid out upon it, Egyptian bulls that had been sacrificed and great hogs, and some of them were being flayed and others were being cut up; and two gold vases had been dedicated set with jewels, the rarest and most beautiful that India can provide. So he went to the priest and said: "What is all this; for someone is making a very handsome gift to the god?" And the priest replied: "You may rather be surprised at a man's offering all this without having first put up a prayer in our fane, and without having stayed with us as long as other people do, and without having gained his health from the god, and without obtaining all the things he came to ask for. For he appears to have come only yesterday, yet he is sacrificing on this lavish scale. And he declares that he will sacrifice more victims, and dedicate more gifts, if Asclepius will hearken to him. And he is one of the richest men in existence; at any rate he owns in Cilicia an estate bigger than all the Cilicians together possess. And he is supplicating the god to restore to him one of his eyes that has fallen out." But Apollonius fixed his eyes upon the ground, as he was accustomed to do in later life, and asked: "What is his name?" And when he heard it, he said: "It seems to me, O Priest, that we ought not to welcome this fellow in the Temple: for he is some ruffian who has come here, and that he is afflicted in this way is due to some sinister reason: nay, his very conduct in sacrificing on such a magnificent scale before he has gained anything from the god is not that of a genuine votary, but rather of a man who is begging himself off for the penalty of some horrible and cruel deed." This was what Apollonius said: and Asclepius appeared to the priest by night, and said: "Send away so and so at once with all his possessions, and let him keep them, for he deserves to lose the other eye as well." The priest accordingly made inquiries about the Cilician and learned that his wife by a former marriage borne a daughter, and he had fallen in love with the maiden and had seduced her, and was living with her in open sin. For the mother had surprised the two in bed, and had put out both her eyes and one of his by stabbing them with her brooch-pin.

CHAPTER XI

AGAIN he inculcated the wise rule that in our sacrifices or dedications we should no go beyond the just mean, in the following way. On one occasion several people had flocked to the Temple, not long after the expulsion of the Cilician, and he took the occasion to ask the priest the following questions: "Are then," he said, "the gods just?" "Why, of course, most just," answered the priest. "Well, and are they wise?" "And what," said the other, "can be wiser than the godhead?" "But do they know the affairs of men, or are they without experience of them?" "Why," said the other, "this is just the point in which the gods excel mankind, for the latter, because of their frailty, do not understand their own concerns, whereas the gods have the privilege of understanding the affairs both of men and of themselves." "All your answers," said Apollonius, "are excellent, O Priest, and very true. Since then, they know everything, it appears to me that a person who comes to the house of God and has a good conscience, should put up the following prayer: 'O ye gods, grant unto me that which I deserve.' For," he went on, "the holy, O Priest, surely deserve to receive blessings, and the wicked the contrary. Therefore the gods, as they are beneficent, if they find anyone who is healthy and whole and unscarred by vice, will send him on his way, surely, after crowning him, not with golden crowns, but with all sorts of blessings; but if they find a man branded with sin and utterly corrupt, they will hand him over and leave him to justice, after inflicting their wrath upon him all the more, because he dared to invade their Temple without being pure." And at the same moment he looked towards Asclepius, and said: "O Asclepius, the philosophy you teach is secret and congenial to yourself, in that you suffer not the wicked to come hither, not even if they pour into your lap all the wealth of India and Sardes. For it is not out of reverence for the divinity that they sacrifice these victims and suspend these offerings, but in order to purchase a verdict, which you will not concede to them in your perfect justice." And much similar wisdom he delivered himself of in this Temple, while he was still a youth.

CHAPTER XII

THIS tale also belongs to the period of his residence in Aegae. Cilicia was governed at the time by a ruffian addicted to infamous forms of passion. No sooner did he hear the beauty of Apollonius spoken of, than he cast aside the matters he was busy upon (and he was just then holding a court in Tarsus), and hurrying off to Aegae pretended he was sick and must have the help of Asclepius. There he came upon Apollonius walking alone and prayed him to recommend him to the god. But he replied: "What recommendation can you want from anyone if you are good? For the gods love men of virtue and welcome them without any instructions." "Because, to be sure," said the other, "the god, O Apollonius, has invited you to be his guest, but so far has not invited me." "Nay," answered Apollonius, "'tis my humble merits, so far as a young man can display good qualities, which have been my passport to the favor of Asclepius, whose servant and companion I am. If you too really care for uprightness, go boldly up to the god and tender what prayer you will." "By heaven, I will," said the other, "if you will allow me to address you one first." "And what prayer," said Apollonius, "can you make to me?" "A prayer which can only be offered to the beautiful, and which is that they may grant to others participation in their beauty and not grudge their charms." This he said with a vile leer and voluptuous air and all the usual wriggles of such infamous debauchees; but Apollonius with a stern fierce glance at him, said: "You are mad, you scum." The other not only flamed up at these words, but threatened to cut off his head, whereat Apollonius laughed at him and cried out loud, "Ha," naming a certain day. And in fact it was only three days later that the ruffian was executed by the officers of justice on the high road for having intrigued with Archelaus the king of Cappadocia against the Romans. These and many similar incidents are given by Maximus of Aegae in his treatise, a writer whose reputation won him a position in the emperor's Secretariat.

CHAPTER XIII

NOW when he heard that his father was dead, he hurried to Tyana, and with his own hands buried him hard by his mother's sepulcher, for she too had died not long before; and he divided the property, which was very ample, with his brother, who was an incorrigibly bad character and given to drunk. Now the latter had reached his twenty-third year; Apollonius, on the other hand, was only twenty, and the law subjected him to guardians. He therefore spent afresh some time in Aegae, and turned the temple into a Lyceum and Academy, for it resounded with all sorts of philosophical discussions. After that he returned to Tyana, by this time grown to manhood and his own master. Someone said to him that it was his duty to correct his brother and convert him from his evil ways; whereupon he answered: "This would seem a desperate enterprise; for how can I who am the younger one correct and render wise an older man? but so far as I can do anything, I will heal him of these bad passions." Accordingly he gave to him the half of his own share of the property, on the pretense that he required more than he had, while he himself needed little; and then he pressed him and cleverly persuaded him to submit to the counsels of wisdom, and said: "Our father has departed this life, who educated us both and corrected us, so that you are all that I have left, and I imagine, I am all that you have left. If therefore I do anything wrong, please advise me and cure me of my faults; and in turn if you yourself do anything wrong, suffer me to teach you better." And so he reduced his brother to a reasonable state of mind, just as we break in skittish and unruly horses by stroking and patting them; and he reformed him from his faults, numerous as they were, for he was the slave of play and of wine, and he serenaded courtesans and was vain of his hair, which he dressed up and dyed, strutting about like an arrogant dandy. So when all was well between him and his brother, he at once turned his attention to his other relatives, and conciliated such of them as were in want by bestowing on them the rest of his property, leaving only a trifle to himself; for he said that Anaxagoras of Clazomenae kept his philosophy for cattle rather than for men when he abandoned his fields to flocks and goats, and that Crates of Thebes, when he threw his money into the sea benefited neither man nor beast. And as Pythagoras was commended for his saying that "a man should have no intercourse except with his own wife," he declared that this was intended by Pythagoras for others than himself, for that he was resolved never to wed nor have any connexion whatever with women. In laying such restraint on himself he surpassed Sophocles, who only said that in reaching old age he had escaped from a mad and cruel master; but Apollonius by dint of virtue and temperance never even in his youth was so overcome. While still a mere stripling, in full enjoyment of his bodily vigor, he mastered and gained control of the maddening passion. And yet there are those who accuse him falsely of an addiction to venery, alleging that he fell a victim of such sins and spent a whole year in their indulgence among the Scythians, the facts being that he never once visited Scythia nor was ever carried away by such passions. Not even Euphrates ever accused the sage of venery, though he traduced him otherwise and composed lying treatises against him, as we shall show when we come to speak of him below. And his quarrel with Apollonius was that the latter rallied him for doing anything for money and tried to wean him of his love of filthy lucre and of huckstering his wisdom. But these matters I must defer to the times to which they belong.

CHAPTER XIV

ON one occasion, Euxenus asked Apollonius why so noble a thinker as he and one who was master of a diction so fine and nervous did not write a book. He replied: "I have not yet kept silence". And forthwith he began to hold his tongue from a sense of duty, and kept absolute silence, though his eyes and his mind were taking note of very many things, and though most things were being stored in his memory. Indeed, when he reached the age of a hundred, he still surpassed Simonides in point of memory, and he used to chant a hymn addressed to memory, in which it is said that everything is worn and withered away by time, whereas time itself never ages, but remains immortal because of memory. Nevertheless his company was not without charm during the period of his silence; for he would maintain a conversation by the expression of his eyes, by gestures of his hands and nodding his head; nor did he strike men as gloomy or morse; for he retained his fondness for company and cheerfulness. This part of his life he says was the most uphill work he knew, since he practiced silence for five whole years; for he says he often had things to say and could not do so, and he was often obliged not to hear things the hearing of which would have enraged him, and often when he was moved and inclined to break out in a rebuke to others, he said to himself: "Bear up then, my heart and tongue;" and when reasoning offended him he had to give up for the time the refuting of it.

CHAPTER XV

THESE years of silence he spent partly in Pamphylia and partly in Cilicia; and though his paths lay through such effeminate races as these, he never spoke nor was even induced to murmur. Whenever, however, he came on a city engaged in civil conflict (and many were divided into fractions over spectacles of a low kind), he would advance and show himself, and by indicating part of his intended rebuke by manual gesture or by look on his face, he would put an end to all the disorder, and people hushed their voices, as if they were engaged in the mysteries. Well, it is not so very difficult to restrain those who have started a quarrel about dances and horses, for those who are rioting about such matters, if they turn their eyes to a real man, blush and check themselves and easily recover their senses; but a city hard pressed by famine is not so tractable, nor so easily brought to a better mood by persuasive words and its passion quelled. But in the case of Apollonius, mere silence on his part was enough for those so affected. Anyhow, when he came to Aspendus in Pamphylia (and this city is built on the river Eurymedon, lesser only than two others about there), he found vetches on sale in the market, and the citizens were feeding upon this and on anything else they could get; for the rich men had shut up all the grain and were holding it up for export from the country. Consequently an excited crowd of all ages had set upon the governor, and were lighting a fire to burn him alive, although he was clinging to the statues of the Emperor, which were more dreaded at that time and more inviolable than the Zeus in Olympia; for they were statues of Tiberius, in whose reign a master is said to have been held guilty of impiety, merely because he struck his own slave when he had on his person a silver drachma coined with the image of Tiberius. Apollonius then went up to the governor and with a sign of his hand asked him what was the matter; and he answered that he had done no wrong, but was indeed being wronged quite as much as the populace; but, he said, if he could not get a hearing, he would perish along with the populace. Apollonius then turned to the bystanders, and beckoned to them that they must listen; and they not only held their tongues from wonderment at him, but they laid the brands they had kindled on the altars which were there. The governor then plucked up courage and said: "This man and that man," and he named several, "are to blame for the famine which has arisen; for they have taken away the grain and are keeping it, one in one part of the country and another in another." The inhabitants of Aspendus thereupon passed the word to one another to make for these men's estates, but Apollonius signed with his head, that they should do no such thing, but rather summon those who were to blame and obtain the grain from them with their consent. And when, after a little time the guilty parties arrived, he very nearly broke out in speech against them, so much was he affected by the tears of the crowd; for the children and women had all flocked together, and the old men were groaning and moaning as if they were on the point of dying by hunger. However, he respected his vow of silence and wrote on a writing board his indictment of the offenders and handed it to the governor to read out aloud; and his indictment ran as follows: "Apollonius to the grain dealers of Aspendus. The earth is mother of us all, for she is just; but you, because you are unjust have pretended that she is your mother alone; and if you do not stop, I will not permit you to remain upon her." They were so terrified by these words, that they filled the marketplace with grain and the city revived.

CHAPTER XVI

AFTER the term of his silence was over he also visited the great Antioch, and passed into the Temple of Apollo of Daphne, to which the Assyrians attach the legend of Arcadia. For they say that Daphne, the daughter of Ladon, there underwent her metamorphosis, and they have a river flowing there, the Ladon, and a laurel tree is worshipped by them which they say is the one substituted for the maiden; and cypress trees of enormous height surround the Temple, and the ground sends up springs both ample and placid, in which they say Apollo purifies himself by ablution. And there it is that the earth sends up a shoot of cypress, they say in honor of Cyparissus, an Assyrian youth; and the beauty of the shrub lends credence to the story of his metamorphosis. Well, perhaps I may seem to have fallen into a somewhat juvenile vein to approach my story by such legendary particulars as these, but my interest is not really mythology. What then is the purport of my narrative? Apollonius, when he beheld a Temple so graceful and yet the home of no serious studies, but only of men half-barbarous and uncultivated, remarked: "O Apollo, change these dumb dogs into trees, so that at least as cypresses they may become vocal." And when he saw the Ladon, he said: "It is not your daughter alone that underwent a change, but you too, so far as one can see, have become a barbarian after being a Hellene and an Arcadian." And when he was minded to converse, he avoided the frequented regions and the disorderly, and said, that it was not a rabble he wanted but real men; and he resorted to the more solemn places, and lived in such Temples as were not shut up. At sunrise, indeed, he performed certain rites by himself, rites which he only communicated to those who had disciplined themselves by a four years' spell of silence; but during the rest of the day, in case the city was a Greek one, and the sacred rituals familiar to a Greek, he would call the priests together and talk wisely about the gods, and would correct them, supposing they had departed from the traditional forms. If, however, the rites were barbarous and peculiar, then he would find out who had founded them and on what occasion they were established, and having learnt the sort of cult it was, he would make suggestions, in case he could think of any improvement upon them, and then he would go in quest of his followers and bid them ask any questions they liked. For he said that it was the duty of philosophers of his school to hold converse at the earliest dawn with the gods, but as the day advanced, about the gods, and during the rest of the day to discuss human affairs in friendly intercourse. And having answered all the questions which his companions addressed to him, and when he had enough of their society, he would rise and give himself up for the rest to haranguing the general public, not however before midday, but as far as possible just when the day stood still. And when he thought he had enough of such discussion, he would be anointed and rubbed, and then fling himself into cold water, for he called hot baths the old age of men. At any rate when the people of Antioch were shut out of them because of the enormities committed there, he said: "The emperor, for your sins, has granted you a new lease of life." And when the Ephesians wanted to stone their governor because he did warm their baths enough he said to them: "You are blaming your governor because you get such a sorry bath; but I blame you because you take a bath at all."

CHAPTER XVII

THE literary style which he cultivated was not dithyrambic or tumid and swollen with poetical words, nor again was it far-fetched and full of affected Atticisms; for he thought that an excessive degree of Atticising was unpleasant. Neither did he indulge in subtleties, nor spin out his discourses; nor did anyone ever hear him dissembling to an ironical way, nor addressing to his audience methodical arguments; but when he conversed he would assume an oracular manner and use the expressions, "I know," or "It is my opinion," or, "Where are you drifting to?" or, "You must know." And his sentences where short and crisp, and his words were telling and closely fitted to the things he spoke of, and his words had a ring about them as of the dooms delivered by a sceptred king. And when a certain quibbler asked him, why he asked himself no questions, he replied: "Because I asked questions when I was a stripling; and it is not my business to ask questions now, but to teach people what I have discovered." "How then," the other asked him afresh, "O Apollonius, should the sage converse?" "Like a law-giver," he replied, "for it is the duty of the law-giver to deliver to the many the instructions of whose truth he has persuaded himself." This was the line he pursued during his stay in Antioch, and he converted to himself the most unrefined people.

CHAPTER XVIII

AFTER this he formed the scheme of an extensive voyage, and had in mind the Indian race and the sages there, who are called Brahmans and Hyrcanians; for he said that it was a young man's duty to go abroad to embark upon foreign travel. But he made quite a windfall of the Magi, who live in Babylon and Susa. For he would take the opportunity to acquaint himself thoroughly with their lore while he was on his way. And he announced his intention to his followers, who were seven in number; but when they tried to persuade him to adopt another plan, in hopes of drawing him off from his resolution, he said: "I have taken the gods into counsel and have told you their decision; and I have made trial of you to see if you are strong enough to undertake the same things as myself. Since therefore you are so soft and effeminate, I wish you very good health and that you may go on with your philosophy; but I must depart whither wisdom and the gods lead me." Having said this he quitted Antioch with two attendants, who belonged to his father's house, one of them a shorthand writer and the other a calligraphist.

CHAPTER XIX

AND he reached the ancient city of Nineveh, where he found an idol set up of barbarous aspect, and it is, they say, Io, the daughter of Inachus, and horns short and, as it were, budding project from her temples. While he was staying there and forming wiser conclusions about the image than could the priests and prophets, one Damis, a native of Nineveh, joined him as a pupil, the same, as I said at the beginning, who became the companion of his wanderings abroad and his fellow-traveller and associate in all wisdom, and who has preserved to us many particulars of the sage. He admired him, and having a taste for the road, said: "Let us depart, Apollonius, you follow God, and I you; for I think you will find that I can serve you. I can't say you how much more, but at least I've been to Babylon, and I know all the cities there are, because I have been up there not long ago, and also the villages in which there is much good to be found; and moreover, I know the languages of the various barbarous races, and there are several, for example the Armenian tongue, and that of the Medes and Persians, and that of the Kadusii, and I am familiar with all of them." "And I," said Apollonius, "my good friend, understand all languages, though I never learnt a single one." The native of Nineveh was astonished at this answer, but the other replied: "You need not wonder at my knowing all human languages; for, to tell you the truth, I also understand all the secrets of human silence." Thereupon the Assyrian worshipped him, when he heard this, and regarded him as a demon; and he stayed with him increasing in wisdom and committing to memory whatever he learnt. This Assyrian's language, however, was of a mediocre quality, for he had not the gift of expressing himself, having been educated among the barbarians; but to write down a discourse or a conversation and to give impressions of what he heard or saw and to put together a journal of such matters—that he was well able to do, and carried it out as well as the best. At any rate the volume which he calls his scrap-book, was intended to serve such a purpose by Damis, who was determined that nothing about Apollonius should be passed over in silence, nay, that his most casual and negligent utterances should also be written down. And I may mention the answer which he made to one who caviled and found fault with this journal. It was a lazy fellow and malignant who tried to pick holes in him, and remarked that he recorded well enough a lot of things, for example, the opinions and ideas of his hero, but that in collecting such trifles as these he reminded him of dogs who pick up and eat the fragments which fall from a feast. Damis replied thus: "If banquets there be of gods, and gods take food, surely they must have attendants whose business it is that not even the parcels of ambrosia that fall to the ground should be lost."

CHAPTER XX

SUCH was the companion and admirer that he had met with, and in common with him most of his travels and life were passed. And as they fared on into Mesopotamia, the tax-gatherer who presided over the Bridge (*Zeugma*) led them into the registry and asked them what they were taking out of the country with them. And Apollonius replied: "I am taking with me temperance, justice, virtue, continence, valor, discipline." And in this way he strung together a number of feminine nouns or names. The other, already scenting his own perquisites, said: "You must then write down in the register these female slaves." Apollonius answered: "Impossible, for they are not female slaves that I am taking out with me, but ladies of quality."

Now Mesopotamia is bordered on one side by the Tigris, and on the other by the Euphrates, rivers which flow from Armenia and from the lowest slopes of Taurus; but they contain a tract like a continent, in which there are some cities, though for the most part only villages, and the races that inhabit them are the Armenian and the Arab. These races are so shut in by the rivers that most of them, who lead the life of nomads, are so convinced that they are islanders, as to say that they are going down to the sea, when they are merely on their way to the rivers, and think that these rivers border the earth and encircle it. For they curve around the continental tract in question, and discharge their waters into the same sea. But there are people who say that the greater part of the Euphrates is lost in a marsh, and that this river ends in the earth. But some have a bolder theory to which they adhere, and declare that it runs under the earth to turn up in Egypt and mingle itself with the Nile. Well, for the sake of accuracy and truth, and in order to leave out nothing of the things that Damis wrote, I should have liked to relate all the incidents that occurred on their journey through these barbarous regions; but my subject hurries me on to greater and more remarkable episodes. Nevertheless, I must perforce dwell upon two topics: on the courage which Apollonius showed, in making a journey through races of barbarians and robbers, which were not at that time even subject to the Romans, and at the cleverness with which after the matter of the Arabs he managed to understand the language of the animals. For he learnt this on his way through these Arab tribes, who best understand and practice it. For it is quite common for the Arabs to listen to the birds prophesying like any oracles, but they acquire this faculty of understanding them by feeding themselves, so they say, either on the heart or liver of serpents.

CHAPTER XXI

HE left Ctesiphon behind, and passed on to the borders of Babylon; and here was a frontier garrison belonging to the king, which one could not pass by without being questioned who one was, and as to one's city, and one's reason for coming there. And there was a satrap in command of this post, a sort of "Eye of the King," I imagine; for the Mede had just acceded to the throne, and instead of being content to live in security, he worried himself about things real and imaginary and fell into fits of fear and panic. Apollonius then and his party were brought before this satrap, who had just set up the awning on his wagon and was driving out to go somewhere else. When he saw a man so dried up and parched, he began to bawl out like a cowardly woman and hid his face, and could hardly be induced to look up at him. "Whence do you come to us," he said, "and who sent you?" as if he was asking questions of a spirit. And Apollonius replied: "I have sent myself, to see whether I can make men of you, whether you like it or not." He asked a second time who he was to come trespassing like that into the king's country, and Apollonius said: "All the earth is mine, and I have a right to go all over it and through it." Whereupon the other said: "I will torture you, if you don't answer my questions." "And I hope," said the other, "that you will do it with your own hands, so that you may be tested by the touchstone of a true man." Now the eunuch was astonished to find that Apollonius needed no interpreter, but understood what he said without the least trouble or difficulty.

"By the gods," he said, "who are you?" this time altering his tone to a whine of entreaty. And Apollonius replied: "Since you have asked me civilly this time and not so rudely as before, listen, I will tell you who I am: I am Apollonius of Tyana, and my road leads me to the king of India, because I want to acquaint myself with the country there; and I shall be glad to meet your king, for those who have associated with him say that he is no bad fellow, and certainly he is not, if he is this Vardanes who has lately recovered the empire which he had lost." "He is the same," replied the other, "O divine Apollonius; for we have heard of you a long time ago, and in favor of so wise a man as you he would, I am sure, step down off his golden throne and send your party to India, each of you mounted on a camel. And I myself now invite you to be my guest, and I beg to present you with these treasures." And at the moment he pointed out a store of gold to him saying: "Take as may handfuls as you like, fill your hands, not once, but ten times." And when Apollonius refused the money he said: "Well, at any rate you will take some of the Babylonian wine, which the king bestows on us, his ten satraps. Take a jar of it, with some roast steaks of bacon and venison and some meal and bread and anything else you like. For the road after this, for many stades, leads through villages which are ill-stocked with provision." And here the eunuch caught himself up and said: "Oh! ye gods, what have I done? For I have heard that this man never eats the flesh of animals, nor drinks wine, and here I am inviting him to dine in a gross and ignorant manner." "Well," said Apollonius, "you can offer me a lighter repast and give me bread and dried fruits." "I will give you," said the other, "leavened bread and palm dates, like amber and of good size. And I will also supply you with vegetables, the best which the gardens of the Tigris afford." "Well," said Apollonius, "the wild herbs which grow free are nicer than those which are forced and artificial." "They are nicer," said the satrap, "I admit, but our land in the direction of Babylon is full of wormwood so that the herbs which grow in it are disagreeably bitter." In the end Apollonius accepted the satrap's offer, and as he was on the point of going away, he said: "My excellent fellow, don't keep your good manners to the end another time, but begin with them." This by way of rebuking him for saying that he would torture him, and for the barbaric language which he had heard to begin with.

CHAPTER XXII

AFTER they had advanced twenty stades they chanced upon a lioness that had been slain in a chase; and the brute was bigger than any they had ever seen; and the villagers rushed and cried out, and to tell the truth, so did the huntsmen, when they saw what an extraordinary thing lay before them. And it really was a marvel; for when it was cut asunder they found eight whelps within it. And the lioness becomes mother in this way. They carry their young for six months, but they bring forth young only three times; and the number of the whelps at the first birth is three and at the second two, and if the mother makes a third attempt, it bears only one whelp, but I believe a very big one and preternaturally fierce. For we must not believe those who say that the whelps of a lioness make their way out into the world by clawing through their mother's womb; for nature seems to have created the relationship of offspring to mother for their nourishment with a view to the continuance of the race. Apollonius then eyed the animal for a long time, with attention, and then he said: "O Damis, the length of our stay with the king will be a year and eight months; for neither will he let us go sooner than that, nor will it be to our advantage to quit him earlier. And you may guess the number of months from that of the whelps, and that of the years from the lioness; for you must compare wholes with wholes." And Damis replied: "But what of the sparrows of Homer, what do they mean, the ones which the dragon devoured in Aulis, which were eight in number, when he seized their mother for a ninth? Calchas surely explained these to signify nine years and predicted that the war with Troy would last so long; so take care that Homer may not be right and Calchas, too, and that our stay may not extend to nine years abroad." "Well," replied Apollonius, "Homer was surely quite right in comparing the nestlings to years, for they are already hatched out and in the world; but what I had in mind were incomplete animals that were not yet born, and perhaps never would have been born; how could I compare them to years? For things that violate nature can hardly come to be; and they anyhow quickly pass to destruction, even if they do come to existence. Follow my arguments, and let us go, first praying to the gods who reveal thus much to us."

CHAPTER XXIII

AND as he advanced into the Cissian country and was already close to Babylon, he was visited by a dream, and the god who revealed it to him fashioned its imagery as follows: there were fishes which had been cast up from the sea on to the land, and they were gasping, and uttering a lament almost human, and bewailing that they had quitted their element; and they were begging a dolphin that was swimming past the shore to help them in their misery, just like human beings who are weeping in a foreign land. Apollonius was not in the least frightened by his dream, and proceeded to conjecture its meaning and drift; but he was determined to give Damis a shock, for he found that he was the most nervous of men. So he related his vision to him, and feigned as if it foreboded evil. But Damis began to bellow as if he had seen the dream himself, and tried to dissuade Apollonius from going any further, "Lest," he said, "we also like fishes get thrown out of our element and perish, and have to weep and wail in a foreign land. Nay, we may even be reduced to straits, and have to go down on our knees to some potentate or king, who will flout us as the dolphins did the fishes." Then Apollonius laughed and said: "You've not become a philosopher yet, if you are afraid of this sort of thing. But I will explain to you the real drift of the dream. For this land of Cissia is habited by the Eretrians, who were brought up here from Euboea by Darius five hundred years ago, and they are said to have been treated at their capture like the fishes that we saw in the dream; for they were netted in, so they say, and captured one and all. It would seem then that the gods are instructing me to visit them and tend their needs, supposing I can do anything for them. And perhaps also the souls of the Greeks whose lot was cast in this part of the world are enlisting my aid for their land. Let us then go and diverge from the highroad and ask only about the well, hard by where the settlement is." Now this well is said to consist of a mixture of pitch and oil and water, and if you draw up a bucket and pour it out, these three elements divide and part themselves from one another. That he really did visit Cissia, he himself acknowledges in a letter which he wrote to the sophist of Clazomenae; for he was so kind an loyal, that when he saw the Eretrians, he remembered the sophist and wrote to him an account of what he had seen, and of what he had done for them; and all through this letter he urges the sophist to take pity on the Eretrians, and prays him, every time that he is declaiming a discourse about them, not to deprecate even the shedding of tears over their fate.

CHAPTER XXIV

AND the record which Damis left about the Eretrians is in harmony with this. For they live in the country of the Medes, not far distant from Babylon, a day's journey for a fleet traveler; but their country is without cities; for the whole of Cissia consists of villages, except for a race of nomads that also inhabits it, men who seldom dismount from their horses. And the settlement of the Eretrians is in the center of the rest, and the river is carried round it in a trench, for they say that they themselves diverted it round the village in order to form a rampart of defense against the barbarians of the country. But the soil is drenched with pitch, and is bitter to plant in; and the inhabitants are very short lived, because the pitch in the water forms a sediment in most of their bowels. And they get their sustenance off a bit of rising ground on the confines of their village, where the ground rises above the tainted country; on this they sow their crops and regard it as their land. And they say that they have heard from the natives that 780 of the Eretrians were captured, not of course all of them fighting men; for there was a certain number of women and old men among them; and there was, I imagine, a certain number of children too, for the greater portion of the population of Eretria had fled to Caphereus and to the loftiest peaks of Euboea. But anyhow the men who were brought up numbered about 400, and there were ten women perhaps; but the rest, who had started from Ionia and Lydia, perished as they were marching up. And they managed to open a quarry on the hill; and as some of them understood the art of cutting stone, they built temples in the Greek style and a market-place large enough for their purpose; and they dedicated various altars, two to Darius, and one to Xerxes, and several to Daridaeus. But up to the time of Daridaeus, 88 years after their capture, they continued to write in the manner of the Greeks, and what is more, their ancient graves are inscribed with the legend: "So and so, the son of so and so." And though the letters are Greek, they said that

they never yet had seen the like. And there were ships engraved on the tombstones, to show that the various individuals had lived in Euboea, and engaged either in seafaring trade, or in that of purple, as sailors or as dyers; and they say that they read an Elegiac inscription written over the sepulcher of some sailors and seafarers, which ran thus:
Here, we who once sailed over the deep-flowing billows of the Aegaean sea
Are lying in the midst of the plain of Ecbatana.
Farewell, once-famed fatherland of Eretria, farewell Athens,
Ye neighbor of Euboea, farewell thou darling sea.

Well, Damis says that Apollonius restored the tombs that had gone to ruin and closed them up, and that he poured out libations and made offering to their inmates, all that religion demands, except that he did not slay or sacrifice any victim; then after weeping and in an access of emotion, he delivered himself of the following apostrophe in their midst:

"Ye Eretrians, who by the lot of fortune have been brought hither, ye, even if ye are far from your own land, have at least received burial; but those who cast you hither perished unburied round the shores of your island ten years after yourself; for the gods brought about this calamity in the Hollows of Euboea."

And Apollonius at the end of his letter to the sophist writes as follows: "I also attended, O Scopelianus, to your Eretrians, while I was still a young man; and I gave what help I could both to their dead and their living." What attention then did he show to their living? This—the barbarians in the neighborhood of the hill, when the Eretrians sowed their seed upon it, would come in summertime and plunder their crops, so that they had to starve and see the fruits of their husbandry go to others. When therefore he reached the king, he took pains to secure for them the sole use of the hill.

CHAPTER XXV

I FOUND the following to be an account of the sage's stay in Babylon, and of all we need to know about Babylon. The fortifications of Babylon extend 480 stadia and form a complete circle, and its wall is three half *plethrons* high, but less than a *plethron* I in breadth. And it is cut asunder by the river Euphrates, into halves of similar shape; and there passes underneath the river an extraordinary bridge which joins together by an unseen passage the palaces on either bank. For it is said that a woman, Medea, was formerly queen of those parts, who spanned the river underneath in a manner in which no river was ever bridged before; for she got stones, it is said, and copper and pitch and all that men have discovered for use in masonry under water, and she piled these up along the banks of the river. Then she diverted the stream into lakes; and as soon as the river was dry, she dug down two fathoms, and made a hollow tunnel, which she caused to debouch into the palaces on either bank like a subterranean grotto; and she roofed it on a level with the bed of the stream. The foundations were thus made stable, and also the walls of the tunnel; but as the pitch required water in order to set as hard as stone, the Euphrates was let in again on the roof while still soft, and so the junction stood solid. And the palaces are roofed with bronze, and a glitter goes off from them; but the chambers of the women and of the men and the porticos are adorned partly with silver, and partly with golden tapestries or curtains, and partly with solid gold in the form of pictures; but the subjects embroidered on the stuffs are taken by them from Hellenic story, Andromedas being represented, and Amymonae, and you see Perseus frequently. And they delight in Orpheus, perhaps out of regard for his peaked cap and breeches, for it cannot be for his music or the songs with which he charmed and soothed others. And woven into the pattern you perceive Datis tearing up Naxos out of the sea, and Artaphernes beleaguering Eretria, and such battles of Xerxes as he said he won. For there is, of course, the occupation of Athens and Thermopylae, and other pictures still more to the Median taste, such as rivers drained from off the land and a bridge over the sea and the piercing of Athos. But they say that they also visited a man's apartment of which the roof had been carried up in the form of a dome, to resemble in a manner the heavens, and that it was roofed with lapis lazuli, a stone that is very blue and like heaven to the eye; and there were images of the gods, which they worship, fixed aloft, and looking like golden figures shining out of the ether. And it is here that the king gives judgment, and golden wrynecks are hung from the ceiling, to remind him of Adrastea, the goddess of justice, and to engage him not to exalt himself above humanity. These figures the Magi themselves say they arranged; for they have access to the palace, and they call them the tongues of the gods.

CHAPTER XXVI

WITH respect to the Magi, Apollonius has said all there is to be said, how he associated with them and learned some things from them, and taught them others before he went away. But Damis is not acquainted with the conversations which the sage held with the Magi, for the latter forbade him to accompany him in his visits to them; so he tells us merely that he visited the Magi at mid-day and about midnight, and he says that he once asked his master: "What of the Magi?" and the latter answered: "They are wise men, but not in all respects."

CHAPTER XXVII

BUT of this later on. When then he arrived at Babylon, the satrap in command the great gates, having learnt that he had come to see the country, held out a golden image of the king, which everyone must kiss before he is allowed to enter the city. Now an ambassador coming from the Roman Emperor has not this ceremony imposed upon him, but anyone who comes from the barbarians or just to look at the country, is arrested with dishonor unless he has first paid his respect to this image. Such are the silly duties committed to satraps among the barbarians. When therefore Apollonius saw the image, he said: "Who is that?" And on being told that it was the king, he said: "This king whom you worship would acquire a great boon, if I merely recommended him as seeming honorable and good to me." And with these words he passed through the gate. But the satrap was astonished, and followed him, and taking hold of his hand, he asked him through an interpreter his name and his family and what was his profession and why he came thither; and he wrote down the answers in a book and also a description of his dress and appearance, and ordered him to wait there.

CHAPTER XXVIII

BUT he himself ran off to the persons whom they are pleased to call "Ears of the King," and described Apollonius to them, after first telling them both that he refused to do homage and that he was not the least like other men. They bade him bring him along, and show him respect without using any violence; and when he came the head of the department asked him what induced him to flout the king, and he answered: "I have not yet flouted him." "But would you flout him?"

was the next question. "Why, of course I will," said Apollonius, "if on making his acquaintance I find him to be neither honorable nor good." "Well, and what presents do you bring for him?" Apollonius answered afresh that he brought courage and justice and so forth. "Do you mean," said the other, "to imply that the king lacks these qualities?" "No, indeed," he answered, "but I would fain teach him to practice them, in case he possesses them." "And surely it was by practicing these qualities," said the other, "that he has recovered the kingdom, which you behold, after he had lost it, and has restored his house,—no light task this nor easy." "And how many years is it since he recovered his kingdom?"

"This is the third year since," answered the other, "which year began about two months ago." Apollonius, then as was his custom, upheld his opinion and went on: "O bodyguard, or whatever I ought to call you, Darius the father of Cyrus and Artaxerxes was master of these royal domains, I think, for sixty years, and he is said, when he felt that his end was at hand, to have offered a sacrifice to Justice and to have addressed her thus: 'O lady mistress, or whosoever thou art.' This shows that he had long loved justice and desired her, but as yet knew her not, nor deemed that he had won her; he brought up his two sons so foolishly that they took up arms against one another, and one was wounded and the other killed by his fellow. Well, here is a king perhaps who does not even know how to keep his seat on the throne, and you would have me believe that he combines already all virtues, and you extol him, though, if he does turn out fairly good, it is you and not I that will gain thereby."

The barbarian then glanced at his neighbor and said: "Here is a windfall! 'tis one of the gods who has brought this man here; for as one good man associating with another improves him, so he will much improve our king, and render him more temperate and gracious; for these qualities are conspicuous in this man." They accordingly ran into the palace and told everybody the good news, that there stood at the king's gates a man who was wise and a Hellene, and a good counselor.

CHAPTER XXIX

WHEN these tidings were brought to the king, he happened to be sacrificing with the Magi, for religious rites are performed under their supervision. And he called one of them and said: "The dream is come true, which I narrated to you when you visited me in my bed."

Now the dream which the king had dreamed was as follows: he thought that he was Artaxerxes, the son of Xerxes, and that he had altered and assumed the latter's form; and he was very much afraid lest some change should come over his affairs, for so he interpreted his change of appeareance. But when he heard that it was a Hellene, and a wise man, that had come, he remembered about Themistocles of Athens, who had once come from Greece and had lived with Artaxerxes, and had not only derived great benefit from the king, but had conferred great benefit himself. So he held out his right hand and said: "Call him in, for it wake the best of beginnings, if he will join with me in my sacrifice and prayer."

CHAPTER XXX

ACCORDINGLY Apollonius entered escorted by a number of people, for they had learnt that the king was pleased with the newcomer and though that this would gratify him; but as he passed into the palace, he did not glance at anything that others admired, but he passed them by as if he was still traveling on the highroad, and calling Damis to him he said: "You asked me yesterday what was the name of the Pamphylian woman who is said to have been intimate with Sappho, and to have composed the hymns which they sing in honor of Artemis of Perga, in the Aeolian and Pamphylian modes." "Yes, I did ask you," said Damis, "but you did not tell me her name." "I did not tell you it, my good fellow, but I explained to you about the keys in which the hymns are written, and I told you about the names; and how the Aeolian strains were altered into the highest key of all, that which is peculiar to the Pamphylians. After that we turned to another subject, for you did not ask me again about the name of the lady. Well, she is called—this clever lady is—Damophyle, and she is said, like Sappho, to have had girlfriends and to have composed poems, some of which were love-songs and others hymns. The particular hymn to Artemis was transposed by her, and the singing of it derives from Sapphic odes." How far then he was from being astonished at the king and his pomp and ceremony, he showed by the fact that he did not think such things worth looking at, but went on talking about other things, as if he did not think the palace worth a glance.

CHAPTER XXXI

NOW the king caught sight of Apollonius approaching, for the vestibule of the Temple was of considerable length, and insisted to those by him that he recognized the sage; and when he came still nearer he cried out with a loud voice and said: "This is Apollonius, whom Megabates, my brother, said he saw in Antioch, the admired and respected of serious people; and he depicted him to me at that time just such a man as now comes to us." And when Apollonius approached and saluted him, the king addressed him in the Greek language and invited him to sacrifice with him; and it chanced that he was on the point of sacrificing to the Sun as a victim a horse of the true Nisaean breed, which he had adorned with trappings as if for a triumphal procession. But Apollonius replied: "Do you, O king, go on with your sacrifice, in your own way, but permit me to sacrifice in mine." And he took up a handful of frankincense and said: "O thou Sun, send me as far over the earth as is my pleasure and thine, and may I make the acquaintance of good men, but never hear anything of bad ones, nor they of me." And with these words he threw the frankincense into the fire, and watched to see how the smoke of it curled upwards, and how it grew turbid, and in how many points it shot up; and in a manner he caught the meaning of the fire, and watched how it appeared of good omen and pure. Then he said: "Now, O king, go on with your sacrifice in accordance with your own traditions, for my traditions are such as you see."

CHAPTER XXXII

AND he quitted the scene of sacrifice in order not to be present at the shedding of blood. But after the sacrifice was over he approached and said: "O king, do you know the Greek tongue thoroughly, or have you a smattering of it perhaps, in order to be able to express yourself and appear polite in case any Greek arrives?" "I know it thoroughly," replied the king, "as well as I do my native language; so say you what you like, for this I suppose is the reason why you put the question to me." "It was my reason," said the other; "so listen. The goal of my voyage is India, but I had no intention of passing you by; for I heard that you were such a man as from a slight acquaintance I already perceive you to be, and was desirous also of examining the wisdom which is indigenous among you and is cultivated by the Magi, and of finding out whether they are such wise theologians as they are reported to be. Now my own system of wisdom is that of Pythagoras, a man of Samos, who taught me to worship the gods in the way you see, and to be aware of them whether they are seen or not seen, and to be frequent in my converse with them, and to dress myself in this land-wool; for it was never worn by sheep, but is the spotless product of spotless parents, the gift of water and of earth, namely linen. And the very fashion of letting my hair grow long, I have learnt from Pythagoras as part of his discipline, and also it is a result of his wisdom that I keep myself pure from animal food. I cannot therefore become either for you or for anybody else a companion in drinking or an associate in idleness and luxury; but if you have problems of conduct that are difficult and hard to settle, I will furnish you with solutions, for I not only know matters of practice and duty, but I even know them beforehand." Such was the conversation which Damis declares the sage to have held; and Apollonius himself composed a letter containing them, and has sketched out in his epistles much else of what he said in conversation.

CHAPTER XXXIII

SINCE the king said that he was more pleased and delighted with his arrival than if he had added to his own possessions the wealth of Persia and India, and added that Apollonius must be his guest and share with him the royal roof, Apollonius remarked: "Supposing, O king, that you came to my country of Tyana and I invited you to live where I live, would you care to do so?" "Why no," answered the king, "unless I had a house to live in that was big enough to accommodate not only my escort and bodyguard, but myself as well, in a handsome manner." "Then," said the other, "I may use the same argument to you; for if I am housed above my rank, I shall be ill at ease, for superfluity distresses wise men more than deficiency distresses you. Let me therefore be entertained by some private person who has the same means as myself, and I will visit with you as often as you like." The king conceded this point, lest he should be betrayed into doing anything that might annoy him, and Apollonius took up his quarters with a gentleman of Babylon of good character and besides high-minded. But before he had finished dinner one of the eunuchs presented himself and addressed him thus: "The king," he said, "bestows upon you ten presents, and leaves you free to name them; but he is anxious that you should not ask for small trifles, for he wishes to exhibit to you and to us his generosity." Apollonius commended the message, and asked: "Then when am I to ask for them?" And the messenger replied: "To-morrow," and at once went off to all the king's friends and kinsmen and bade them be present when the sage should prefer his demand and receive the honor. But Damis says that he expected him to ask for nothing, because he had studied his character and knew that he offered to the gods the following prayer: "O ye gods, grant unto me to have little and to want nothing." However, as he saw him much preoccupied and, as it were, brooding, he determined that he was going to ask and anxiously turning over in his mind, what he should ask. But at eventide: "Damis," said Apollonius, "I am thinking over with myself the question of why the barbarians have regarded eunuchs as men sufficiently chaste to be allowed the free entry of the women's apartments." "But," answered the other, "O Apollonius, a child could tell you. For inasmuch as the operation has deprived them of the faculty, they are freely admitted into those apartments, no matter how far their wishes may go." "But do you suppose the operation has removed their desires or the further aptitude?" "Both," replied Damis, "for if you extinguish in a man the unruly member that lashes the body to madness, the fit of passion will come on him no more." After a brief pause, Apollonius said: "To-morrow, Damis, you shall learn that even eunuchs are liable to fall in love, and that the desire which is contracted through the eyes is not extinguished in them, but abides alive and ready to burst into a flame; for that will occur which will refute your opinion. And even if there were really any human art of such tyrannical force that it could expel such feelings from the heart, I do not see how we could ever attribute to them any chastity of character, seeing that they would have no choice, having been by sheer force and artificially deprived of the faculty of falling in love. For chastity consists in not yielding to passion when the longing and impulse is felt, and in the abstinence which rises superior to this form of madness." Accordingly Damis answered and said: "Here is a thing that we will examine another time, O Apollonius; but we had better consider now that answer you can make to-morrow to the king's magnificent offer. For you will perhaps ask for nothing at all, but you should be careful and be on your guard lest you should seem to decline any gift the king may offer, as they say, out of mere empty pride, for you see the land that you are in and that we are wholly in his power. And you must be on your guard against the accusation of treating him with contempt, and understand, that although we have sufficient means to carry us to India, yet what we have will not be sufficient to bring us back thence, and we have no other supply to fall back upon."

CHAPTER XXXIV

AND by such devices he tried to wheedle Apollonius into not refusing to take anything he might be offered; but Apollonius, as if by way of assisting him in his argument, said: "But, O Damis, are you not going to give me some examples? Let me supply you with some: Aeschines, the son of Lysanias, went off to Dionysius in Sicily in quest of money, and Plato is said thrice to have traversed Charybdis in quest of the wealth of Sicily, and Aristippus of Cyrene, and Helicon of Cyzicus, and Phyton of Rhegium, when he was in exile, buried their noses so deep in the treasure-houses of Dionysius, that they could barely tear themselves away. Moreover they tell of how Eudoxus of Cnidus once arrived in Egypt and both admitted that he had come there in quest of money, and conversed with the king about the matter. And not to take away more characters, they say that Speusippus, the Athenian, was so fond of money, that he reeled off festal songs, when he romped off to Macedonia, in honor of Cassander's marriage, which were frigid compositions, and that he sang these songs in public for the sake of money. Well, I think, O Damis, that a wise man runs more risk than do sailors and soldiers in action, for envy is ever assailing him, whether he holds his tongue or speaks, whether he exerts himself or is idle, whether he passes by anything or takes care to visit anyone, whether he addresses others or neglects to address them. And so a man must fortify himself and understand that a wise man who yields to laziness or anger or passion, or love of drink, or who commits any other action prompted by impulse and inopportune, will probably find his fault condoned; but if he stoops to greed, he will not be pardoned, but render himself odious with a combination of all vices at once. For surely they will not allow that he could be the slave of money, unless he was already the slave of his stomach or of fine raiment or of wine or of riotous living. But you perhaps imagine that it is a lesser thing to go wrong in Babylon than to go wrong at Athens or at the Olympian or Pythian games; and you do not reflect that a wise man finds Hellas everywhere, and that a sage will not regard or consider any place to be a desert or barbarous, because he, at any rate, lives under the eyes of virtue, and although he only sees a few men, yet he is himself looked at by ten thousand eyes. Now if you came across an athlete, Damis, one of those who practice and train themselves in wrestling and boxing, surely you would require him, in case he were contending in the Olympic games, or went to Arcadia, to be both noble in character and good; nay, more, of the Pythian or Nemean contest were going on, you would require him to take care of his physique, because these games are famous and the race-courses are made much of in Hellas; would you then, if Philip were sacrificing with Olympic rites after capturing certain cities, or if his son Alexander were holding games to celebrate his victories, tell the man forthwith to neglect the training of his body and to leave off being keen to win, because the contest was to be held in Olynthus or in Macedonia or in Egypt, rather than among the Hellenes, and on your native race-courses?" These then were the arguments by which Damis declares that he was so impressed as to blush at what he had said, and to ask Apollonius to pardon him for having through imperfect acquaintance with him, ventured to tender him such advice, and use such arguments. But the sage caught him up and said: "Never mind, for it was not by way of rebuking and humbling you that I have spoken thus, but in order to give you some idea of my own point of view."

CHAPTER XXXV

NOW when the eunuch arrived and summoned him before the king, he said: "I will come as soon as I have duly discharged my religious duties." Accordingly he sacrificed and offered his prayer, and then departed, and everyone looked at him and wondered at his bearing. And when he had come within, the king said: "I present you with ten gifts, because I consider you such a man as never before has come hither from Hellas." And he answered and said: "I will not, O king, decline all your gifts; but there is one which I prefer to may tens of gifts, and for that I will most eagerly solicit." And he at one told the story of the Eretrians, beginning it from the time of Datis. "I ask then," he said, "that these poor people should not be driven away from their borders and from the hill, but should be left to cultivate the span of earth, which Darius allowed them; for it is very hard if they are not to be allowed to retain the land which was substituted for their own when they were driven out of the latter." The king then consented and said: "The Eretrians were, until yesterday, the enemies of myself and of my fathers; for they once took up arms against us, and they have been neglected in order that their race might perish; but henceforth they shall be written among my friends, and they shall have, as a satrap, a good man who will judge their country justly. But why," he said, "will you not accept the other nine gifts?" "Because," he answered, "I have not yet, O king, made any friends here." "And do you yourself require nothing?" said the king. "Yes," he said, "I need dried fruits and bread, for that is a repast which delights me and which I find magnificent."

CHAPTER XXXVI

WHILE they were thus conversing with one another a hubbub was heard to proceed from the palace, of eunuchs and women shrieking all at once. And in fact an eunuch had been caught misbehaving with one of the royal concubines just as if he were an adulterer. The guards of the harem were now dragging him along by the hair in the way they do royal slaves. The senior of the eunuchs accordingly declared that he had long before noticed he had an affection for this particular lady, and had already forbidden him to talk to her or touch her neck or hand, or assist her toilette, though he was free to wait upon all the other members of the harem; yet he had now caught him behaving as if he were the lady's lover. Apollonius thereupon glanced at Damis, as if to indicate that the argument they had conducted on the point that even eunuchs fall in love, was now demonstrated to be true; but the king remarked to the bystanders: "Nay, but it is disgraceful, gentlemen, that, in the presence of Apollonius, we should be enlarging on the subject of chastity rather than he. What then, O Apollonius, do you urge us to do with him?" "Why, to let him live, of course," answered Apollonius to the surprise of them all. Whereon the king reddened, and said: "Then you do not think he deserves to die may times for thus trying to usurp my rights?" "Nay, but my answer, O king, was suggested not by any wish to condone his offense, but rather to mete out to him a punishment which will wear him out. For if he lives with this disease of impotence on him, and can never take pleasure in eating or drinking, nor in the spectacles which delight you and your companions, and if his heart will throb as he often leaps up in his sleep, as they say is particularly the case of people in love,—is there any form of consumption so wasting as this, any form of hunger so likely to enfeeble his bowels? Indeed, unless he be one of those who are ready to live at any price, he will entreat you, O king, before long even to slay him, or he will slay himself, deeply deploring that he was not put to death straight away this very day." Such was the answer rendered on this occasion by Apollonius, one so wise and humane, that the king was moved by it to spare the life of his eunuch.

CHAPTER XXXVII

ONE day the king was going to hunt the animals in the parks in which the barbarians keep lions and bears and leopards, and he asked Apollonius to accompany him on the chase, but the latter replied: "You have forgotten, O king, that I never attend you, even when you are sacrificing. And moreover, it is no pleasure to me to attack animals that have been ill-treated and enslaved in violation of their nature." And the king asking him what was the most stable and secure way of governing, Apollonius answered:

"To respect many, and confide in few." And on one occasion the governor of Syria sent a mission about two villages, which, I think, are close to the Bridge, alleging that these villages had long ago been subject to Antiochus and Seleucus, but at present they were under his sway, and belonged to the Romans, and that, whereas the Arabians and Armenians did not disturb these villages, yet the king had traversed so great a distance in order to exploit them, as if they belonged to himself, rather than to the Romans. The king sent the embassy aside, and said: "O Apollonius, these villages were given to my forefathers by the kings whom I mentioned, that they might sustain the wild animals, which are taken by us in our country and sent to theirs across the Euphrates, and they, as if they had forgotten this fact, have espoused a policy that is new and unjust. What then do you think are the intentions of the embassy?" Apollonius replied: "Their attention, O king, is moderate and fair, seeing that they only desire to obtain from you, with your consent, places which, as they are in their territory, they can equally well retain without it." And he added his opinion that it was a mistake to quarrel with the Romans over villages so paltry that probably bigger ones were owned even by private individuals; he also said that it was a mistake to go to war even over large issues. And when the king was ill he visited him, and discoursed so weightily and in such a lofty strain of the soul, that the king recovered, and said to his courtiers, that Apollonius had so wrought upon him that he now felt a contempt, not only for his kingdom, but also for death.

CHAPTER XXXVIII

ONE day the king was showing to him the grotto under the Euphrates, and asked him what he though of so wonderful a thing.

Apollonius in answer belittled the wonder of the work, and said: "It would be a real miracle, O king, if you went dry-shod through a river as deep as this and as unfordable." And when he was shown the walls of Ecbatana, and was told that they were the dwelling-place of gods, he remarked: "They are not the dwelling place of gods at all, and I am not sure that they are of real men either; for, O king, the inhabitants of the city of Lacedaemon do not dwell within walls, and have never fortified their city." Moreover, on one occasion the king had decided a suit for some villages and was boasting to Apollonius of how he had listened to the one suit for two whole days. "Well," said the other, "you took a mighty long time, anyhow, to find out what was just." And when the revenues from the subject country came in on one occasion in great quantities at once, the king opened his treasury and showed his wealth to the sage, to induce him to fall in love with wealth; but he admired nothing that he saw and said: "This, for you, O king, represents wealth, but to me it is mere chaff." "How, then," said the other, "and in what manner can I best make use of it?" "By spending it," he said, "for you are king."

CHAPTER XXXIX

HE had addressed many such sayings to the king, and found him ready to do what he advised him; when finding out that he had enough of the society of the Magi, he said to Damis: "Come, let us start for India. For the people who visited the lotus-eaters in their ships were seduced from their own home-principles by the food; but we, without tasting any of the victuals of this land, have remained here a longer time than is right and fitting." "And I," said Damis, "am more than of your opinion; but as I bore in mind the period of time which you discovered by the help of the lioness, I was waiting on for it to be completed. Now it has not yet all of it expired, for we have so far only spent a year and four months; however, if we can depart at once, would it be as well?" "But," said the other, "the king will not let us go, O Damis, before the eighth month has passed; for you, I think, see that he is a worthy man and too superior a person to be ruling over barbarians."

CHAPTER XL

WHEN at last they were resolved on their departure and the king had consented that they should go away, Apollonius remembered the presents, which he had put off till he should have acquired friends, and he said: "O excellent king, I have in no way remunerated my host and I owe a great reward to the Magi; do you therefore attend to them, and oblige me by bestowing your favors on men who are both wise and wholly devoted to yourself." The king then was more than delighted, and said: "For you I will to-morrow make their estate enviable and will see that they have been granted great favors; but since you ask for nothing that is mine, I hope you will at least allow these gentlemen to accept from me money and what else they like," and he pointed to Damis and his companions. And when they too declined the offer, Apollonius said: "You see, O king, how many hands I have, and how closely they resemble one another." "But do you anyhow take a guide," said the king, "and camels on which to ride; for the road is too long by far for you to walk the whole of it." "Be it so," said Apollonius, "O king: for they say that the road is a difficult one for him who is not mounted, and moreover this animal is easily fed and finds his pasture easily where there is no herbage. And, methinks, we must lay in a supply of water also, and take it in bottles, like wine." "Yes," said the king, "for three days the country is waterless, but after that there are plenty of rivers and springs; but you must take the road over the Caucasus, for there you will find plenty of the necessities of life and the country is friendly." And the king then asked him what he would bring back to him from his destination; and he answered: "A graceful gift, O king, for if I am turned into a wiser man by the society of people yonder, I shall return to you here a better man than I now am." When he said this the king embraced him and said: "May you come back, for that will indeed be a great gift."

BOOK II

CHAPTER I

IN the summer our travelers, together with their guide, left Babylon and started out, mounted on camels; and the king had supplied them with the camel-driver, and plenty of provisions, as much as they wanted. The country through which they traveled was fertile; and the villages received them very respectfully, for the leading camel bore upon his forehead a chain of gold, to intimate to all who met them that the king was sending on their way some of his own friends. And as they approached the Caucasus they say that they found the land becoming more fragrant.

CHAPTER II

WE may regard this mountain as the beginning of the Taurus, which extends through Armenia and Cilicia as far as Pamphylia and Mycale, and it ends at the sea on the shore of which the Carians live, and we may regard this as the extreme end of the Caucasus, and not as its beginning, as some people say. For the height of Mycale is not very great, whereas the peaks of the Caucasus are so lofty that the sun is cloven asunder by them. And it encompasses with the rest of the Taurus the whole of Scythia which borders on India, and skirts Maeotis and the left side of the Pontus, a distance almost of 20,000 stades; for no less than this is the extent of land enclosed by the elbow of the Caucasus. As to the statement made about such part of the Taurus as is in our country, to the effect that it projects beyond Armenia,—it was long disbelieved, but has received definite confirmation from the conduct of the leopards, which I know are caught in the spice-bearing region of Pamphylia. For these animals delight in fragrant odors, and scenting their smell from afar off they quit Armenia and traverse the mountains in search of the tear or gum of the Styrax, whenever the winds blow from its quarter and the trees are distilling. And they say that a pard was once caught in Pamphylia which was wearing a chain round its neck, and the chain was of gold, and on it was inscribed in Armenian lettering: "The king Arsaces to the Nysian god." Now the king of Armenia was certainly at that time Arsaces, and he, I imagine, finding the pard, had let it go free in honor of Dionysus because of its size. For Dionysus is called Nysian by the Indians and by all the

Oriental races from Nysa in India. And this animal had been for a time under the restraint of a man, and would let you pat with your hand and caress it; bit when it was goaded to excitement by the springtime, for in that season pards begin to rut, it would rush into the mountains, from longing to meet the male, decked as it was with the ring; and it was taken in the lower Taurus whither it had been attracted by the fragrance of the gum. And the Caucasus bounds India and Media, and stretches down by another arm to the Red Sea.

CHAPTER III

AND legends are told of this mountain by the barbarians, which also have an echo in the poems of the Greeks about it, to the effect that Prometheus, because of his love of man, was bound there, and that Heracles—another Heracles, for of course the Theban is not meant— could not brook the ill-treatment of Prometheus, and shot the bird which was feeding upon his entrails. And some say that he was bound in a cave, which as a matter of fact is shown in a foot-hill of the mountain; and Damis says that his chains still hung from the rocks, though you could not easily guess at the material of which they were made, but others say that they bound him on the peak of the mountain; and it has two summits, and they say that his hands were lashed to them, although they are distant from one another not less than as stade[2], so great was his bulk. But the inhabitants of the Caucasus regard the eagle as a hostile bird, and burn out the nests which they build among the rocks by hurling into them fiery darts, and they also set snares for them, declaring that they are avenging Prometheus; to such an extent are their imaginations dominated by the fable.

CHAPTER IV

HAVING passed the Caucasus our travelers say they saw men four cubits height, and they were already black, and that when they passed over the river Indus they saw others five cubits high. But on their way to this river our wayfarers found the following incidents worth of notice. For they were traveling by bright moonlight, when the figure of an *empusa* or hobgoblin appeared to them, that changed from one form into another, and sometimes vanished into nothing. And Apollonius

---

[2] 606 English feet.

realized what it was, and himself heaped abuse on the hobgoblin and instructed his party to do the same, saying that this was the right remedy for such a visitation. And the phantasm fled away shrieking even as ghosts do.

CHAPTER V

AND as they were passing over the summit of the mountain, going on foot, for it was very steep, Apollonius asked of Damis the following question. "Tell me," he said, "where we were yesterday." And he replied: "On the plain." "And today, O Damis, where are we?" "In the Caucasus," said he, "if wholly I mistake not." "Then when were you lower down than you are now?" he asked again, and Damis replied: "That's a question hardly worth asking. For yesterday we were traveling through the valley below, while today we are close up to heaven." "Then you think," said the other, "O Damis, that our road yesterday lay low down, whereas our road today lies high up?" "Yes, by Zeus," he replied, "unless at least I'm mad." "In what respect then," said Apollonius, "do you suppose that our roads differ from one another, and what advantage has todays' path for you over that of yesterday?" "Because," said Damis, "yesterday I was walking along where a great many people go, but today, where are very few." "Well," said the other, "O Damis, can you not also in a city turn out of the main street and walk where you will find very few people?" "I did not say that," replied Damis, "but that yesterday we were passing through villages and populations, whereas today we are ascending through an untrodden and divine region: for you heard our guide say that the barbarians declare this tract to be the home of the gods." And with that he glanced up to the summit of the mountain. But Apollonius recalled his attention to the original question by saying: "Can you tell me then, O Damis, what understanding of divine mystery you get by walking so near the heavens?" "None whatever," he replied. "And yet you ought," said Apollonius. "When your feet are placed on a platform so divine and vast as this, you ought henceforth to publish more accurate conceptions of the heaven and about the sun and moon, since you think, I suppose, that you will even lay a rod to them as you stand as close to the heavens here." "Whatever," said he, "I knew about God's nature yesterday, I equally know today, and so far no fresh idea has occurred to me concerning him." "So then," replied the other, "you are, O Damis, still below, and have won nothing from being high up, and you are as far from heaven as you were yesterday. And my question which I asked you to begin with was a fair one, although you thought that I asked it in order to make fun of you." "The truth is," replied Damis, "that I thought I should anyhow go down from the mountain wiser than I came up it, because I had heard, O Apollonius, that Anaxagoras of Clazomenae observed the heavenly bodies from the mountain Mimas in Ionia, and Thales of Miletus from Mycale which was close by his home; and some are said to have used as their observation mount Pangaeus and others Athos. But I have come up a greater height than any of these, and yet shall go down again no wiser than I was before." "For neither did they," replied Apollonius: "and such lookouts show you indeed a bluer heaven and bigger stars and the sun rising out of the night; but all these phenomena were manifest long ago to shepherds and goatherds, but neither Athos will reveal to those who climb up it, nor Olympus, so much extolled by the poets, in what way God cares for the human race and how he delights to be worshipped by them, nor reveal the nature of virtue and of justice and temperance, unless the soul scan these matters narrowly, and the soul, I should say, if it engages on the task pure and undefiled, will sour much higher than this summit of Caucasus."

CHAPTER VI

AND having passed beyond the mountain, they at once came upon elephants with men riding on them; and these people dwell between the Caucasus and the river Cophen, and they are rude in their lives and they are nomad riders on the herds of elephants; some of them however rode on camels, which are used by Indians for carrying dispatches, and they will travel 1,000 stades a day without ever bending the knee or lying down anywhere. One of the Indians, then, who was riding on such a camel, asked the guide where they were going, and when he was told the object of their voyage, he informed the nomads thereof; and they raised a shout of pleasure, and bade them approach, and when they came up they offered them wine which they had made out of palm dates and honey from the same tree, and steaks from the flesh of lions and leopards which they had just flayed. And our travelers accepted everything except the flesh, and then started off for India and betook themselves eastwards.

CHAPTER VII

AND as they were taking breakfast by a spring of water, Damis poured out a cup of the Indians' wine, and said: "Here's to you, Apollonius, on the part of Zeus the Savior; for it is a long time since you have drunk any wine. But you will not, I am sure, refuse this as you do wine that is made from the fruit of the vine." And withal he poured out a libation, because he had mentioned the name of Zeus. Apollonius then gave a laugh and said: "Do we not also abstain from money, O Damis?" "Yes, by Zeus," said the other, "as you have often demonstrated to us." "Shall we then," said the other, "abstain from the use of a golden drachma and a silver piece, and be proof against temptation by any such coin, although we see not private individuals only, but kings as well, agape for money, and then if anyone offers us a brass coin for a silver coin, or a gilded one and a counterfeit, shall we accept it, merely because it not what it pretends to be, and what the many itch to have? And be sure the Indians have coins of orichalcus and black brass, with which, I suppose, all who come the Indian haunts must purchase everything; what then? Supposing the nomads, good people as they are, offered us money, would you in that case, Damis, seeing me decline it, have advised me better and have explained that what is coined by the Romans or by the king of Media is really money, whereas this is another sort of stuff polished up among the Indians? And what would you think of me, if you could persuade me of such things? Would you not think I was a cheat and abandoned my philosophy as thoroughly as cowardly soldiers do their shields? And yet, when you have thrown away your shield you can procure another that is quite as good as the first, in the opinion of Archilochus. But how can one who has dishonored and cast away philosophy, ever recover her? And in this case Dionysus might will pardon one who refuses all wine whatever, but if I chose date wine in preference to that made of grapes, he would be aggrieved, I am sure, and say that this gift had been scorned and flouted. And we are not far away from this god, for you hear the guide saying that the mountain of Nysa is close by, upon which Dionysus works, I believe, a great many miracles. Moreover, drunkenness, Damis, invades men not from drinking the wine of grapes alone, for they are equally well roused to frenzy by date wine. Anyhow we have seen a great many Indians overcome by this wine, some of them dancing till they fell, and others singing drowsily, just like the people among us, who end drinking bouts at night and don't go home till dawn. And that you yourself regard this drink as genuine wine, is clear from the fact that you poured out a libation of it to Zeus and offered up the prayers which usually accompany wine. And this, Damis, is the defense which I have to make of myself against you; for neither do I wish to dissuade you from drinking, nor these companions of ours either; nay, I would allow you also to eat meat; for the abstinence from these things has, I perceive, profited you nothing, though it has profited me in the philosophic profession which I have made from my boyhood." The companions of Damis welcomed this speech and took to their good cheer with a will, thinking that they would find the journey easier if they lived rather better.

CHAPTER VIII

THEY crossed the river Cophen, themselves in boats, but the camels by a ford on foot; for the river has not yet reached its full size here. They were now in a continent subject to the king, in which the mountain of Nysa rises, covered to its very top with plantations, like the mounntain of Tmolus in Lydia, and you can ascend it, because paths been made by cultivators. They say then that when they ascended it, they found the shrine of Dionysus, which it is said Dionysus founded in honor of himself, planting round it a circle of laurel trees which encloses just as much ground as suffices to contain a moderate sized temple. He also surrounded the laurels with a border of ivy and vines; and he set up inside an image of himself, knowing that in time the trees would grow together and make themselves into a kind of roof; and this had now formed itself, so that neither rain can wet nor wind blow upon the shrine. And there were sickles and wine-presses and their furniture dedicated to Dionysus, as if to one who gathers grapes, all made of gold and silver. And the image resembled a youthful Indian, and was carved out of polished white stone. And when Dionysus celebrates his orgies and shakes Nysa, the cities underneath the mountain hear the noise and exult in sympathy.

CHAPTER IX

NOW the Hellenes disagree with the Indians, and the Indians among themselves, concerning this Dionysus. For we declare that the Theban Dionysus made an expedition to India in the role both of soldier and of reveler, and we base our arguments, among other things, on the offering at Delphi, which is secreted in the treasuries there. And it is a disk of silver bearing the inscription: "Dionysus the son of Semele and of Zeus, from the men of India to the Apollo of Delphi." But the Indians who dwell in the Caucasus and along the river Cophen say that he was an Assyrian visitor when he came to them, who knew the religious rites of the Theban. But those who inhabit the district between the Indus and the Hydraotes and the continental region beyond, which ends at the river Ganges, declare that Dionysus was son of the river Indus, and that the Dionysus of Thebes having become his disciple adopted the thyrsus and devoted himself to the orgies; that this Dionysus on saying that he was the son of Zeus and had lived safe inside his father's thigh until he was born, gained from this Dionysus a mountain called Merus or "Thigh" on which Nysa borders, and planted Nysa in honor of Dionysus with the vine of which he had brought the suckers from Thebes; and that it was there that Alexander held his orgies. But the inhabitants of Nysa deny that Alexander ever went up the mountain, although he was eager to do so, being an ambitious person and fond of old-world things; but he was afraid lest his Macedonians, if they got among vines, which they had not seen for a long time, would fall into a fit of home-sickness or recover their taste for wine, after they had become accustomed to water only. So they say he passed by Nysa, making his vow to Dionysus, and sacrificing at the foot of the mountain. Well I know that some people will take amiss what I write, because the companions of Alexander on his campaigns did not write down the truth in reporting this, but I at any rate insist upon the truth, and hold that, if they had respected it more, they would never have deprived Alexander of the praise due to him in this matter; for, in my opinion, it was a greater thing that he never went up, in order to maintain the sobriety of his army, than that he should have ascended the mountain and have himself held a revel there, which is what they tell you.

CHAPTER X

DAMIS says that he did not see the rock called the "Birdless" (*Aornus*), which is not far distant from Nysa, because this lay off their road, and their guide feared to diverge from the direct path. But he says he heard that it had been captured by Alexander, and was called "Birdless," not because it rises 9,000 feet, for the sacred birds fly higher than that; but because on the summit of the rock there is, they say, a cleft which draws into itself the birds which fly over it, as we may see at Athens also in the vestibule of the Parthenon, and in several places in Phrygia and Lydia. And this is why the rock was called and actually is "Birdless".

CHAPTER XI

AND as they made their way to the Indus they met a boy of about thirteen years old mounted on an elephant and striking the animal. And when they wondered at the sight, Apollonius said: "Damis, what is the business of a good horseman?" "Why, what else," he replied, "than to sit firm upon the horse, and then control it, and turn it with the bit, and punish it when it is unruly, and to take care that the horse does not plunge into a chasm or a ditch or a hole, especially when he is passing over a marsh or a clay bog?" "And shall we require nothing else, Damis, of a good horseman?" said Apollonius. "Why, yes," he said, "when the horse is galloping up a hill he must slacken the bit; and when he is going down hill he must not let the horse have his way, but hold him in; and he must caress his ears and man; and in my opinion a clever rider is not always whipping, and I should commend any one who rode in this way." "And what is needful for a soldier who rides a charger?" "The same things," he said, "O Apollonius, and in addition the ability to hurl and avoid missiles and to pursue and to retire, and crowd the enemies together without letting his horse be frightened by the rattling of shields or the flashing of the helmets, or by the noise made when the men raise their war-cry and give a whoop; this, I think all belongs to good horsemanship." "What then will you say of this boy who is riding on the elephant?" "He is much more wonderful, Apollonius. For it seems to me a superhuman feat for such a tiny mite to manage so huge an animal and guide it with the crook, which you see him digging into the elephant like an anchor, without fearing either the look of the brute or its height, or its enormous strength; and I would not have believed it possible, I swear by Athena, if I had heard another telling it, and had not seen it." "Well then," said Apollonius, "if anyone wanted to sell us this boy, would you buy him, Damis?" "Yes, by Zeus," he said, "and I would give everything I have to possess him. For it seems to me the mark of a liberal and splendid nature, to be able to capture like a citadel the greatest animal which earth sustains, and then govern it as its master." "What then would you do with the boy," said the other, "unless you bought the elephant as well?" "I would set him," said

Damis, "to preside over my household and over my servants, and he would rule them much better than I can." "And are you not able," said Apollonius, "to rule your own servants?" "About as able to do so," replied Damis, "as you are yourself, Apollonius. For I have abandoned my property, and am going about, like yourself, eager to learn and to investigate things in foreign countries." "But if you did actually buy the boy, and if you had two horses, one of them a racer, and the other a charger, would you put him, O Damis, on these horses?" "I would perhaps," he answered, "upon the racer, for I see others doing the same, but how could he ever mount a war-horse accustomed to carry armor? For he could not either carry a shield, as knights must do; or wear a breast-plate or helmet; and how could he wield a javelin, when he cannot use the shaft of a bolt or of an arrow, but he would in military matters be like a stammerer." "Then," said the other, "there is, Damis, something else which controls and guides this elephant, and not the driver alone, whom you admire almost to the point of almost worshipping." Damis replied: "What can that be, Apollonius? For I see nothing else upon the animal except the boy." "This animal," he answered, " is docile beyond all others; and when he has once been broken in to serve man, he will put up with anything at the hands of man, and he makes it his business to be tractable and obedient to him, and he loves to eat out of his hands, in the way little dogs do; and when his master approaches he fondles him with his trunk, and he will allow him to thrust his head into his jaws, and he holds them as wide open as his master likes, as we have seen among the nomads. But of a night the elephant is said to lament his state of slavery, yes by heaven, not by trumpeting in his ordinary way, but by wailing mournfully and piteously. And if a man comes upon him when he is lamenting in this way, the elephant stops his dirge at once as if he were ashamed. Such control, O Damis, has he over himself, and it is his instinctive obedience which actuates him rather than the man who sits upon and directs him."

CHAPTER XII

AND when they came to the Indus, they saw a herd of elephants crossing the river, and they say they heard this account of the animals. Some of them are marsh elephants, others again mountain elephants, and there is third kind which belong to the plain: and they are captured for use in war. For indeed they go into battle, saddled with towers big enough to accommodate ten or fifteen Indians all at once; and from these towers the Indians shoot their bows and hurl their javelins, just as if they were taking aim from gate towers. And the animal itself regards his trunk as a hand and uses it to hurl weapons. And the Indian elephants are as much bigger as those of Libya, as these are bigger than the horses of Nisa. And other authorities have dwelt on the age of the animals, and say that they are very long-lived; but our party too say that they came on an elephant near Taxila, the greatest city in India, who was anointed with myrrh by the natives and adorned with fillets. For, they said, this elephant was one of those who fought on the side of Porus against Alexander; and, as it had made a brave fight, Alexander dedicated it to the Sun. And it had, they say, gold rings around its tusks or horns, whichever you call them, and an inscription was on them written in Greek, as follows: "Alexander the son of Zeus dedicates Ajax to the Sun." For he had given this name to the elephant, thinking so great an animal deserved a great name. And the natives reckoned that 350 years had elapsed since the battle, without taking into account how old the elephant was when he went into battle.

CHAPTER XIII

AND Juba, who was once sovereign of the Libyan race, says that formerly the knights of Libya fought with one another on elephants, and division of these had a tower engraved upon their tusks, but the others nothing. And when night interrupted the fray the animals which were so marked had, he says, got the worst of it, and fled into Mount Atlas; but he himself 400 years afterwards caught one of the fugitives and found the cavity of the stamp still fresh on the tusk and not yet worn away by time. This Juba is of opinion that the tusks are horns, because they grow just where the temples are, and there is no grinding of one upon another, and they remain as they grew and do not, like teeth, fall out and then grow afresh. But I cannot accept this view; for horns, if not all, at any rate those of stags, do fall out and grow afresh, but the teeth, although in the case of men those which may fall out, will every one of them grow again, on the other hand there is not a single animal whose tusk or dog-tooth falls out naturally, nor in which, when it has fallen out, it will come again. For nature implants these tusks in their jaws for the sake of defense. And moreover, a circular ridge is formed year by year at the base of the horns, as we see in the case of goats and sheep and oxen; but a tusk grows out quite smooth, and unless something breaks it, it always remains so, for it consists of a material and substance as hard as stone. Moreover the carrying of horns is confined to animals with cloven hoofs, but this animal has five nails and the foot branches into more toes than two, and since these are not squeezed into a hoof, the elephant has a pliable sole. And in the case of all animals that have horns, nature supplies cavernous bones and causes the horn to grow from outwards, whereas she makes the elephant tusk full and equally massive throughout; and when in the lathe you lay bare the interior, you find a very thin tube piercing the center of it, as is the case with teeth. Now the tusks of the marsh elephants are dark in color and porous and difficult to work, because they are hollowed out into many cavities, and often knots are formed in them which oppose difficulties to the craftsman's tool; but the tusks of the mountain kind, though smaller than these, are pretty white and there is nothing about them difficult to work; but best of all are the tusks of the elephants of the plain, for these are very large and very white and so pleasant to turn and carve that the hand can shape them into whatever it likes.

If I may also describe the characters of these elephants; those which come from the marshes, and are taken there, are considered to be stupid and flighty by the Indians; but those which come from the mountains they regard as vicious and treacherous and, unless they want something, not to be relied upon by man; but the elephants of the plain are said to be good and tractable, and fond of learning tricks; for they will write and dance, and will sway themselves to and fro and leap up and down from the ground to the sound of the pipe.

CHAPTER XIV

AND Apollonius saw a herd, I think, of about thirty elephants crossing over the River Indus, and they were following as their leader the smallest among them; but the bigger ones had picked up their young ones on their projecting tusks, where they held them fast by twining their trunks around them. Said Apollonius: "No one, O Damis, has instructed them to do this, but they act of their own instinctive wisdom and cleverness; and you see how, like baggage-porters, they have picked up their young, and have them bound fast on, and so carry them along." "I see," he said, "Apollonius, how cleverly and with what sagacity they do this. What then is the sense of this silly speculation indulged in by those who idly dispute whether the affection that men feel for their young is natural or not, when these very elephants, by their conduct, proclaim that it is so, and that it comes to them by nature? For they have certainly not learnt to do so from men, as have other creatures; for these have never yet shared the life of men, but have been endowed by nature with their love of their offspring, and this is why they provide for them and feed their young." "And," said Apollonius, "you need not, Damis, confine your remarks to elephants; for this animal is only second to man, in my opinion, in understanding and foresight; but I am thinking rather of bears, for they are the fiercest of all animals, and yet they will do anything for their whelps; and also of wolves, among which, although they are so addicted to plunder, yet the female protects its young ones, and the male brings her food in order to save the life of the whelps. And I also equally have in mind the panther, which, from the warmth of its temperament, delights to become a mother, for that is the time when it is determined to rule the male and be mistress of the household; and the male puts up with anything and everything from her, subordinating everything to the welfare of the offspring. And there is also told a story of the lioness, how she will make a lover of the panther and receive him in the lion's lair in the plain; but when she is going to bring forth her young she flees into the mountains to the haunts of the panthers; for she brings forth young ones that are spotted, and that is why she hides her young and nurses them in winding thickets, pretending that she is spending the day out hunting. For if the lion detected the trick, he would tear the whelps in pieces and claw her offspring as illegitimate. You have read not doubt, also, of one of Homer's lions, and of how he made himself look terrible in behalf of his own whelps and steeled himself to do battle for them. And they say the tigress, although she is the cruelest animal, will in this country and also on the Read Sea approach the ships, to demand back her whelps; and if she gets them back, she goes off mightily delighted; but if the ships sail away, they say that she howls along the sea-coast and sometimes dies outright. And who does not know the ways of birds, how that the eagles and the storks will not build their nests until they have fixed in them, the one an eagle-stone, and other a stone of light, to help the hatching out of the eggs and to drive away the snakes. And if we look at creatures in the sea, we need not wonder at the dolphins loving their offspring, for they are superior creatures; but shall we not admire the whales and seals and the viviparous species? For I once saw a seal that was kept shut up at Aegae in the circus, and she mourned so deeply for her whelp, which had died after being born in confinement, that she refused food for three days together, although she is the most voracious of animals. And the whale takes up its young ones into the cavities of its throat, whenever it is fleeing from a creature stronger than itself. And a viper has been seen licking the serpents which it had borne, and caressing them with her tongue, which she shoots out for the purpose. But we need not entertain, Damis, the silly story that the young of vipers are brought into the world without mothers; for that is a thing which is consistent neither with nature nor with experience."

Damis then resumed the conversation by saying: "You will allow me then to praise Euripides, for this iambic line which he puts into the mouth of Andromache:

'And in the case of all men, then, their life lay in their children.'"

"I admit," said Apollonius, "that that is said cleverly and divinely; but much cleverer and truer would have been the verse, if it had included all animals." "Then you would like," said Damis, "O Apollonius, to rewrite the line so that we might sing it as follows:

'And in the case of all animals, then, their life lay in their children.'
and I agree with you, for it is better so."

CHAPTER XV

"BUT tell me this: did we not, at the beginning our conversation, declare that the elephants display wisdom and intelligence in what they do?" "Why certainly," he replied, "we did say so, Damis; for if intelligence did not govern this animal, neither would it subsist, nor the populations among which it lived." "Why then," said Damis, "do they conduct their passage over the river in a way so stupid and inconvenient to themselves? For as you see, the smallest one is leading the way, and he is followed by a slightly larger one, then comes another still larger than he, and the biggest ones come last of all. But surely they ought to travel in the opposite fashion, and make the biggest ones a wall and rampart in front of themselves." "But," replied Apollonius, "in the first place they appear to be running away from men who are pursuing them, and whom we shall doubtless come across, as they follow the animals' tracks; and they must and ought to use their best strength to fortify their rear against attack, as is done in war; so that you may regard this maneuver as tactically excellent on the part of the brutes. Secondly, as they are crossing a river, if their biggest ones went first, that would not enable the rest of the herd to judge whether the water is shallow enough for all to pass; for the tallest ones would find the passage practicable and easy, but the others would find it dangerous and difficult, because they would not rise above the level of the stream. But the fact that the smallest is able to get across is a sign in itself to the rest that there is no difficulty. And moreover, if the bigger ones went in first, they would deepen the river for the small ones, for the mud is forced to settle down into ruts and trenches, owing to the heaviness of the animal and the thickness of his feet; whereas the larger ones are in no way prejudiced by the smaller ones, crossing in front, because they sink in less deeply."

CHAPTER XVI

"AND I have read in the discourse of Juba that elephants assist one another when they are being hunted, and that they will defend one that is exhausted, and if they can remove him out of danger, they anoint his wounds with the tears of the aloe tree, standing round him like physicians." Many such learned discussions were suggested to them as one occasion after another worth speaking of arose.

CHAPTER XVII

AND the statements by Nearchus and Pythagoras, about the river Acesines, to the effect that it debauches into the Indus, and that snakes breed in it seventy cubits long, were, they say, fully verified by them; but I will defer what I have to say till I come to speak about dragons, on whose capture Damis gives an account. But when they reached the Indus and were inclined to pass over the river, they asked the Babylonian whether he knew anything of the river, and questioned him about how to get across it. But he said that he had never navigated it, nor did he know whence he they could get a boat on it. "Why then," said they, "did you not hire a guide?" "Because," he said, "I have one who will direct us." And with that, he showed them a letter, written to that effect, and this gave them occasion to marvel afresh at the humanity and foresight of Vardanes. For he had addressed the letter in question to the satrap of the Indus, although he was not subject to his dominion; and in it he reminded him of the good service he had done him, but declared that he would not ask any recompense for the same, "for," he said, "it is not my habit to ask for a return of favors." But he said he would be very grateful, if he could give a welcome to Apollonius and send him on wherever he wished to go. And he had given gold to the guide, so that in case he found Apollonius in want thereof, he might give it him and save him from looking to the generosity of anyone else. And when the

Indian received the letter, he declared that he was highly honored, and would interest himself in the sage as much as if the king of India had written in his behalf; and he lent his official boat for him to embark in and other vessels on which the camels were ferried across, and he also sent a guide to the whole of the country which is bordered by the Hydraotes, and he wrote to his own king, begging him not to treat with less respect than Vardanes a man who was a Greek and divine.

CHAPTER XVIII

THUS they crossed the Indus at a point where it was nearly 40 stades broad, for such is the size of its navigable portion; and they write the following account of this river. They say that the Indus arises in the Caucasus and is bigger at its source than any of the other rivers of Asia; and as it advances it absorbs into itself several navigable rivers and, like the Nile, it floods the land of India and brings down soil over it, and so provides the Indians with land to sow in the manner of the Egyptians. Now it is said that there is snow on the hills in Ethiopia and in the land of the Catadupi, and I do not choose to contradict, out of respect for the authorities; nevertheless, I cannot agree with them, when I consider how the Indus effects the same results as the Nile, without any snow falling on the country that rises behind and above it. And moreover I know that God has set the Ethiopian and the Indian at the two extremes or horns of the entire earth, making black the latter who dwell where the sun rises no less than the former who dwell where it sets; now how should this be the case of the inhabitants, unless they enjoyed summer heat even in the winter? But where the sun warms the earth all over through the year, how can one suppose that it ever snows? And how could it ever snow there so hard, as to supply the rivers there with water, and make them rise above their normal levels? But even if there were frequent snowfalls in regions so exposed to the sun, how could the melted snow ever cover such an expanse as to resemble a sea? And how could it ever supply a river which deluges the whole of Egypt?

CHAPTER XIX

AND as they were being conveyed across the Indus, they say that they came across many river-horses and many crocodiles; and they say that the vegetation on the Indus resembles that which grows along the Nile, and that the climate of India is sunny in winter, but suffocating in summer; but to counteract this Providence has excellently contrived that it should often rain in their country. And they also say that they learned from the Indians that the king was in the habit of coming to this river when it rose in the appropriate seasons, and would sacrifice to the river black bulls and horses; for white is less esteemed by the Indians than black, because, I imagine, the latter is their own color; and when he has sacrificed, they say that he plunges into the river a measure of gold made to resemble that which is used in measuring wheat. And why the king does this, the Indians, they say, have no idea; but they themselves conjectured that this measure was sunk in the river, either to secure the plentiful harvest, whose yield the farmers use such a measure to gauge, or to keep the river within its proper bounds and prevent it from rising to such heights as that it would drown the land.

CHAPTER XX

AND after they had crossed the river, they were conducted by the satrap's guide direct to Taxila, where the Indian had his royal palace. And they say that on that side of the Indus the dress of the people consists of native linen, with shoes of byblus and a hat when it rains; but that the upper classes there are appareled in byssus; and that the byssus grows upon a tree of which the stem resembles that of the white poplar, and the leaves those of the willow. And Apollonius says that he was delighted with the byssus, because it resembled his sable philosopher's cloak. And the byssus is imported into Egypt from India for many sacred uses. Taxila, they tell us, is about as big as Nineveh, and was fortified fairly well after the manner of Greek cities; and here was the royal residence of the personage who then ruled the empire of Porus. And they saw a Temple, they saw, in front of the wall, which was not far short of 100 feet in size, made of porphyry, and there was constructed within it a shrine, somewhat small as compared with the great size of the Temple which is surrounded with columns, but deserving of notice. For bronze tablets were nailed into each of its walls on which were engraved the exploits of Porus and Alexander. But the pattern was wrought with orichalcus and silver and gold and black bronze, of elephants, horses, soldiers, helmets, shields, but spears, and javelins and swords, were all made of iron; and the composition was like the subject of some famous painting by Zeuxis or Polygnotus and Euphranor, who delighted in light and shade; and, they say, here also was an appearance of real life, as well as depth and relief. And the metals were blended in the design, melted in like so many colors; and the character of the picture was also pleasing in itself, for Porus dedicated these designs after the death of the Macedonian, who is depicted in the hour of victory, restoring Porus who is wounded, and presenting him with India which was now his gift. And it is said that Porus mourned over the death of Alexander, and that he lamented him as generous and a good prince; and as long as Alexander was alive after his departure from India, he never used the royal diction and style, although he had license to do so, nor issued kingly edicts to the Indians, but figured himself as satrap full of moderation, and guided every action by the wish to please Alexander.

CHAPTER XXI

MY argument does not allow me to pass over the accounts written of this Porus. For when the Macedonian was about to cross the river, and some of Porus' advisers wished him to make an alliance with the kings on the other side of the Hyphasis and the Ganges, urging that the invader would never face a general coalition against him of the whole of India, he replied: "If the temper of my subjects is such that I cannot save myself without allies, then for me it is better not to be king." And when someone announced to him that Alexander had captured Darius, he remarked, "a king but not a man." And when the mule driver had caparisoned the elephant on which he meant to fight, he replied: "Nay, I shall carry him, if I prove myself the same man I used to be." And when they counseled him to sacrifice to the river, and induce it to reject the rafts of the Macedonians, and make it impassable to Alexander, he said: "It ill befits those who have arms to resort to imprecation." And after the battle, in which his conduct struck Alexander as divine and superhuman, when one of his relations said to him: "If you had only paid homage to him after he had crossed, O Porus, you would not yourself have been defeated in battle, nor would so many Indians have lost their lives, nor would you yourself have been wounded," he said: "I knew from my report that Alexander was so fond of glory that, if I did homage to him, he would regard me as a slave, but if I fought him, as a king. And I much preferred his admiration to his pity, not was I wrong in my calculation. For by showing myself to be such a man as Alexander found me, I both lost and won everything that day." Such is the character which historians give to this Indian, and they say that he was the handsomest of his race, and in stature taller than any man since the

Trojan heroes, but that he was quite young, when he went to war with Alexander.

CHAPTER XXII

WHILE he was waiting in the Temple,—and it took a long time for the king to be informed that strangers had arrived,—Apollonius said: "O Damis, is there such a thing as painting?" "Why yes," he answered, "if there be any such thing as truth." "And what does this art do?" "It mixes together," replied Damis, "all the colors there are, blue with green, and white with black, and red with yellow." "And for what reason," said the other, "does it mix these? For it isn't merely to get a color, like dyed wax." "It is," said Damis, "for the sake of imitation, and to get a likeness of a dog, or a horse, or a man, or a ship, or of anything else under the sun; and what is more, you see the sun himself represented, sometimes borne upon a four horse car, as he is said to be seen here, and sometimes again traversing the heaven with his torch, in case you are depicting the ether and the home of the gods." "Then, O Damis, painting is imitation?" "And what else could it be?" said he: "for if it did not effect that, it would voted to be an idle playing with colors." "And," said the other, "the things which are seen in heaven, whenever the clouds are torn away from one another, I mean the centaurs and stag-antelopes, yes, and the wolves too, and the horses, what have you got to say about them? Are we not to regard them as works of imitation?" "It would seem so," he replied. "Then, Damis, God is a painter, and has left his winged chariot, upon which he travels, as he disposes of affairs human and divine, and he sits down on these occasions to amuse himself by drawing these pictures, as children make figures in the sand." Damis blushed, for he felt that his argument was reduced to such an absurdity. But Apollonius, on his side, had no wish to humiliate him, for he was not unfeeling in his refutations of people, and said: "But I am sure, Damis, you did not mean that; rather that these figures flit through the heaven not only without meaning, but, so far as providence is concerned, by mere chance; while we who by nature are prone to imitation rearrange and create them in these regular figures." "We may, he said, "rather consider this to be the case, O Apollonius, for it is more probable, and a much sounder idea." "Then, O Damis, the mimetic art is twofold, and we may regard the one kind as an employment of the hands and mind in producing imitations, and declare that this is painting, whereas the other kind consists in making likenesses with the mind alone." "Not twofold," replied Damis, "for we ought to regard the former as the more perfect and more complete kind, being anyhow painting and a faculty of making likenesses with the help both of mind and hand; but we must regard the other kind as a department that, since its possessor perceives and imitates with the mind, without having the delineative faculty, and would never use his hand in depicting its objects." "Then," said Apollonius, "you mean, Damis, that the hand may be disabled by a blow or by disease?" "No," he answered, "but it is disabled, because it has never handled pencil nor any instrument or color, and has never learned to draw." "Then," said the other, "we are both of us, Damis, agreed that man owes his mimetic faculty to nature, but his power of painting to art. And the same would appear to be true of plastic art. But, methinks, you would not confine painting itself to the mere use of colors, for a single color was often found sufficient for this purpose by our older painters; and as the art advanced, it employed four, and later, yet more; but we must also concede the name of a painting to an outline drawn without any color at all, and composed merely of shadow and light. For in such designs we see a resemblance, we see form and expression, and modesty and bravery, although they are altogether devoid of color; and neither blood is represented, nor the color of a man's hair or beard; nevertheless these compositions in monochrome are likenesses of people either tawny or white, and if we drew one of these Indians with a pencil without color, yet he would be known for a negro, for his flat nose, and his stiff curling locks and prominent jaw, and a certain gleam about his eyes, would give a black look to the picture and depict an Indian to the eyes of all those who have intelligence. And for this reason I should say that those who look at works of painting and drawing require a mimetic faculty; for no one could appreciate or admire a picture of a horse or of a bull, unless he had formed an idea of the picture represented. Nor again could one admire a picture of Ajax, by the painter Timomachus, which represents him in a state of madness, unless one had conceived in one's mind first an idea or notion of Ajax, and had entertained the probability that after killing the flocks in Troy he would sit down exhausted and even meditate suicide. But these elaborate works of Porus we cannot, Damis, regard as works of brass founding alone, for they are cast in brass; so let us regard them as the *chefs d' œuvre* of a man who is both painter and brass-founder at once, and as similar to the work of Hephaestus upon the shield of Achilles, as revealed in Homer. For they are crowded together in that work too men slaying and slain, and you would say that the earth was stained with gore, though it is made of brass."

CHAPTER XXIII

WHILE the sage was engaged in this conversation, messengers and an interpreter presented themselves from the king, to say that the king would make him his guest for three days,[3] because the laws did not allow of strangers residing in the city for a longer time; and accordingly they conducted him into the palace. I have already described the way in which the city is walled, but they say that it was divided up into narrow streets in the same irregular manner as in Athens, and that the houses were built in such a way that if you look at them from outside they had only one story, while if you went into one of them, you at once found subterranean chambers extending as far below the level of the earth as did the chambers above.

CHAPTER XXIV

AND they say that they saw a Temple of the Sun in which was kept loose a sacred elephant called Ajax, and there were images of Alexander made of gold, and others of Porus, though the latter were of black bronze. But on the walls of the Temple there were red stones, and gold glittered underneath, and gave off a sheen as bright as sunlight. But the statue was compacted of pearls arranged in the symbolic manner affected by all barbarians in their shrines.

CHAPTER XXV

AND in the palace they say that they saw no magnificent chambers, nor any bodyguards or sentinels, but, considering what is usual in the houses of magnates, a few servants, and three or four people who wished, so I suppose, to converse with the king. And they say that they admired this arrangement more than they did the pompous splendor of Babylon, and their esteem was enhanced when they went within. For the men's chambers and the porticoes and the whole of the vestibule were in a very chaste style.

---

[3] Compare the proverb "Saepe dies post tres vilescit piscis et hospes," and cp. W. Robertson Smith, *Religion of the Semites*, 1901, p. 270.

CHAPTER XXVI

SO the Indian was regarded by Apollonius as a philosopher, and addressing him through an interpreter, he said: "I am delighted, O king, to find you living like a philosopher." "And, I" said the other, "am delighted that you should think of me thus." "And," said Apollonius, "is this customary among you, or was it you yourself established your government on so modest a scale?" "Our customs," said the king, "are dictated by moderation, and I am still more moderate in my carrying them out; and though I have more than other men, yet I want little, for I regard most things as belonging to my own friends." "Blessed are you then in your treasure," said Apollonius, "if you rate your friends more highly than gold and silver, for out of them grows up for you a harvest of blessings." "Nay more," said the king, "I share my wealth also with my enemies. For the barbarians who live on the border of this country were perpetually quarreling with us and making raids into my territories, but I keep them quiet and control them with money, so that my country is patrolled by them, and instead of their invading my dominions, they themselves keep off the barbarians that are on the other side of the frontier, and are difficult people to deal with." And when Apollonius asked him, whether Porus also had paid them subsidy, he replied: "Porus was as fond of war as I am of peace." By expressing such sentiments he quite disarmed Apollonius, who was so captivated by him, that once, when he was rebuking Euphrates for his want of philosophic self-respect, he remarked: "Nay, let us at least reverence Phraotes the Indian," for this was the name of the Indian. And when a satrap, for the great esteem in which he held the monarch, desired to bind on his brow a golden mitre adorned with various stones, he said: "Even if I were an admirer of such things, I should decline them now, and cast them off my head, because I have met with Apollonius. And how can I now adorn myself with ornaments which I never before deigned to bind upon my head, without ignoring my guest and forgetting myself?" Apollonius also asked him about his diet, and he replied: "I drink just as much wine as I pour out in libation to the Sun; and whatever I take in the chase I give to others to eat, for I am satisfied with the exercise I get. But my own meal consists of vegetables and of the pith and fruit of date palms, and of all that a well-watered garden yields in the way of fruit. And a great deal of fruit is yielded to me by the trees which I cultivate with these hands." When Apollonius heard this, he was more than gratified, and kept glancing at Damis.

CHAPTER XXVII

AND when they had conversed a good deal about which road to take to the Brahmans, the king ordered the guide from Babylon to be well entertained, as it was customary so to treat those who came from Babylon; and the guide from the satrap, to be dismissed after being given provisions for the road. Then he took Apollonius by the hand, and having bidden the interpreter to depart, he said: "You will then, I hope, choose me for your boon companion." And he asked question of him in the Greek tongue. But Apollonius was surprised, and remarked: "Why did you not converse with me thus, from the beginning?" "I was afraid," said the king, "of seeming presumptuous, seeming, that is, not to know myself and not to know that I am a barbarian by decree of fate; but you have won my affection, and as soon as I saw that you take pleasure in my society, I was unable to keep myself concealed. But that I am quite competent in the Greek speech I will show you amply." "Why then," said Apollonius, "did you not invite me to the banquet, instead of begging me to invite you?" "Because," he replied, "I regard you as my superior, for wisdom has more of the kingly quality about it." And with that he led him and his companions to where he was accustomed to bathe. And the bathing-place was a garden, a stade in length, in the middle of which was dug out a pool, which was fed by fountains of water, cold and drinkable; and on each side there were exercising places, in which he was accustomed to practice himself after the manner of the Greeks with javelin and quoit-throwing; for physically he was very robust, both because he was still young, for he was only seven-and-twenty years old, and because he trained himself in this way. And when he had had enough exercise, he would jump into the water and exercised himself in swimming. But when they had taken their bath, they proceeded into the banqueting chamber with wreaths upon their heads; for this is the custom of the Indians, whenever they drink wine in the palace.

CHAPTER XXVIII

AND I must on no account omit to describe the arrangement of the banquet, since this has been clearly described and recorded by

Damis. The king then banquets upon a mattress, and as many as five of his nearest relations with him; but all the rest join in the feast sitting upon chairs. And the table resembles an altar in that it is built up to the height of a man's knee in the middle of the chamber, and allows rooms for thirty to dispose themselves around it like a choir in a close circle. Upon it laurels are strewn, and other branches which are similar to the myrtle, but yield to the Indians their balm. Upon it are served up fish and birds, and there are also laid upon it whole lions and gazelles and swine and the loins of tigers; for they decline to eat the other parts of this animal, because they say that, as soon as it is born, it lifts up its front paws to the rising Sun. Next, the master of ceremonies rises and goes to the table, and he selects some of the viands for himself, and cuts off other portions, and then he goes back to his own chair and eats his full, constantly munching bread with it. And when they all have had enough, goblets of silver and gold are brought in, each of which is enough for ten banqueters, and out of these they drink, stooping down like animals that are being watered. And while they are drinking, they have brought in performers of various dangerous feats, not undeserving of serious study. For a boy, like one employed by dancing-girls, would be tossed lightly aloft, and at the same moment an arrow is aimed at him, up in the air, and when he was a long way from the ground, the boy would, by a tumblers' leap, raise himself above the weapon, and if he missed his leap, he was sure to be hit. For the archer, before he let fly, went round the banqueters and showed them the point of his weapon, and let them try the missile themselves. Shooting through a ring, too, or hitting a hair with an arrow, or for a man to mark the outline of his own son with arrows, as he stands in front of a board, keeps them occupied at their banquets, and they aim straight, even when they are drinking.

CHAPTER XXIX

WELL, the companions of Damis marveled at the accuracy of their eye, and were surprised at the exactness with which they aimed their weapons; but Apollonius, who ate with the king, since they agreed in diet, was less interested in these feats and said to the king: "Tell me, O King, how you acquired such a command of the Greek tongue, and whence you derived all your philosophical attainments in this place? For I don't imagine that you owe them to teachers, for it is not likely that there are, in India, any who could teach it." The king smiled and said:

"In old days they would ask men who arrived by sea whether they were pirates, so common did they consider that way of living, hard though it is; but so far as I can make out, you Greeks ask your visitors whether they are not philosophers, so convinced you are that everyone you meet with must needs possess the divinest of human attainments. And that philosophy and piracy are one and the same thing among you, I am well aware; for they say that a man like yourself is not to be found anywhere; but that most of your philosophers are like people who have despoiled another man of his garment and then have dressed themselves up in it, although it does not fit them, and proceed to strut about trailing another man's garment. Nay, by Zeus, just as robbers live in luxury, well knowing that they lie at the mercy of justice, so are they, it is said, addicted to gluttony and riotous living and to delicate apparel. And the reason is this: you have laws, I believe, to the effect that if a man is caught forging money, he must die, and the same if anyone illegally enrolls a child upon the register, or there is some penalty, I know not what; but people who utter counterfeit philosophy or corrupt her are not, I believe, restrained among you by any law, nor is there any authority set to suppress them.

CHAPTER XXX

NOW among us few engage in philosophy, and they are sifted and tried as follows: A young man so soon as he reaches the age of eighteen, and this I think is accounted the time of full age among you also, must pass across the river Hyphasis to the men who you are set upon visiting, after first making a public statement that he will become a philosopher, so that those who wish to may exclude him, if he does not approach the study in a state of purity. And by pure I mean, firstly, in respect of his parentage, that no disgraceful deed can be proved against either his father or his mother; next that their parents in turn, and the third generation upwards, are equally pure, that there was no ruffian among them, no debauchee, nor any unjust usurer. And when no scar or reproach can be proved against them, nor any other stain whatever, then it is time narrowly to inspect the young man himself and test him, to see firstly, whether he has a good memory, and secondly, whether he is modest and reserved in disposition, and does not merely pretend to be so, whether he is addicted to drink, or greed, or a quack, or a buffoon, or rash, or abusive, to see whether he is obedient to his father, to his mother, to his teachers, to his school-masters, and above all, if he makes no bad use of his personal attractions. The particulars then of his parents and of their progenitors are gathered from witnesses and from the public archives. For whenever an Indian dies, there visits his house a particular authority charged by the law to make a record of him, and of how he lived. And if this officer lies or allows himself to be deceived, he is condemned by the law and forbidden ever to hold another office, on the ground that he has counterfeited a man's life. But the particulars of the youths themselves are duly learnt by inspection of them. For in many cases a man's eyes reveal the secrets of his character, and in many cases there is material for forming a judgment and appraising his value in his eyebrows and cheeks, for from these features the dispositions of people can be detected by wise and scientific men, as images are seen in a looking-glass. For seeing that philosophy is highly esteemed in this country, and it is held in honor by the Indians, it is absolutely necessary that those who take to it should be tested and subjected to a thousand modes of proof. Well then, that we study philosophy under direction of teachers, and that admission to philosophy is by examination among us, I have clearly explained; and now I will relate to you my own history.

CHAPTER XXXI

MY grandfather was king, and had the same name as myself; but my father was a private person. For he was left quite young and two of his relations were appointed guardians in accordance with the laws of the Indians. But they did not carry on the king's government honestly on his behalf. No, by the Sun, but so unfairly that their subjects found their regime oppressive and the government fell into bad repute. A conspiracy then was formed against them by some of the magnates, who attacked them and slew them when they were sacrificing to the river Indus. The conspirators than seized upon the reins of government and took control of the State. Now my father's kinsmen entertained apprehensions of him, because he was not yet sixteen years of age, so they sent him across the Hyphasis to the king there. And he has more subjects than I have, and his country is much more fertile than this one. This monarch wished to adopt him, but this my father declined on the ground that he would not struggle with fate that robbed him of his kingdom; but he besought to allow him to take his way to the sages and become a philosopher, for he said that this would make it easier for him to bear the reverses of his house. The king however being anxious to restore him to his father's kingdom, my father said: "If you see that I am become a genuine philosopher, then restore me; but if not, let me remain as I am." The king accordingly went in person to the sages, and said that he would lie under great obligation to them if they would take care of a youth who had already showed such nobility of character, and they, discerning in him something out of the common run, were delighted to impart to him their wisdom, and were glad to educate him when they saw how addicted he was to learning. Now seven years afterwards the king fell sick, and at the very moment when he was dying, he sent for my father, and appointed him co-heir in the government with his own son, and promised his daughter in marriage to him as she was already of marriageable age. And my father, since he saw that the king's son was the victim of flatterers and of wine and of such like vices, and was also full of suspicions of himself, said to him: "Do you keep all this and swill down the whole Empire as your own; for it is ridiculous that one who could not even gain the kingdom which belonged to him should presume to meddle with one which does not; but give me your sister, for this is all I want of yours." So having obtained her in marriage he lived hard by the sage in seven fertile village which the king bestowed upon his sister as her pin-money. I then am the issue of this marriage, and my father after a Greek education brought me to the sages at an age somewhat too early perhaps, for I was only twelve at the time, but they brought me up like their own son; for any that they admit knowing the Greek tongue they are especially fond of, because they consider that in virtue of the similarity of his disposition he already belongs to themselves.

CHAPTER XXXII

AND when my parents had died, which they did almost together, the sages bade me repair to the villages and look after my own affairs, for I was now nineteen years of age. But, alas, my good uncle had already taken away the villages, and didn't even leave me the few acres my father had acquired; for he said that the whole of them belonged to his kingdom, and that I should get more than I deserved if he spared my life. I accordingly raised a subscription among my mother's freedmen, and kept four retainers. And one day when I was reading the play "The Children of Heracles," a man presented himself from my own country, bringing a letter from a person devoted to my father, who urged me to cross the river Hydraotes and confer with him about my present kingdom; for he said there was a good prospect of recovering it, if I did not dawdle. I cannot but think that some god set me on reading this drama at the moment, and I followed the omen; and having crossed the river I learnt that one of the usurpers of the throne was dead, and that the other was besieged in this very palace. Accordingly I hurried forward, and proclaimed to the inhabitants of the villages through which I passed that I was the sons of so and so, naming my father, and that I was come to take possession of my own kingdom; but they received me with open arms and escorted me, recognizing my resemblance to my grandfather, and they had daggers and bows, and our numbers increased from day to day. And when I approached the gates the population received me with such enthusiasm that they snatched up torches off the altar of the Sun and came before the gates and escorted me hither with many hymns in praise of my father and grandfather. But the drone that was within they walled up, although I protested against his being put to such death."

CHAPTER XXXIII

HERE Apollonius interrupted and said: "You have exactly played the part of the restored sons of Heracles in the play, and praised be the gods who have helped so noble a man to come by his own and restored you by their noble intervention. But tell me this about these sages: were they not once actually subject to Alexander, and were they not brought before him to philosophize about the heavens?" "Those were the Oxydracae," he said, "and a race that has always been independent and well equipped for war; and they assert that they deal in wisdom, though they know nothing of value. But the genuine sages live between the Hyphasis and the Ganges, in a country which Alexander never assailed; not I imagine because he was afraid of what was in it, but, I think, because the omens warned him against it. But if he had crossed the Hyphasis, and had been able to take the surrounding country, he could certainly never have taken possession of their castle in which they live, not even if he had had ten thousand like Achilles, and thirty thousand like Ajax behind him; for they do not do battle with those who approach them, but they repulse them with prodigies and thunderbolts which they send forth, for they are holy men and beloved of the gods. It is related, anyhow, that Heracles of Egypt and Dionysus after they had overrun the Indian people with their arms, at last attached them in company, and that they constructed engines of war, and tried to take the place by assault; but the sages, instead of taking the field against them, lay quiet and passive, as it seemed to the enemy; but as soon as the latter approached they were driven off by rockets of fire and thunderbolts which were hurled obliquely from above and fell upon their armor. It was on that occasion, they say, that Hercules lost his golden shield, and the sages dedicated it as an offering, partly out of respect for Hercules' reputation, and partly because of the reliefs upon the shield. For in these Hercules is represented fixing the frontier of the world at Gadira, and using the mountains for pillars, and confining the ocean within its bounds. Thence it is clear that it was not the Theban Hercules, but the Egyptian one, that came to Gadira, and fixed the limits of the world."

CHAPTER XXXIV

WHILE they were thus talking, the strain of the hymn sung to the pipe fell upon their ears, and Apollonius asked the king what was the meaning of their cheerful ode. "The Indians," he answered, "sing their admonitions to the king, at the moment of his going to bed; and they pray that he may have good dreams, and rise up propitious and affable towards his subjects." "And how," said Apollonius, "do you, O king, feel in regard to this matter? For it is yourself I suppose that they honor with their pipes." "I don't laugh at them," he said, "for I must allow it because of the law, although I do not require any admonition of the kind: for in so far as a king behaves himself with moderation and integrity, he will bestow, I imagine, favors on himself rather than on his subjects."

CHAPTER XXXV

AFTER this conversation they laid themselves down to repose; but when a new day had dawned, the king himself went to the chamber in which Apollonius and his companions were sleeping, and gently stroking the bed he addressed the sage, and asked him what he was thinking about. "For," he said, "I don't imagine you are asleep, since you drink water and despise wine." Said the other: "Then you don't think that those who drink water go to sleep?" "Yes," said the king, "they sleep, but with a very light sleep, which just sits upon the tips of their eyelids, as we say, but not upon their minds." "Nay with both do they sleep," said Apollonius, "and perhaps more with the mind than with the eyelids. For unless the mind is thoroughly composed, the eyes will not admit of sleep either. For note how madmen are not able to go to sleep because their mind leaps with excitement, and their thoughts run coursing hither and thither, so that their glances are full of fury and morbid impulse, like those of the dragons who never sleep. Since then, O king," he went on, "we have clearly intimated the use and function of sleep, and what it signifies for men, let us examine whether the drinker of water need sleep less soundly than the drunkard." "Do not quibble," said the king, "for if you put forward the case of a drunkard, he, I admit, will not sleep at all, for his mind is in a state of revel, and whirls him about and fills him with uproar. All, I tell you, who try to go to sleep when in drink seem to themselves to be rushed up on the roof, and then to be dashed down to the ground, and to fall into a whirl, as they say happened to Ixion. Now I do not put the case of a drunkard, but of a man who has merely drunk wine, but remains sober; I wish to consider whether he will sleep, and how much better he will sleep than a man who drinks no wine."

CHAPTER XXXVI

APOLLONIUS then summoned Damis, and said: "'tis a clever man with whom we are discussing and one thoroughly trained in argument." "I see it is so, " said Damis, "and perhaps this is what is meant by the phrase 'catching a Tartar'. But the argument excites me very much, of which he has delivered himself; so it is time for you to wake up and finish it." Apollonius then raised his head slightly and said: "Well I will prove, out of your own lips and following your own argument, how much advantage we who drink water have in that we sleep more sweetly. For you have clearly stated and admitted that the minds of drunkards are disordered and are in a condition of madness; for we see those who are under the spell of drink imagining that they see two moons at once and two suns, while those who have drunk less, even though they are quite sober, while they entertain no such delusions as these, are yet full of exultation and pleasure; and this fit of joy often falls upon them, even though they have not had any good luck, and men in such a condition will plead cases, although they never opened their lips before in a law court, and they will tell you they are rich, although they have not a farthing in their pockets. Now these, O king, are the affections of a madman. For the mere pleasure of drinking disturbs their judgment, and I have known many of them who were so firmly convinced that they were well off, that they were unable to sleep, but leapt up in their slumbers, and this is the meaning of the saying that 'good fortune itself is a reason for being anxious.' Men have also devised sleeping draughts, by drinking or anointing themselves with which, people at once stretch themselves out and go to sleep as if they were dead; but when they wake up from such sleep it is with a sort of forgetfulness, and they imagine that they are anywhere rather than where they are. Now these draughts are not exactly drunk, but I would rather say that they drench the soul and body; for they do not induce any sound or proper sleep, but the deep coma of a man half dead, or the light and distracted sleep of men haunted by phantoms, even though they be wholesome ones; and you will, I think, agree with me in this, unless you are disposed to quibble rather than argue seriously. But those who drink water, as I do see things as they really are, and they do not record in fancy things that are not; and they were never found to be giddy, nor full of drowsiness, or of silliness, nor unduly elated; but they are wide awake and thoroughly rational, and always the same, whether late in the evening or early in the morning when the market is crowded; for these men never nod, even though they pursue their studies far into the night. For sleep does not drive them forth, pressing down like a slave-holder upon their necks, that are bowed down by the wine; but you find them free and erect, and they go to bed with a clear, pure soul and welcome sleep, and are neither buoyed up by the bubbles of their own private luck, nor scared out of their wits by any adversity. For the soul meets both alternatives with equal calm, if it be sober and not overcome by either feeling; and that is why it can sleep a delightful sleep untouched by the sorrows which startle others from their couches.

CHAPTER XXXVII

AND more than this, as a faculty of divination by means of dreams, which is the divines and most godlike of human faculties, the soul detects the truth all the more easily when it is not muddied by wine, but accepts the message unstained and scans it carefully. Anyhow, the explains of dreams and visions, those whom the poets call interpreters of dreams, will never undertake to explain any vision to anyone without having first asked the time when it was seen. For if it was at dawn and in the sleep of morning tide, they calculate its meaning on the assumption that the soul is then in a condition to divine soundly and healthily, because by then it has cleansed itself of the stains of wine.

But if the vision was seen in the first sleep or at midnight, when the soul is still immersed in the lees of wine and muddied thereby, they decline to make any suggestions, and they are wise. And that the gods also are of this opinion, and that they commit the faculty of oracular response to souls which are sober, I will clearly show. There was, O king, a seer among the Greeks called Amphiaros." "I know," said the other; "for you allude, I imagine, to the son of Oecles, who was swallowed up alive by the earth on his way back from Thebes." "This man, O king," said Apollonius, "still divines in Attica, inducing dreams in those who consult him, and the priests take a man who wishes to consult him, and they prevent his eating for one day, and from drinking wine for three, in order that he may imbibe the oracles with his soul in a condition of utter transparency. But if wine were a good drug of sleep, then the wise Amphiaros would have bidden his votaries to adopt the opposite regimen, and would have had them carried into his shrine as full of wine as leather flagons. And I could mention many oracles, held in repute by Greeks and barbarians alike, where the priest utters his responses from the tripod after imbibing water and not wine. So you may consider me also as a fit vehicle of the god, O king, along with all who drink water. For we are rapt by the nymphs and are bacchantic revelers in sobriety." "Well, then," said the king, "you must make me too, O Apollonius, a member of your religious brotherhood." "I would do so," said the other, "provided only you will not be esteemed vulgar and held cheap by your subjects. For in the case of a king a philosophy that is at once moderate and indulgent makes a good mixture, as is seen in your own case; but an excess of rigor and severity would seem vulgar, O king, and beneath your august station; and, what is more, it might be construed by the envious as due to pride."

CHAPTER XXXVIII

WHEN they had thus conversed, for by this time it was daylight, they went out into the open. And Apollonius, understanding that the king had to give audience to embassies and such-like said: "You then, O king, must attend to the business of state, but let me go and devote this hour to the Sun, for I must needs offer up to him my accustomed prayer." "And I pray he may hear your prayer," said the king, "for he will bestow his grace on all who find pleasure in your wisdom; but I will wait for you until you return, for I have to decide some cases in which your presence will very greatly help me."

CHAPTER XXXIX

APOLLONIUS then returned, when the day was already for advanced and asked him about the cases which he had been judging; but he answered: "Today I have not judged any, for the omens did not allow me." Apollonius then replied and said: "It is the case then that you consult the omens in such cases as these, just as you do when you are setting out on a journey or a campaign." "Yes, by Zeus," he said, "for there is a risk in this case, too, of one who is a judge straying from the right line." Apollonius felt that what he said was true, and asked him again what the suit was which he had to decide; "For I see," he said, "that you have given your attention to it and are perplexed what verdict to give." "I admit," said the king, "that I am perplexed; and that is why I want your advice; for one man has sold to another land, in which there lay a treasure as yet undiscovered, and some time afterwards the land, being broken up, revealed a certain chest, which the person who sold the land says belongs to him rather than the other, for that he would never have sold the land, if he had known beforehand that he had a fortune thereon; but the purchaser claims that he acquired everything that he found in land, which thenceforth was his. And, both their contentions are just; and I shall seem ridiculous if I order them to share the gold between them, for any old woman could settle the matter in that way." Apollonius thereupon replied as follows: "The fact that they are quarreling about gold shows that these two men are no philosophers; and you will, in my opinion, give the best verdict if you bear this in mind, that the gods attach the first importance and have most care for those who live a life of philosophy together with moral excellence, and only pay secondary attention to those who have committed no faults and were never found unjust. Now they entrust to philosophers the task of rightly discerning things divine and human as they should be discerned, but to those who merely are of good character they give enough to live upon, so hat they may never be rendered unjust by actual lack of the necessaries of life. It seems then to me, O king, right to weight these men in the balance, as it were, and to examine their respective lives; for I cannot believe that the gods would deprive the one even of his land, unless he was a bad man, or that they would, on the other hand, bestow on the other even what was under the land, unless he was better than the man who sold it." The two claimants came back the next day, and the seller was convicted of being a ruffian who had neglected the sacrifices, which it was his bounden duty to sacrifice to the gods on that land[4]; but the other was found to be a decent man and a most devout worshipper of the gods. Accordingly, the opinion of Apollonius prevailed, and the better of the two men quitted the court as one on whom the gods had bestowed this boon.

CHAPTER XL

WHEN the law-suit had been thus disposed of, Apollonius approached the Indian, and said: " This the third day, O king, that you have made me your guest; and at dawn to-morrow I must quit your land in accordance with the law." "But," said the other, " the law does not yet speak to you thus, for you can remain on the morrow, since you came after midday." "I am delighted," said Apollonius, "with your hospitality, and indeed you seem to me to be straining the law for my sake." "Yes indeed, and I would I could break it," said the king, "in your behalf; but tell me this, Apollonius, did not the camels bring you from Babylon which they say you were riding?" "They did," he said, "and Vardanes gave them us." "Will they then be able to carry you on, after they have come already so many stades from Babylon?" Apollonius made no answer, but Damis said: "O king, our friend here does not understand anything about our journey, nor about the races among which we shall find ourselves in future; but he regards our passage into India as mere child's play, under the impression that he will everywhere have you and Vardanes to help him. I assure you, the true condition of the camels has not been acknowledged to you; for they are in such an evil state that we could carry them rather than they us, and we must have others. For if they collapse anywhere in the wilderness of India, we," he continued, "shall have to sit down and drive off the vultures and wolves from the camels, and as no one will drive them off from us we shall perish too." The king answered accordingly and said: "I will remedy this, for I will give you other camels, and you need four I think, and the satrap ruling the Indus will send back four others to Babylon. But I have a herd of camels on the Indus, all of them white." "And," said Damis, "will you not also give us a guide, O king?" "Yes, of course," he answered, "and I will give a camel to the guide and provisions, and I will write a letter to Iarchas, the oldest of the sages, praying him to welcome Apollonius as warmly as he did myself, and to

---

[4] Or render: the gods of the underworld.

welcome you also as philosophers and followers of a divine man." And forthwith the Indian gave them gold and precious stones and linen and a thousand other such things. And Apollonius said that he had enough gold already, because Vardanes had given it to the guide on the sly; but that he would accept the linen robes, because they were like the cloaks worn by the ancient and genuine inhabitants of Attica. And he took up one of the stones and said: "O rare stone, how opportunely have I found you, and how providentially!" detecting in it, I imagine, some secret and divine virtue. Neither would the companions of Damis accept for themselves the gold; nevertheless they took good handfuls of the gems, in order to dedicate them to the gods, whenever they should regain their own country.

CHAPTER XLI

SO they remained the next day as well, for Indian would not let them go, and he gave them a letter for Iarchas, written in the following terms:—

"King Phroates to Iarchas his master and to his companions, all hail!

Apollonius, wisest of men, yet accounts you still wiser than himself, and is come to learn your lore. Send him away therefore when he knows all that you know yourselves, assured that nothing of your teachings will perish, for in discourse and memory he excels all men. And let him also see the throne, on which I sat, when you, Father Iarchas, bestowed on me the kingdom. And his followers too deserve commendation for their devotion to such a master. Farewell to yourself and your companions."

CHAPTER XLII

AND they rode out of Taxila, and after a journey of two days reached the plain, in which Porus is said to have engaged Alexander: and they say they saw gates therein that enclosed nothing, but had been erected to carry trophies. For there was set up on them a statue of Alexander standing in a four-poled chariot,[5] as he looked when at Issus he confronted the satraps of Darius. And at a short distance from one another there are said to have been built two gates, carrying the one a

---

[5] *i.e.* with eight horses.

statue of Porus, and the other one of Alexander, of both, as I imagine, reconciled to one another after the battle; for the one is in the attitude of one man greeting another, and the other of one doing homage.

CHAPTER XLIII

AND having crossed the river Hydraotes and passed by several tribes, they reached the Hyphasis, and thirty stades away from this they came on altars bearing this inscription: "To Father Ammon and Heracles his brother, and to Athena Providence and to Zeus of Olympus and to the Cabeiri of Samothrace and to the Indian Sun and to the Delphian Apollo."

And they say there was also a brass column dedicated, and inscribed as follows:

"Alexander stayed his steps at this point." The altars we may suppose to be due to Alexander who so honored the limit of his Empire; but I fancy the Indians beyond the Hyphasis erected the column, by way of expressing their pride at Alexander's having gone no further.

BOOK III

CHAPTER I

It is now time to notice the river Hyphasis, and to ask what is its size as it traverses India, and, what remarkable features it possesses. The springs of this river well forth out of the plain, and close to its source its streams are navigable, but as they advance they soon become impossible for boats, because spits of rock alternating with one another, rise up just below the surface; round these the current winds of necessity, so rendering the river unnavigable. And in breadth it approaches to the river Ister, and this is allowed to be the greatest of all the rivers which flow through Europe. Now the woods along the bank closely resemble those of the river in question, and a balm also is distilled from the trees, out of which the Indians make a nuptial ointment; and unless the people attending the wedding have besprinkled the young couple with this balm, the union is not considered complete nor compatible with Aphrodite bestowing her grace upon it. Now they say that the grove in the neighborhood of the river is dedicated to this goddess, as also the fishes called peacock fish which are bred in this river alone, and which have been given the same name as the bird, because their fins are blue, and their scales spotty, and their tails golden, and because they can fold and spread the latter at will. There is also a creature in this river which resembles a white worm. By melting down they make an oil, and from this oil, it appears, there is given off a flame such that nothing but glass can contain it. And this creature may be caught by the king alone, who utilizes it for the capture of cities; for as soon as the fat in question touches the battlements, a fire is kindled which defies all the ordinary means devised by men against combustibles.

CHAPTER II

AND they say that wild asses are also to be captured in these marshes, and these creatures have a horn upon the forehead, with which they butt like a bull and make a noble fight of it; the Indians make this horn into a cup, for they declare that no one can ever fall sick on the day on which he has drunk out of it, nor will any one who has done so be the worse for being wounded, and he will be able to pass through fire unscathed, and he is even immune from poisonous draughts which others would drink to their harm. Accordingly, this goblet is reserved for kings, and the king alone may indulge in the chase of this creature. And Apollonius says that he saw this animal, and admired its natural features; but when Damis asked him if he believed the story about the goblet, he answered: "I will believe it, if I find the king of the Indians hereabout to be immortal; for surely a man who can offer me or anyone else a draught potent against disease and so wholesome, will he not be much more likely to imbibe it himself, and take a drink out of this horn every day even at the risk of intoxication? For no one, I conceive, would blame him for exceeding in such cups."

CHAPTER III

AT this place they say that they also fell in with a woman who was black from her head to her bosom, but was altogether white from her bosom down to her feet; and the rest of the party fled from her believing her to be a monster, but Apollonius clasped the woman by the hand and understood what she was; for in fact such a woman in India is consecrated to Aphrodite, and a woman is born piebald in honor of this goddess, just as is Apis among the Egyptians.

CHAPTER IV

THEY say that from this point they crossed the part of the Caucasus which stretches down to the Red Sea; and this range is thickly overgrown with aromatic shrubs. The spurs then of the mountain bear the cinnamon tree, which resembles the young tendrils of the vine, and the goat gives sure indication of this aromatic shrub; for if you hold out a bit of cinnamon to a goat, she will whine and whimper after your hand like a dog, and will follow you when you go away, pressing her nose against it; and if the goat herd drags her away, she will moan as if she were being torn away from the lotus. But on the steeps of this mountain there grow very lofty frankincense trees, as well as many other species, for example the pepper trees which are cultivated by the apes. Nor did they neglect to record the look and appearance of this tree, and I will repeat exactly their account of it. The pepper tree resembles in general the willow of the Greeks, and particularly in regard to the berry of the fruit; and it grows in steep ravines where it cannot be got at by men, and where a community of apes is said to live in the recesses of the mountain and in any of its glens; and these apes are held in great esteem by the Indians, because they harvest the pepper for them, and they drive the lions off them with dogs and weapons. For the lion, when he is sick, attacks the ape in order to get a remedy, for the flesh of the ape stays the course of his disease; and he attacks it when he is grown old to get a meal, for the lions when they are past hunting stags and wild boars gobble up the apes, and husband for their pursuit whatever strength they have left. The inhabitants of the country, however, are not disposed to allow this, because they regard these animals as their benefactors, and so make war against the lions in behalf of them. For this is the way they go to work in collecting the pepper; the Indians go up to the lower trees and pluck off the fruit, and they make little round shallow pits around the trees, into which they collect the pepper, carelessly tossing it in, as if it had no value and was of no serious use to mankind. Then the monkeys mark their actions from above out of their fastnesses, and when the night comes on they imitate the action of the Indians, and twisting off the twigs of the trees, they bring and throw them into the pits in question; then the Indians at daybreak carry away the heaps of the spice which they have thus got without any trouble, and indeed during the repose of slumber.

CHAPTER V

AFTER crossing the top of the mountain, they say they saw a smooth plain seamed with cuts and ditches full of water, some of which were carried crosswise, whilst others were straight; these are derived from the river Ganges, and serve both for boundaries and also are distributed over the plain, when the soil is dry. But they say that this soil is the best in India, and constitutes the greatest of the territorial divisions of that country, extending in length towards the Ganges a journey of fifteen days and of eighteen from the sea to the mountain of the apes along which it skirts. The whole soil of the plain is a dead level, black and fertile of everything; for you can see on it standing grain as high as reeds and you can also see beans three times as large as the Egyptian kind, as well as sesame and millet of enormous size. And they say that nuts also grow there, of which many are treasured up in our temples here as objects of curiosity. But the vines which grow there are small, like those of the Lydians and Maeones; their vintage however is not only drinkable, but has a fine bouquet from the first. They also say that they came upon a tree there resembling the laurel, upon which there grew a cup or husk resembling a very large pomegranate; and inside the cup there was a kernel as blue as the cups of the hyacinth, but sweeter to the taste than any of the fruits the seasons bring.

CHAPTER VI

NOW as they descended the mountain, they say they came in for a dragon hunt, which I must needs describe. For it is utterly absurd for those who are amateurs of hare-hunting to spin yarns about the hare as to how it is caught or ought to be caught, and yet that we should omit to describe a chase as bold as it is wonderful, and in which the sage, of whom I have written this account, was careful to set on record: The whole of India is girt with dragons of enormous size; for not only the marshes are full of them, but the mountains as well, and there is not a single ridge without one. Now the marsh kind are sluggish in their habits and are thirty cubits long, and they have no crest standing up on their heads, but in this respect resemble the she-dragons. Their backs however are very black, with fewer scales on them than the other kinds; and Homer has described them with deeper insight than have most poets, for he says that the dragon that lived hard by the spring in Aulis had a tawny back; but other poets declare that the congener of this one in the grove of Nemea also had a crest, a feature which we could not verify in regard to the marsh dragons.

CHAPTER VII

AND the dragons along the foothills and the mountain crests make their way into the plains after their quarry, and get the better all round of those in the marshes; for indeed they reach a greater length, and move faster than the swiftest rivers, so that nothing escapes them. These actually have a crest, of moderate extent and height when they are young; but as they reach their full size, it grows with them and extends to a considerable height, at which time also they turn red and get serrated backs. This kind also have beards, and lift their necks on high, while their scales glitter like silver; and the pupils of their eyes consist of a fiery stone, and they say that this has an uncanny power for many secret purposes. The plain specimen falls the prize of the hunters whenever it draws into its folds an elephant; for the destruction of both creatures is the result, and those who capture the dragons are rewarded by getting the eyes and skin and teeth. In most respects the tusks resemble the largest swine's, but they are slighter in build and twisted, and have a point as unabraded as sharks' teeth.

CHAPTER VIII

Now the dragons of the mountains have scales of a golden color, and in length excel those of the plain, and they have bushy beards, which also are of a golden hue; and their eyebrows are more prominent than those of the plain, and their eye is sunk deep under the eyebrow, and emits a terrible and ruthless glance. And they give off a noise like the clashing of brass whenever they are burrowing under the earth, and from their crests, which are all fiery red, there flashes a fire brighter than a torch. They also can catch the elephants, though they are themselves caught by the Indians in the following manner. They embroider golden runes on a scarlet cloak, which they lay in front of the animal's burrow after charming them the runes to cause sleep; for this is the only way to overcome the eyes of the dragon, which are otherwise inflexible, and much mysterious lore is sung by them to overcome him. These runes induce the dragon to stretch his neck out of his burrow and fall asleep over them: then the Indians fall upon him as he lies there, and dispatch him with blows of their axes, and having cut off the head they despoil it of its gems. And they say that in the heads of the mountain dragons there are stored away stones of flowery color, which flash out all kinds of hues, and possess a mystical power as resided in the ring, which they say belonged to Gyges. But often the Indian, in spite of his axe and his cunning, is caught by the dragon, who carries him off into his burrow, and almost shakes the mountains as he disappears. These are also said to inhabit the mountains in the neighborhood of the Red Sea, and they say that they heard them hissing terribly and that they saw them go down to the shore and swim far out into the sea. It was impossible however to ascertain the number of years that this creature lives, nor would my statements be believed. This is all I know about dragons.

CHAPTER IX

THEY tell us that the city under the mountain is of great size and is called Paraca, and that in the center of it are enshrined a great many heads of dragons, for the Indians who inhabit it are trained from their boyhood in this form of sport. And they are also said to acquire an understanding of the language and ideas of animals by feeding either on the heart or the liver of the dragon. And as they advanced they thought they heard the pipe of some shepherd marshaling his flock, but it turned out to be a man looking after a herd of white hinds, for the Indians use these for milking, and find their milk very nutritious.

CHAPTER X

FROM this point their road led for four days across a rich and well cultivated country, till they approached the castle of the sages, when their guide bade his camel crouch down, and leapt off it in such an agony of fear that he was bathed in perspiration. Apollonius however quite understood where he was come to, and smiling at the panic of the Indian, said: "It seems to me that this fellow, were he a mariner who had reached harbor after a long sea voyage, would worry at being on land and tremble at being in dock." And as he said this he ordered his camel to kneel down, for indeed he was by now well accustomed to do so. And it seems that what scared the guide so much was that he was now close to the sages; for the Indians fear these people more than they do their own king, because the very king to whom the land is subject consults them about everything that he has to say or do, just as people who send to an oracle of a god; and the sages indicate to him what it is expedient for him to do, and what is inexpedient, and dissuade and warn him off with signs from what is inexpedient.

CHAPTER XI

AND they were about to halt in the neighboring village, which is hardly distant a single stade from the eminence occupied by the sages, when they saw a youth run up to them, the blackest Indian they ever saw; and between his eyebrows was a crescent shaped spot which shone brightly. But I learn that at a later time the same feature was remarked in the case of Menon the pupil of Herod the Sophist, who was an Ethiop; it showed while he was a youth, but as he grew up to man's estate its splendor waned and finally disappeared with his youth. But the Indian also wore, they say, a golden anchor, which is affected by Indians as a herald's badge, because it holds all things fast.

CHAPTER XII

THEN he ran up to Apollonius and addressed him in the Greek tongue; and so far this did not seem so remarkable, because all the inhabitants of the village spoke the Greek tongue. But when he addressed him by name and said " Hail so and so," the rest of the party were filled with astonishment, though our sage only felt the more confidence in his mission: for he looked to Damis and said: "We have reached men who are unfeignedly wise, for they seem to have the gift of foreknowledge." And he at once asked the Indian what he must do, because he was already eager for an interview: and the Indian replied: "Your party must halt here, but you must come on just as you are, for the Masters themselves issue this command."

CHAPTER XIII

THE word *Masters* at once had a Pythagorean ring for the ears of Apollonius and he gladly followed the messenger.

Now the hill the summit of which is inhabited by the sages is, according to the account of our travelers, of about the same height as the Acropolis of Athens; and it rises straight up from the plain, though its natural position equally secures it from attack, for the rock surrounds it on all sides. On many parts of this rock you see traces of cloven feet and outlines of beards and of faces, and here and there impressions of backs as of persons who had slipped and rolled down. For they say that Dionysus, when he was trying to storm the place together with Heracles, ordered the Pans to attack it, thinking that they would be strong enough to stand the shock; but they were thunderstruck by the sages and fell one, one way, and another, another; and the rocks as it were took the print of the various postures in which they fell and failed. And they say that they saw a cloud floating round the eminence on which the Indians live and render themselves visible or invisible at will. Whether there were any other gates to the eminence they say they did not know; for the cloud around it did not anywhere allow them to be seen, whether there was an opening in the rampart, or whether on the other hand it was a close-shut fortress.

CHAPTER XIV

APOLLONIUS says that he himself ascended mostly on the south side of the ridge, following the Indian, and that the first thing he saw was a well four fathoms deep, above the mouth of which there rose a sheen of deep blue light; and at midday when the sun was stationary about it, the sheen of light was always drawn up on high by the rays, and in its ascent assumed the look of a glowing rainbow. But he learnt afterwards that the soil underneath the well was composed of realgar, but that they regarded the water as holy and mysterious, and no one either drank it or drew it up, but it was regarded by the whole land of India all around as binding in oaths. And near this there was a crater, he says, of fire, which sent up a lead-colored flame, though it emitted no smoke or any smell, nor did this crater ever overflow, but emitted just matter enough not to bubble over the edges of the pit. It is here that the Indians purify themselves of involuntary sins, wherefore the sages call the well, the well of testing, and the fire, the fire of pardon. And they say that they saw there two jars of black stone, of the rains and of the winds respectively. The jar of the rains, they say, is opened in case the land of India is suffering from drought, and sends up clouds to moisten the whole country; but if the rains should be in excess they are stopped by the jar being shut up. But the jar of the winds plays, I imagine, the same role as the bag of Aeolus: for when they open this jar ever so little, they let out one of the winds, which creates a seasonable breeze by which the country is refreshed. And they say that they came upon statues of Gods, and they were not nearly so much astonished at finding Indian or Egyptian Gods as they were by finding the most ancient of the Greek Gods, a statue of Athena Polias and of Apollo of Delos and of Dionysus of Limnae and another of him of Amyclae, and others of similar age. These were set up by these Indians and worshipped with Greek rites. And they say that they are inhabiting the heart of India, as they regard the mound as the navel of this hill, and on it they worship fire with mysterious rites, deriving the fire, according to their own account, from the rays of the sun; and to the Sun they sing a hymn every day at midday.

CHAPTER XV

APOLLONIUS himself describes the character of these sages and of their settlement upon the hill; for in one of his addresses to the

Egyptians he says, "I saw Indian Brahmans living upon the earth and yet not on it, and fortified without fortifications, and possessing nothing, yet having the riches of all men." He may indeed be thought to have here written with too much subtlety; but we have anyhow the account of Damis to effect that they made a practice of sleeping the ground, and that they strewed the ground with such grass as they might themselves prefer; and, what is more, he says that he saw them levitating themselves two cubits high from the ground, not for the sake of miraculous display, for they disdain any such ambition; but they regard any rites they perform, in thus quitting earth and walking with the Sun, as acts of homage acceptable to the God. Moreover, they neither burn upon an altar nor keep in stoves the fire which they extract from the sun's rays, although it is a material fire; but like the rays of sunlight when they are refracted in water, so this fire is seen raised aloft in the air and dancing in the ether. And further they pray to the Sun who governs the seasons by his might, that the latter may succeed duly in the land, so that India may prosper; but of a night they intreat the ray of light not to take the night amiss, but. to stay with them just as they have brought it down. Such then was the meaning of the phrase of Apollonius, that "the Brahmans are upon earth and yet not upon earth." And his phrase "fortified without fortifications or walls," refers to the air or vapor under which they bivouac, for though they seem to live in the open air, yet they raise up a shadow and veil themselves in it, so that they are not made wet when it rains and they enjoy the sunlight whenever they choose. And the phrase "without possessing anything they had the riches of all men," is thus explained by Damis: All the springs which the Bacchanals see leaping up from the ground under their feet, whenever Dionysus stirs them and earth in a common convulsion, spring up in plenty for these Indians also when they are entertaining or being entertained. Apollonius therefore was right in saying that people provided as they are with all they want offhand and without having prepared anything, possess what they do not possess. And on principle they grow their hair long, as the Lacedaemonians did of old and the people of Thurium and Tarentum, as well as the Melians and all who set store by the fashions of Sparta; and they bind a white turban on their heads, and their feet are naked for walking and they cut their garments to resemble the *exomis* [6]. But the material of which they make

---

[6] An overmantle leaving one arm and shoulder bare. Buddhist monks still wear a similar garment. The so-called wool was asbestos.

their raiment is a wool that springs wild from the ground, white like that of the Pamphylians, though it is of softer growth, and a grease like olive oil distills from off it. This is what they make their sacred vesture of, and if anyone else except these Indians tries to pluck it up, the earth refuses to surrender its wool. And they all carry both a ring and a staff of which the peculiar virtues can effect all things, and the one and the other, so we learn, are prized as secrets.

CHAPTER XVI

WHEN Apollonius approached, the rest of the sages welcomed him and shook hands; but Iarchas sat down on a high stool—and this was of black copper and chased with golden figures, while the seats of the others were of copper, but plain and not so high, for they sat lower down than Iarchas—and when he saw Apollonius, Iarchas greeted him in the Greek tongue and asked for the Indian's letter. And as Apollonius showed astonishment at his gift of prescience, he took pains to add that a single letter was missing in the epistle, namely a *delta*, which had escaped the writer; and this was found to be the case. Then having read the epistle, he said " What do you think of us, O Apollonius? " "Why," replied the latter, "how can you ask, when it is sufficiently shown by the fact that I have taken a Jamey to see you which was never till now accomplished by any of the inhabitants of my country." "And what do you think we know more than yourself?" "I," replied the other, "consider that your lore is profounder and much more divine than our own; and if I add nothing to my present stock of knowledge while I am with you, I shall at least have learned that I have nothing more to learn." Thereupon the Indian replied and said: "Other people ask those who arrive among them, who they are that come, and why, but the first display we make of our wisdom consists in showing that we are not ignorant who it is that comes. And you may test this point to begin with." And to suit his word he forthwith recounted the whole story of Apollonius' family both on his father's and his mother's side, and he related all his life in Aegae, and how Damis had joined him, and any conversations that they had had on the road, and anything they had found out through the conversation of others with them. All this, just as if he had shared their voyage with them, the Indian recounted straight off, quite clearly and without pausing for breath. And when Apollonius was astounded and asked him how he came to know it all, he replied: "And you too are come to share in this wisdom, but you are not yet an adept." "Will you teach me, then," said the other, "all this wisdom?" "Aye, and gladly, for that is a wiser course than grudging and hiding matters of interest; and moreover, O Apollonius, I perceive that you are well endowed with memory, a goddess whom we love more than any other of the divine beings." "Well," said the other, "you have certainly discerned by your penetration my exact disposition." "We," said the other, "O Apollonius, can see all spiritual traits, for we trace and detect them by a thousand signs. But as it is nearly midday, and we must get ready our offerings for the Gods, let us now employ ourselves with that, and afterwards let us converse as much as you like; but you must take part in all our religious rites." "By Zeus," said Apollonius, "I should be wronging the Caucasus and the Indus, both of which I have crossed in order to reach you, if I did not feast myself on your rites to the full." "Do so," said the other, "and let us depart."

CHAPTER XVII

ACCORDINGLY they betook themselves to a spring of water, which Damis, who saw it subsequently, says resembles that of Dirce in Boeotia; and first they stripped, and then they anointed their heads with an amber-like drug, which imparted such a warmth to these Indians, that their bodies steamed and the sweat ran off them as profusely as if they were washing themselves with fire; next they threw themselves into the water and, having so taken their bath, they betook themselves to the temple with wreaths upon their heads and full of sacred song. And they stood round in the form of a chorus, and having chosen Iarchas as conductor they struck the earth, uplifting their rods, and the earth arched itself like a billow of the sea and raised them up two cubits high into the air. But they sang a song resembling the paean of Sophocles which they sing at Athens in honor of Asclepius. But when they had alighted upon the ground, Iarchas called the stripling who carried the anchor and said: "Do you look after the companions of Apollonius." And he went off swifter than the quickest of the birds, and coming back again said: "I have looked after them." Having fulfilled then the most of their religious rites, they sat down to rest upon their seats, but Iarchas said to the stripling: "Bring out the throne of Phraotes for the wise Apollonius that he may sit upon it to converse with us."

CHAPTER XVIII

And when he had taken his seat, he said: "Ask whatever you like, for you find yourself among people who know everything." Apollonius then asked him whether they knew themselves also, thinking that he, like the Greeks, would regard self-knowledge as a difficult matter. But the other, contrary to Apollonius' expectations, corrected him and said: "We know everything, just because we begin by knowing ourselves; for no one of us would be admitted to this philosophy unless he first knew himself." And Apollonius remembered what he had heard Phraotes say, and how he who would become a philosopher must examine himself before he undertakes the task; and he therefore acquiesced in this answer, for he was convinced of its truth in his own case also. He accordingly asked a fresh question, namely, who they considered themselves to be; and the other answered "We consider ourselves to be Gods." Apollonius asked afresh: "Why?" "Because," said the other, "we are good men." This reply struck Apollonius as so instinct with trained good sense that he subsequently mentioned it to Domitian in his defense of himself.

CHAPTER XIX

HE therefore resumed his questions and said: "And what view do you take of the soul?" "That," replied the other, "which Pythagoras imparted to you, and which we imparted to the Egyptians." "Would you then say," said Apollonius, "that as Pythagoras declared himself to be Euphorbus, so you yourself, before you entered your present body, were one of the Trojans or Achaeans or someone else?" And the Indian replied: "Those Achaean sailors were the ruin of Troy, and your talking so much about it is the ruin of you Greeks. For you imagine that the campaigners against Troy were the only heroes that ever were, and you forget other heroes both more numerous and more divine, whom your own country and that of the Egyptians and that of the Indians have produced. Since then you have asked me about my earlier incarnation, tell me, whom you regard as the most remarkable of the assailants or defenders of Troy." "I," replied Apollonius, "regard Achilles, the son of Peleus and Thetis, as such, for he and no other is celebrated by Homer as excelling all the Achaeans in personal beauty and size, and he knows of mighty deeds of his. And he also rates very highly such men as Ajax and Nireus, who were only second to him in beauty and courage, and are celebrated as such in his poems." "With him," said the other, "O Apollonius, I would have you compare my own ancestor, or rather my ancestral body, for that was the light in which Pythagoras regarded Euphorbus.

CHAPTER XX

"THERE was then," he said, "a time when the Ethiopians, an Indian race, dwelt in this country, and when Ethiopia as yet was not; but Egypt stretched its borders beyond Meroe and the cataracts, and on the one side included in itself the fountains of the Nile, and on the other was only bounded by the mouths of the river. Well, at that time of which I speak, the Ethiopians lived here, and were subject to King Ganges, and the land was sufficient for their sustenance, and the gods watched over them; but when they slew this king, neither did the rest of the Indians regard them as pure, nor did the land permit them to remain upon it; for it spoiled the seed which they sowed in it before it came into ear, and it inflicted miscarriages on their women, and it gave a miserable feed to their flocks; and wherever they tried to found a city, it would give way sink down under their feet. Nay more, the ghost of Ganges drove them forward on their path, a haunting terror to their multitude, and it did not quit them until they atoned to earth by sacrificing the murderers who had shed the king's blood with their hands. Now this Ganges it seems, was ten cubits high, and in personal beauty excelled any man the world had yet seen, and he was the son of the river Ganges; and when his own father inundated India, he himself turned the flood into the Red Sea, and effected a reconciliation between his father and the land, with the result that the latter brought forth fruits in abundance for him when living, and also avenged him after death. And since Homer brings Achilles to Troy in Helen's behalf, and relates how he took twelve cities by sea and eleven on land, and how he was carried away by wrath because he had been robbed of a woman by the king, on which occasion, in my opinion, he showed himself merciless and cruel, let us contrast the Indian in similar circumstances. He on the contrary set himself to found sixty cities, which are the most considerable of those hereabouts—and I would like to know who would regard the destruction of cities as a better title to fame than the rebuilding of them—and he also repulsed the Scythians who once invaded this land across the Caucasus. Surely it is better to prove yourself a good man by liberating your country than to bring slavery upon a city, and that too on behalf of a woman who probably was never really carried off against her will. And he had formed an alliance with the king of the country, over which Phraotes now rules, although that other had violated every law and principle of morality by carrying of his wife, he yet did not break his oath, and so stable, he said, was his pledged word, that, in spite of the injury he had suffered, he would not do anything to harm that other.

CHAPTER XXI

"AND I could enumerate many more merits of this great man, if I did not shrink from pronouncing a panegyric upon myself; for I may tell you I am the person in question, as I clearly proved when I was four years old. For this Ganges on one occasion fixed seven swords made of adamant in the earth, to prevent any monster approaching our country; now the gods ordered us to sacrifice if we came where he had implanted these weapons, though without indicating the spot where he had fixed them. I was a mere child, and yet I led the interpreters of their will to a trench, and told them to dig there, for it was there I said that they had been laid.

CHAPTER XXII

"AND you must not be surprised at my transformation from one Indian to another; for here is one," and he pointed to a stripling of about twenty years of age, "who in natural aptitude for philosophy excels everyone, and he enjoys good health as you see, and is furnished with an excellent constitution; moreover he can endure fire and all sorts of cutting and wounding, yet in spite of all these advantages he detests philosophy." "What then," said Apollonius, "O Iarchas, is the matter with the youth? For it is a terrible thing you tell me, if one so well adapted by nature to the pursuit refuses to embrace philosophy, and has no love for learning, and that although he lives with you." "He does not live with us," replied the other, "but he has been caught like a lion against his will, and confined here, but he looks askance, at us when we try to domesticate him and caress him. The truth is this stripling was once Palamedes of Troy, and he found his bitterest enemies in Odysseus and Homer; for the one laid an ambush against him of people by whom he was stoned to death, while the other denied him any place in his Epic; and because neither the wisdom with which he was endowed was of any use to him, nor did he meet with any praise from Homer, to whom nevertheless many people of no great importance owe their renown, and because he was outwitted by Odysseus in spite of his innocence, he has conceived an aversion to philosophy, and deplores his ill-luck. And he is Palamedes, for indeed he can write without having learned his letters."

CHAPTER XXIII

WHILE they were thus conversing, a messenger approached Iarchas and said: "The King will come early in the afternoon to consult you about his own business." And Iarchas replied: "Let him come, for he too will go away all the better for making acquaintance of a man from Hellas." And after this, he went on with his former discourse. He accordingly asked Apollonius the question: "Will you tell us," he said, "about your earlier incarnation, and who you were before the present life?" And he replied: "Since it was an ignoble episode, I do not remember much of it." Iarchas therefore took him up and said: "Then you think it ignoble to have been the pilot of an Egyptian vessel, for I perceive that this is what you were?" "What you say," said Apollonius, "is true, Iarchas; for that is really what I was; but I consider this profession not only inglorious but also detestable, and though of as much value to humanity as that of a prince or the leader of an army, nevertheless it bears an evil repute by the reason of those who follow the sea; at any rate the most noble of the deeds which I performed no one at the time saw fit to praise." "Well, and what would you claim for yourself in the way of noble achievement? Is it your having doubled the capes of Malea and Sunium, by checking your ship when it was drifting out of its course, and your having discerned so accurately the quarters from which the winds would blow both fore and aft, or you getting your boat past the reefs in the Hollows of Euboea, where any number of ships' ornamental signs show sticking up?"

CHAPTER XXIV

BUT Apollonius replied: "Since you tempt me to talk about pilotage, I would have you hear what I consider to have been my soundest exploit at that time. Pirates at one time infested the Phoenician Sea, and were hanging about the cities to pick up information about the cargoes which different people had. The agents of the pirates spied out accordingly a rich cargo which I had on board my ship, and having taken me aside in conversation, asked me what was my share in the freight; and I told them that it was a thousand drachmas, for there were four people in command of the ship. 'And,' said they, 'have you a house?' 'A wretched hut,' I replied, 'on the Island of Pharos, where once upon a time Proteus used to live.' 'Would you like then,' they went on, 'to acquire a landed estate instead of the sea, and a decent house instead of your hut, and ten times as much for the cargo as you are going to get now? And to get rid of a thousand misfortunes which beset pilots owing to the roughness of the sea?' I replied that I would gladly do so, but that I did not aspire to become a pirate just at a time when I had made myself more expert than I ever had been, and had won crowns for my skill in my profession. However they persevered and promised to give me a purse of ten thousand drachmas, if I would be their man and do what they wanted. Accordingly I egged them on to talk by promising not to fail them, but to assist them in every way. Then they admitted that they were agents of the pirates, and besought me not to deprive them of a chance of capturing the ship, and instead of sailing away to the city whenever I weighed anchor thence, they arranged that I should cast anchor under the promontory, under the lee of which the pirate ships were riding; and they were willing to swear that they would not only not kill myself, but spare the life of any for whom I interceded. I for my part did not consider it safe to reprehend them, for I was afraid that if they were driven to despair, they would attack my ship on the high seas and then we would all be lost somewhere at sea; accordingly I promised to assist their enterprise, but I insisted upon their taking oath to keep their promise truly. They accordingly made oath, for our interview took place in a temple, and then I said: 'You betake yourselves to the ships of the pirates at once, for we will sail away by night.' And they found me all the more plausible from the way I bargained about the money, for I stipulated that it must all be paid me in current cash, though not before they had captured the ship. They therefore went off, but I put straight out to sea after doubling the promontory." "This then," said Iarchas, "O Apollonius, you consider the behavior of a just man?" "Why yes," said Apollonius, "and of a humane one too! for I consider it was a rare combination of virtues for one who was a mere sailor to refuse to sacrifice men's lives, or to betray the interests of merchants, so rising superior to all bribes of money."

CHAPTER XXV

THEREUPON the Indian smiled and said: "You seem to think that mere abstention from injustice constitutes justice, and I am of opinion that all Greeks do the same. For as I once learned from the Egyptians that come hither, governors from Rome are in the habit of visiting your country, brandishing their axes naked over your heads, before they know they have bad men to rule or not; but you acknowledge them to be just if they merely do not sell justice. And I have heard that the slave merchants yonder do exactly the same; for when they come to you with convoys of Carian slaves and are anxious to recommend their characters to you, they make it a great merit of the slaves that they do not steal. In the same way do you recommend on such grounds the rulers whose sway you acknowledge, and after decorating them with such praises as you lavish upon slaves, you send them away, objects, as you imagine, of universal admiration. Nay more, your cleverest poets will not give you leave to be just and good, even if you want to. For here was Minos, a man who exceeded all men in cruelty, and who enslaved with his navies the inhabitants of continent and islands alike, and yet they honor him by placing in his hand a scepter of justice and give him a throne in Hades to be umpire of spirits; while at the same time they deny food and drink to Tantalus, merely because he was a good man and inclined to share with his friends the immortality bestowed upon them by the Gods. And some of them hang stones over him, and rain insults of a terrible kind upon this divine and good man; and I would much rather that they had represented him as swimming in a lake of nectar, for he regaled men with that drink humanely and ungrudgingly." And as he spoke he pointed out a statue which stood upon his left hand, on which was inscribed the name "Tantalus". Now this statue was four cubits high, and represented a man of fifty years who was clad in the fashion of Argolis, though he differed in his cloak, that being like a Thessalian's, and he held a cup sufficient at least for one thirsty man and drank your health therefrom, and in the goblet was a liquor, an unmixed draught which frothed and foamed, though without bubbling over the edge of the cup. Now I will presently explain what they consider this cup to be, and for what reason they drink from it. In any case, however, we must suppose that Tantalus was assailed by the poets for not giving rein to his tongue, but because he shared the nectar with mankind; but we must not suppose that he was really the victim of the gods' dislike, for, had he been hateful to them, he would never have been judged by the Indians to be a good man, for they are most religious people and never transgress any divine command."

CHAPTER XXVI

While they were still discussing this topic, a hubbub down below in the village struck their ears, for it seems the king had arrived equipped in the height of Median fashion and full of pomp. Iarchas then, not too well pleased, remarked: "If it were Phraotes who was halting here, you would find a dead silence prevailing everywhere as if you were attending a mystery." From this remark Apollonius realized that the king in question was not only inferior to Phraotes in a few details, but in the whole of philosophy; and as he saw that the sages did not bestir themselves to make any preparations or provide for the king's wants, though he was come at midday, he said: "Where is the king going to stay?" "Here," they replied, "for we shall discuss by night the objects for which he is come, since that is the best time for taking counsel." "And will a table be laid for him when he comes," said Apollonius. "Why, of course," they answered, "a rich table too, furnished with everything which this place provides". "Then," said he, "you live richly?" "We," they answered, "live in a slender manner, for although we might eat as much as we like, we are contented with little; but the king requires a great deal, for that is his pleasure. But he will not eat any living creature, for it is wrong to do here, but only dried fruits and roots and the seasonable produce of the Indian land at this time of year, and whatever else the new year's seasons will provide."

CHAPTER XXVII

"BUT see," said he, "here he is." And just then the king advanced together with his brother and his son, ablaze with gold and jewels. And Apollonius was about to rise and retire, when Iarchas checked him from leaving his throne, and explained to him that it was not their custom for him to do so. Damis himself says that he was not present on this occasion, because on that day he was staying in the village, but he heard from Apollonius what happened and wrote it in his book. He says then that when they had sat down, the king extended his hand as if in prayer to the sages and they nodded their assent as if they were conceding his request; and he was transported with joy at the promise, just as if he had come to the oracle of a God. But the brother of the king and his son, who was a very pretty boy, were not more considered than if they had been the slaves of the others, that were mere retainers. After that the Indian rose from his place, and in a formal speech bade the king take food, and he accepted the invitation and that most cordially. Thereupon four tripods stepped forth like those of the Pythian Temple, but of their own accord, like those which advanced in Homer's poem , and upon them were cup-bearers of black brass resembling the figures of Ganymede and of Pelops among the Greeks. And the earth strewed beneath them grass softer than any mattress. And dried fruits and bread and vegetables and the dessert of the season all came in, served in order, and set before them more agreeably that if cooks and waiters had provided it; now two of the tripods flowed with wine, but the other two supplied, the one of them a jet of warm water and the other of cold. Now the precious stones imported from India are employed in Greece for necklaces and rings because they are so small, but among the Indians they are turned into decanters and wine coolers, because they are so large, and into goblets of such size that from a single one of them four persons can slake their thirst at midsummer. But the cup-bearers of bronze drew a mixture, he says, of wine and water made in due proportions; and they pushed cups round, just as they do in drinking bouts. The sages, however, reclined as we do in a common banquet, not that any special honor was paid to the king, although great importance would be attached to him among Greeks and Romans, but each took the first place that he chanced to reach.

CHAPTER XXVIII

AND when the wine had circulated, Iarchas said: "I pledge you to drink the health, O king, of a Hellene," and he pointed to Apollonius, who was reclining just below him, and he made a gesture with his hand to indicate that he was a noble man and divine. But the king said: "I have heard that he and the persons who are halting in the village belong to Phraotes."

"Quite, right," he answered, "and true is what you heard: for it is Phraotes who entertains him here also." "What," asked the king, "is his mode of life and pursuit?" "Why, what else," replied Iarchas, "except that of that king himself?" "It is no great compliment you have paid him," answered the king, "by saying that he has embraced a mode of life which has denied even to Phraotes the chance of being a noble man." Thereupon Iarchas remarked: "You must judge more reasonably, O king, both about philosophy and about Phraotes: for as long as you were a stripling, your youth excused in you such extravagances. But now that you have already reached man's estate, let us avoid foolish and facile utterances." But Apollonius, who found an interpreter in Iarchas said: "And what have you gained, O king, by refusing to be a philosopher?" "What have I gained? Why, the whole of virtue and the identification of myself with the Sun." Then the other, by way of checking his pride and muzzling him, said: "If you were a philosopher, you would not entertain such fancies." "And you," replied the king, "since you are a philosopher, what is your fancy about yourself, my fine fellow?" "That I may pass," replied Apollonius, "for being a good man, if only I can be a philosopher." Thereupon the king stretched out his hand to heaven and exclaimed: "By the Sun, you come here full of Phraotes." But the other hailed this remark as a godsend, and catching him up said: "I have not taken this long journey in vain, if I am become full of Phraotes. But if you should meet him presently, you will certainly say that he is full of me; and he wished to write to you in my behalf, but since he declared that you were a good man, I begged him not to take the trouble of writing, seeing that in his case no one sent a letter commending me."

CHAPTER XXIX

THIS put a stop to the incipient folly of the king for having heard that he himself was praised by Phraotes, he not only dropped his suspicions, but lowering his tone he said: "Welcome, goodly stranger." But Apollonius answered: "And my welcome to you also, O king, for you appear to have only just arrived." "And who," asked the other, "attracted you to us?" "These gentlemen here, who are both Gods and wise men." "And about myself, O stranger"; said the king, "what is said among Hellenes?" "Why, as much," said Apollonius, "as is said about the Hellenes here." "As for myself, I find nothing in the Hellenes," said the other, "that is worth speaking of." "I will tell them that," said Apollonius, "and they will crown you at Olympia."

CHAPTER XXX

AND stooping towards Iarchas he said: "Let him go on like a drunkard, but do you tell me why do you not invite to the same table as yourself, nor hold worthy of other recognition those who accompany this man, though they are his brother and son, as you tell me?" "Because," said Iarchas," they reckon to be kings one day themselves, and by being made themselves to suffer disdain they must be taught not to disdain others." And remarking that the sages were eighteen in number, he again asked Iarchas, what was the meaning of their being just so many and no more. "For," he said, "the number eighteen is not a square number, nor is it one of the numbers held in esteem and honor, as are the numbers ten and twelve and sixteen and so forth." Thereupon the Indian took him up and said: "Neither are we beholden to number nor number to us, but we owe our superior honor to wisdom and virtue; and sometimes we are more in number than we now are, and sometimes fewer. And indeed I have heard that when my grandfather was enrolled among these wise men, the youngest of them all, they were seventy in number but when he reached his 130th year, he was left here all alone, because not one of them survived him at that time, nor was there to be found anywhere in India a nature that was either philosophic or noble. The Egyptians accordingly wrote and congratulated him warmly on being left alone for four years in his tenure of this throne, but he begged them to cease reproaching the Indians for the paucity of their sages. Now we, O Apollonius, have heard from the Egyptians of the custom of the Eleans, and that the Hellanodicæ, who preside over the Olympic games, are ten in number; but we do not approve of the rule imposed in the case of these men; for they leave the choice of them to the lot, and the lot has no discernment, for a worse man might be as easily chosen by lot as a better one. On the other hand would they not make a mistake; if they had made merit the qualification and chosen them by vote? Yes, a parallel one, for if you are on no account to exceed the number ten, there may more than ten just men, and you will deprive some of the rank which their merits entitle them to, while if on the other hand there are not so many as ten, then none will be thought to be really qualified. Wherefore the Eleans would be much wiser-minded if they allowed the number to fluctuate, merely preserving the same standard of justice."

CHAPTER XXXI

WHILE they were thus conversing, the king kept trying to interrupt them, constantly breaking off their every sentence by his silly and ignorant remarks. He accordingly again asked them what they were conversing about, and Apollonius replied: "We are discussing matters important and held in great repute among the Hellenes; though you would think of them but slightly, for you say that you detest everything Hellenic." "I do certainly detest them," he said, "but nevertheless I want to hear; for I imagine you are talking about those Athenians the slaves of Xerxes." But Apollonius replied: "Nay we are discussing other things; but since you have alluded to the Athenians in a manner both absurd and false, answer me this question: Have you, O King, any slaves?" "Twenty thousand," said the other, "and not a single one of them did I buy myself, but they were all born in my household." Thereupon Apollonius, using Iarchas as his interpreter, asked him afresh whether he was in the habit of running away from his slaves or his slaves from him. And the king by way of insult answered him: "Your very question is worthy of a slave, nevertheless I will answer it: a man who runs away is not only a slave but a bad one to boot, and his master would never run away from him, when he can if he likes both torture and card him." "In that case," said Apollonius, "O king, Xerxes has been proved out of your mouth to have been a slave of the Athenians, and like a bad slave to have run away from them; for when he was defeated by them in the naval action in the Straits, he was so anxious about his bridge of boats over the Hellespont that he fled in a single ship." "Yes, but he anyhow burned Athens with his own hands," said the king. And Apollonius answered: "And for that act of audacity, O king, he was punished as never yet was any other man. For he had to run away from those whom he imagined he had destroyed; and when I contemplate the ambitions with which Xerxes set out on his campaign I can conceive that some were justified in exalting him and saying that he was Zeus; but when I contemplate his flight, I arrive at the conviction that he was the most ill-starred of men. For if he had fallen at the hands of the Hellenes, no one would have earned a brighter fame than he. For to whom would the Hellenes have raised and dedicated a loftier tomb? What jousts of armed men, what contests of musicians would not have been instituted in honor of him? For, if men like Melicertes and Palaemon and Pelops the Lydian immigrant, the former of whom died in childhood at the breast, while Pelops enslaved Arcadia and Argolis and the land within the Isthmus,—if these were commemorated by the Greeks as Gods, what would not have been done for Xerxes by men who are by nature more enthusiastic admirers of the virtues, and who consider that they praise themselves in praising those whom they have defeated?"

CHAPTER XXXII

THESE words of Apollonius caused the king to burst into tears, and he said: "Dearest friend, in what an heroic light do you represent these Hellenes to me." "Why then, O king, were you so hard upon them?" "The visitors who come hither from Egypt, O guest," replied the king, "malign the race of Hellenes, and while declaring that they themselves are holy men and wise, and the true law-givers who fixed all the sacrifices and rites of initiation which are in vogue among the Greeks, they deny to the latter any and every sort of good quality, declaring them to be ruffians, and a mixed herd addicted to every sort of anarchy, and lovers of legend and miracle mongers, and though indeed poor, yet making their poverty not a title of dignity, but a mere excuse for stealing. But now that I have heard this from you and understand how fond of honor and how worthy the Hellenes are, I am reconciled for the future to them and I engage both that they shall have my praise and that I will pray all I can for them, and will never set trust in another Egyptian." But Iarchas remarked: "I too, O king, was aware that your mind had been poisoned by these Egyptians; but I would not take the part of the Hellenes until you met some such counselor as this. But since you have been put right by a wise man, let us now proceed to quaff the good cheer provided by Tantalus, and let us sleep over the serious issues which we have to discuss tonight. But at another time I will fill you full with Hellenic arguments, and no other race is so rich in them; and you will delight in them whenever you come hither." And forthwith he set an example to this fellow guests, by stooping the first of them all to the goblet which indeed furnished an ample draught for all; for the stream refilled itself plenteously, as if with spring waters welling up from the ground; and Apollonius also drank, for this cup is instituted by the Indians as a cup of friendship; and they feign that Tantalus is the wine-bearer who supplies it, because he is considered to have been the most friendly of men.

CHAPTER XXXIII

AND when they had drunk, the earth received them on the couches which she had spread for them; but when it was midnight they rose up and first they sang a hymn to the ray of light, suspended aloft in the air as they had been at midday; and then they attended the king, as much as he desired. Damis, however, says that Apollonius was not present at the king's conversation with them, because he thought that the interview had to do with secrets of state. Having then at daybreak offered his sacrifice, the king approached Apollonius and offered him the hospitality of his palace, declaring that he would send him back to Greece an object of envy to all. But he commended him for his kindness, nevertheless he excused himself from inflicting himself upon one with whom he was on no sort of equality; moreover, he said that he had been longer abroad than he liked, and that he scrupled to give his friends at home cause to think they were being neglected. The king thereupon said that he entreated him, and assumed such an undignified attitude in urging his request, that Apollonius said: "A king who insists upon his request in such terms at the expense of his dignity, is laying a trap." Thereupon Iarchas intervened and said: "You wrong, O king, this sacred abode by trying to drag away from it a man against his will; and moreover, being one of those who can read the future, he is aware that his staying with you would not conduce to his own good, and would probably not be in any way profitable to yourself."

CHAPTER XXXIV

THE king accordingly went down into the village, for the law of the sages did not allow a king to be with them more than one day; but Iarchas said to the messenger: "We admit Damis also hither to our mysteries; so let him come, but do you look after the rest of them in the village." And when Damis arrived, they sat down together, as they were wont to do, and they allowed Apollonius to ask questions; and he asked them of what they thought the cosmos was composed; but they replied: "Of elements." "Are there then four?" he asked. "Not four," said Iarchas, "but five." "And how can there be a fifth," said Apollonius, "alongside of water and air and earth and fire?" "There is the ether," replied the other, "which we must regard as the stuff of which gods are made; for just as all mortal creatures inhale the air, so do immortal and divine natures inhale the ether." Apollonius again asked which of the elements came first into being, and Iarchas answered: "All are simultaneous, for a living creature is not born bit by bit." "Am I," said Apollonius, "to regard the universe as a living creature?" "Yes," said the other, "if you have a sound knowledge of it, for it engenders all living things." "Shall I then," said Apollonius, "call the universe female, or of both the male and the opposite gender?" "Of both genders," said the other, "for by commerce with itself it fulfills the role both of mother and father in bringing forth living creatures; and it is possessed by a love for itself more intense than any separate being has for its fellow, a passion which knits it together into harmony. And it is not illogical to suppose that it cleaves unto itself; for as the movement of an animal dictates the function of its hands and feet, in co-operation with a soul in it by which it is set in motion, so we must regard the parts of the universe also as adapting themselves through its inherent soul to all creatures which are brought forth or conceived. For example, the sufferings so often caused by drought are visited on us in accordance with the soul of the universe, whenever justice has fallen into disrepute and is disowned by men; and this animal shepherds itself not with a single hand only, but with many mysterious ones, which it has at its disposal; and though from its immense size it is controlled by no other, yet it moves obediently to the rein and is easily guided.

CHAPTER XXXV

"AND the subject is so vast and so far transcends our mental powers, that I do not know any example adequate to illustrate it; but we will take that of a ship, such as the Egyptians construct for our seas and launch for the exchange of Egyptian goods against Indian wares. For there is an ancient law in regard to the Red Sea, which the king Erythras laid down, when he held sway over that sea, to the effect that the Egyptians should not enter it with a vessel of war, and indeed should employ only a single merchant ship. This regulation obliged the Egyptians to contrive a ship equivalent to several at once of those which other races have; and they ribbed the sides of this ship with bolts such as hold a ship together, and they raised its bulwarks and its mast to a great height, and they constructed several compartments, such as are built upon the timber balks which run athwart a ship, and they set several pilots in this boat and subordinated them to the oldest and wisest of their number, to conduct the voyage; and there were several officers on the prow and excellent and handy sailors to man the sails; and in the crew of this ship there was a detachment of armed men, for it is necessary to equip the ship and protect it against the savages of the Gulf that live on the right hand as you enter it, in case they should ever attack and plunder it on the high seas. Let us apply this imagery to the universe, and regard it in the light of a naval construction; for then you must apportion the first and supreme position to God the begetter of this animal, and subordinate posts to the gods who govern its parts; and we may well assent to the statements of the poets, when they say that there are many gods in heaven and many in the sea, and many in the fountains and streams, and many round about the earth, and that there are some even under the earth. But we shall do well to separate from the universe the region under the earth, if there is one, because the poets represent it as an abode of terror and corruption."

CHAPTER XXXVI

AS the Indian concluded this discourse, Damis says that he was transported with admiration and applauded loudly; for he could never have thought that a native of India could show such mastery of the Greek tongue, nor even that, supposing he understood that language, he could have used it with so much ease and elegance. And he praises the look and smile of Iarchas, and the inspired air with which he expressed his ideas, admitting that Apollonius, although he had a delivery as graceful as it was free from bombast, nevertheless gained a great deal by contact with this Indian, and he says that whenever he sat down to discuss a theme, as he very often did, he resembled Iarchas.

CHAPTER XXXVII

AS the rest of the company praised, no less, the contents of Iarchas' speech than the tone in which he spoke, Apollonius resumed by asking him which they considered the bigger, the sea or the land; and Iarchas replied: "If the land be compared with the sea it will be found to be bigger, for it includes the sea in itself; but if it be considered in relation to the entire mass of water, we can show that the earth is the lesser of the two, for it is upheld by the water."

CHAPTER XXXVIII

THIS discussion was interrupted by the appearance among the sages of the messenger bringing in certain Indians who were in want of succor. And he brought forward a poor woman who interceded in behalf of her child, who was, she said, a boy of sixteen years of age, but had been for two years possessed by a devil. Now the character of the devil was that of a mocker and a liar. Here one of the sages asked, why she said this, and she replied: "This child of mine is extremely good-looking, and therefore the devil is amorous of him and will not allow him to retain his reason, nor will he permit him to go to school, or to learn archery, nor even to remain at home, but drives him out into desert places. And the boy does not even retain his own voice, but speaks in a deep hollow tone, as men do; and he looks at you with other eyes rather than with his own. As for myself I weep over all this and I tear my cheeks, and I rebuke my son so far as I well may; but he does not know me. And I made my mind to repair hither, indeed I planned to do so a year ago; only the demon discovered himself using my child as a mask, and what he told me was this, that he was the ghost of man, who fell long ago in battle, but that at death he was passionately attached to his wife. Now he had been dead for only three days when his wife insulted their union by marrying another man, and the consequence was that he had come to detest the love of women, and had transferred himself wholly into this boy. But he promised, if I would only not denounce him to yourselves, to endow the child with many noble blessings. As for myself, I was influenced by these promises; but he has put me off and off for such a long time now, that he has got sole control of my household, yet has no honest or true intentions." Here the sage asked afresh, if the boy was at hand; and she said not, for, although she had done all she could to get him to come with her, the demon had threatened her with steep places and precipices and declared that he would kill her son, "in case," she added, "I haled him hither for trial." "Take courage," said the sage, "for he will not slay him when he has read this." And so saying he drew a letter out of his bosom and gave it to the woman; and the letter, it appears, was addressed to the ghost and contained threats of an alarming kind.

CHAPTER XXXIX

THERE also arrived a man who was lame. He already thirty years old and was a keen hunter of lions; but a lion had sprung upon him and dislocated his hip so that he limped with one leg. However when they massaged with their hands his hip, the youth immediately recovered his upright gait. And another man had had his eyes put out, and he went away having recovered the sight of both of them.

Yet another man had his hand paralyzed; but left their presence in full possession of the limb. And a certain woman had suffered in labor already seven times, but was healed in the following way through the intercession of her husband. He bade the man, whenever his wife should be about to bring forth her next child, to enter her chamber carrying in his bosom a live hare; then he was to walk once round her and at the same moment to release the hare; for that the womb would be extruded together with the fetus, unless the hare was at once driven out.

CHAPTER XL

AND again a certain man who was a father said that he had had several sons, but that they had died the moment they began to drink wine. Iarchas took him up and said: "Yes, and it is just as well they did die; for they would inevitably have gone mad, having inherited, as it appears, from their parents too warm a temperament. Your children," he added, "must therefore abstain from wine, but in order that they may be never led even to desire wine, supposing you should have another boy, and I perceive you had one only six days ago, you must carefully watch the hen owl and find where it builds its nest; then you must snatch its eggs and give them to the child to chew after boiling them properly; for if it is fed upon these, before it tastes wine, a distaste for wine will be bred in it, and it will keep sober by your excluding from its temperament any but natural warmth."

With such lore as this then they surfeited themselves, and they were astonished at the many-sided wisdom of the company, and day after day they asked all sorts of questions, and were themselves asked many in turn.

CHAPTER XLI

BOTH Apollonius and Damis then took part in the interviews devoted to abstract discussions; not so with the conversations devoted to occult themes, in which they pondered the nature of astronomy or divination, and considered the problem of foreknowledge, and handled the problems of sacrifice and of the invocations in which the gods take pleasure. In these Damis says that Apollonius alone partook of the philosophic discussion together with Iarchas, and that Apollonius embodied the results in four books concerning the divination by the stars, a work which Moeragenes has mentioned. And Damis says that he composed a work on the way to offer sacrifice to the several gods in a manner pleasing to them. Not only then do I regard the work on the science of the stars and the whole subject of such divination as transcending human nature, but I do not even know if anyone has these gifts; but I found the treatise on sacrifices in several cities, and in the houses of several learned men; moreover, if anyone should translate[7] it, he would find it to be a grave and dignified composition, and one that rings of the author's personality. And Damis says that Iarchas gave seven rings to Apollonius named after the seven stars, and that Apollonius wore each of these in turn on the day of the week which bore its name.

CHAPTER XLII

AS to the subject of foreknowledge, they presently had a talk about it, for Apollonius was devoted to this kind of lore, and turned most of their conversations on to it. For this Iarchas praised him and said: "My good friend Apollonius, those who take pleasure in divination, are rendered divine thereby and contribute to the salvation of mankind. For here we have discoveries which we must go to a divine oracle in order to make; yet these, my good friend, we foresee of our unaided selves and foretell to others things which they know not yet. This I regard as the gift of one thoroughly blessed and endowed with the same mysterious power as the Delphic Apollo. Now the ritual insists that those who visit a shrine with a view to obtaining a response, must purify themselves first, otherwise they will be told to "depart from the temple." Consequently I consider that one who would foresee events must be healthy in himself, and must not have his soul stained with any sort of defilement nor his character scarred with the wounds of any sins; so he will pronounce his predictions with purity, because he will understand himself and the sacred tripod in his breast, and with ever louder and clearer tone and truer import will he utter his oracles. Therefore you need not be surprised, if you comprehend the science, seeing that you carry in your soul so much ether."

CHAPTER XLIII

AND with these words he turned to Damis and said playfully: "And you, O Assyrian, have you no foreknowledge of anything, especially as you associate with such a man as this?" "Yes, by Zeus," answered Damis, "at any rate of the things that are necessary for myself;

---

[7] In Bk. IV. ch. 19, we are told that this book was written in the Cappadocian tongue. Hence the need of translation.

for when I first met with Apollonius here, he at once struck me as full of wisdom and cleverness and sobriety and of true endurance; but when I saw that he also had a good memory, and that he was very learned and entirely devoted to the love of learning, he became to me something superhuman; and I came to the conclusion that if I stuck to him I should be held a wise man instead of an ignoramus and a dullard, and an educated man instead of a savage; and I saw that, if I followed him and shared his pursuits, I should visit the Indians and visit you, and that I should be turned into a Hellene by him and be able to mix with the Hellenes. Now of course you set your oracles, as they concern important issues, on a level with those of Delphi and Dodona and of any other shrine you like; as for my own premonitions, since Damis is the person who has them, and since his foreknowledge concerns himself alone, we will suppose that they resemble the guesses of an old beggar wife foretelling what will happen to sheep and such like."

CHAPTER XLIV

ALL the sages laughed of course at this sally, and when their laughter had subsided, Iarchas led back the argument to the subject of divination, and among the many blessings which that art had conferred upon mankind, he declared the gift of healing to be the most important. "For," said he, "the wise sons of Asclepius would have never attained to this branch of science, if Asclepius had not been the son of Apollo; and as such had not in accordance with the latter's responses and oracles concocted and adapted different drugs to different diseases; these he not only handed on to his own sons, but he taught his companions what herbs must be applied to running wounds, and what to parched and dry wounds, and in what doses to administer liquid drugs for drinking, by means of which dropsical patients are drained and bleeding is checked, and diseases of decay and the cavities due to their ravages are put an end to. And who," he said, "can deprive the art of divination of the credit of discovering simples which heal the bites of venomous creatures, and in particular of using the virus itself as a cure for many diseases? For I do not think that men without the forecasts of a prophetic wisdom would ever have ventured to mingle with medicines that save life these most deadly of poisons."

CHAPTER XLV

And inasmuch as the following conversation also has been recorded by Damis as having been held upon this occasion with regard to the mythological animals and fountains and men met with in India, I must not leave it out, for there is much to be gained by neither believing nor yet disbelieving everything. Accordingly Apollonius asked the question, whether there was there an animal called the man-eater (*martichoras*); and Iarchas replied: "And what have you heard about the make of this animal? For it is probable that there is some account given of its shape."

"There are," replied Apollonius, "tall stories current which I cannot believe; for they say that the creature has four feet, and that his head resembles that of a man, but that in size it is comparable to a lion; while the tail of this animal puts out hairs a cubit long and sharp as thorns, which it shoots like arrows at those who hunt it."

And he further asked about the golden water which they say bubbles up from a spring, and about the stone which behaves like a magnet, and about the men who live underground and the pigmies also and the shadow-footed men; and Iarchas answered his questions thus: "What have I to tell you about animals or plants or fountains which you have seen yourself on coming here? For by this time you are as competent to describe these to other people as I am; but I never yet heard in this country of an animal that shoots arrows or of springs of golden water."

CHAPTER XLVI

However about the stone which attracts and binds to itself other stones you must not be skeptical; for you can see the stone yourself if you like, and admire its properties. For the greatest specimen is exactly of the size of this finger nail," and here he pointed to his own thumb, "and it is conceived in a hollow in the earth at a depth of four fathoms; but it is so highly endowed with spirit, that the earth swells and breaks open in many places when the stone is conceived in it. But no one can get hold of it, for it runs away, unless it is scientifically attracted; but we alone can secure, partly by performance of certain rites and partly by certain forms of words, this *pantarbe*, for such is the name given to it.

Now in the night-time it glows like the day just as fire might, for it is red and gives out rays; and if you look at it in the daytime it smites your eyes with a thousand glints and gleams. And the light within it is a spirit of mysterious power, for it absorbs to itself everything in its neighborhood. And why do I say in its neighborhood? Why you can sink anywhere in river or in sea as many stones as you like, and these not even near to one another, but here there; and everywhere; and then if you let down this stone among them by a string it gathers them all together by the diffusion of its spirit, and the stones yield to its influence and cling to it in bunch, like a swarm of bees."

CHAPTER XLVII

And having said this he showed the stone itself and all that it was capable of effecting.

And as to the pigmies, he said that they lived underground, and that they lay on the other side of the Ganges and lived in the manner which is related by all. As to men that are shadow-footed or have long heads, and as to the other poetical fancies which the treatise of Scylax recounts about them, he said that they didn't live anywhere on the earth, and least of all in India.

CHAPTER XLVIII

As to the gold which the griffins dig up, there are rocks which are spotted with drops of gold as with sparks, which this creature can quarry because of the strength of its beak. "For these animals do exist in India," he said, "and are held in veneration as being sacred to the Sun; and the Indian artists, when they represent the Sun, yoke four of them abreast to draw the imaged car; and in size and strength they resemble lions but having this advantage over them that they have wings, they will attack them, and they get the better of elephants and of dragons. But they have no great power of flying, not more than have birds of short flight; for they are not winged as is proper with birds, but the palms of their feet are webbed with red membranes, such that they are able to revolve them, and make a flight and fight in the air; and the tiger alone is beyond their powers of attack, because in swiftness it rivals the winds."

CHAPTER XLIX

"And the phoenix," he said, "is the bird which visits Egypt every five hundred years, but the rest of that time it flies about in India; and it is unique in that it gives out rays of sunlight and shines with gold, in size and appearance like an eagle; and it sits upon the nest; which is made by it at the springs of the Nile out of spices. The story of the Egyptians about it, that it comes to Egypt, is testified to by the Indians also, but the latter add this touch to the story, that the phoenix which is being consumed in its nest sings funeral strains for itself. And this is also done by the swans according to the account of those who have the wit to hear them."

CHAPTER L

In such conversations with the sages Apollonius spent the four months which he passed there, and he acquired all sorts of lore both profane and mysterious. But when he was minded to go on his way they persuaded him to send back to Phraotes with a letter his guide and the camels; and they themselves gave him another guide and camels, and sent him forth on his way, congratulating both themselves and him. And having embraced Apollonius and declared that he would be esteemed a god by the many, not merely after his death, but while he was still alive, they turned back to their place of meditation, though ever and anon they turned towards him, and showed by their action that they parted from him against their will. And Apollonius keeping the Ganges on his right hand, but the Hyphasis on his left, went down towards the sea a journey of ten days from the sacred ridge. And as they went down they saw a great many ostriches, and many wild bulls, and many asses and lions and pards and tigers, and another kind of apes than those which inhabit the pepper trees, for these were black and bushy-haired and were dog-like in features and as big as small men. And in the usual discussion of what they saw they reached the sea, where small factories had been built, and passenger ships rode in them resembling those of the Tyrrhenes. And they say that the sea called Erythra or "red" is of a deep blue color, but that it was so named from a king Erythras, who gave his own name to the sea in question.

CHAPTER LI

Having reached this point, Apollonius sent back the camels to Iarchas together with the following letter:

"Apollonius to Iarchas and the other sages greeting.

"I came to you on foot, and yet you presented me with the sea; but by sharing with me the wisdom which is yours, you have made it mine even to travel through the heavens. All this I shall mention to the Hellenes; and I shall communicate my words to you as if you were present, unless I have in vain drunk the draught of Tantalus. Farewell, ye goodly philosophers."

CHAPTER LII

He then embarked upon the ship and was borne away by a smooth and favorable breeze, and he was struck at the formidable manner in which the Hyphasis discharges itself into the sea at its mouth; for in its later course, as I said before, it falls into rocky and narrow places and over precipices, and breaking its way through these to the sea by a single mouth, presents a formidable danger to those who hug the land too closely.

CHAPTER LIII

They say, moreover, that they saw the mouth of the Indus, and that there was situated on it the city of Patala, round which the Indus flows. It was to this city that the fleet of Alexander came, under the command of Nearchus, a highly trained naval captain. But as for the stories of Orthagoras about the sea called Erythra, to the effect that the constellation of the bear is not to bee seen in it, and that the mariners cast no reckoning at midday, and that the visible stars there vary from their usual positions, this account is endorsed by Damis; and we must consider it to be sound and based on local observations of the heavens. The also mention a small island, of the name of Biblus, in which there is the large cockle, and where there are mussels and oysters and such like organisms, clinging to the rocks and ten times as big as those which we find in Greece. And there is also taken in this region a stone, the pearl in a white shell, wherein it occupies the place of he heart of the oyster.

CHAPTER LIV

And they say they also touched at Pegadae in the country of the Oreitae. As for these people, they have rocks of bronze and sand of bronze, and the dust which the rivers bring down is of bronze. But they regard their land as full of gold because the bronze is of such high quality.

CHAPTER LV

And they say that they came across the people called the Fish-Eaters, whose city is Stobera; and they clothe themselves in the skins of very large fishes, and the cattle there look like fish and eat extraordinary things; for the shepherds feed them upon fish, just as in Caria the flocks are fed on figs. But the Indians of Carman are a gentle race, who live on the edge of a sea so well stocked with fish, that they neither lay them in by stores, not salt them as is done in Pontus, but they just sell a few of them and throw back most they catch panting into the sea.

CHAPTER LVI

They say that they also touched at Balara, which is an emporium full of myrtles and date palms; and they also saw laurels, and the place was well watered by springs. And there were kitchen gardens there, as well as flower gardens, all growing luxuriantly, and the harbors therein were entirely calm. But off there lies a sacred island, which was called Selera, and the passage to it from the mainland was a hundred stades long. Now in this island there lived a Nereid, a dreadful female demon, which would snatch away many mariners and would not even allow ships to fasten a cable to the island.

CHAPTER LVII

It is just as well not to omit the story of the other kind of pearl: since even Apollonius did not regard it as puerile, and it is anyhow a pretty invention, and there is nothing in the annals of sea fishing so remarkable. For on the side of the island which is turned towards the open sea, the bottom is of great depth, and produces an oyster in a white sheath full of fat, for it does not produce any jewel. The inhabitants watch for a calm day, or they themselves render the sea smooth, and this they do by flooding it with oil; and then a man plunges in in order to hunt the oyster in question, and he is in other aspects equipped like those who cut off the sponges from the rocks, but he carries in addition an oblong iron block and an alabaster case of myrrh. The Indian then halts alongside of the oyster and holds out the myrrh before him as a bait; whereupon the oyster opens and drinks itself drunk upon the myrrh. Then its pierced with a long pin and discharges a peculiar liquid called ichor, which the man catches in the iron block which is hollowed out in regular holes. The liquid so obtained petrifies in regular shapes, just like the natural pearl, and it is a white blood furnished by the Red Sea. And they say that the Arabs also who live on the opposite coast devote themselves to catching these creatures. From this point on they found the entire sea full of sharks, and whales gathered there in schools; and the ships, they say, in order to keep off these animals, carry bells at the bow and at the stern, the sound of which frightens away these creatures and prevents them from approaching the ships.

CHAPTER LVIII

And when they sailed as far as the mouth of the Euphrates, they say they sailed up by it to Babylon to see Vardanes, whom the found just as they had found him before. They then came afresh to Nineveh, and as the people of Antioch displayed their customary insolence and took no interest in any affairs of the Hellenes, they went down to the sea at Seleucia, and finding a ship, they sailed to Cyprus and landed at Paphos, where there is the statue of Aphrodite. Apollonius marveled at the symbolic construction of the same, and gave the priests instruction with regard to the ritual of the temple. He then sailed to Ionia, where he excited much admiration and no little esteem among all lovers of wisdom.

BOOK IV

CHAPTER I

And when they saw our sage in Ionia and he had arrived in Ephesus, even the mechanics would not remain at their handicrafts, but followed him, one admiring his wisdom, another his beauty, another his way of life, another his bearing, some of them everything alike about him. Reports also were current about him which originated from various oracles; thus from the oracle at Colophon it was announced that he shared its peculiar wisdom and was absolutely wise, and so forth; from that of Didyma similar rumors emanated, as also from the shrine of Pergamon; for the God urged not a few of these who were in need of health to betake themselves to Apollonius, for this was what "he himself approved and was pleasing to the Fates." Deputations also waited upon him from various cities offering him their hospitality, and asking his advise about life in general as well as about the dedication of altars and images; and he regulated their several affairs in some case by letter, but in others he said would visit them. And the city of Smyrna also sent a deputation, but they would not say what they wanted, though they besought him to visit them; so he asked the legate what they wanted of him, but he merely said, "to see him and to be seen." So Apollonius said: "I will come, but, O ye Muses, grant that we may also like one another."

CHAPTER II

The first discourse then which he delivered was to the Ephesians from the platform of their temple, and its tone was not that of the Socratic school; for he dissuaded and discouraged them from other pursuits, and urged them to fill Ephesus with real study rather than with idleness and revelry such as he found around him there; for they were devoted to dancers and taken up with pantomimes, and the whole city was full of pipers, and full of effeminate rascals, and full of noise. So, though the Ephesians had come over to him, he determined not tot wink at such things, but cleared them out and made them odious to most of them.

CHAPTER III

His other discourses he delivered under the trees which grow hard by the cloisters; and in these he dealt with the question of communism, and taught that they ought to support and be supported by one another. While he was doing so on one occasion, sparrows were sitting quite silent upon the trees, but one of them suddenly set to chirping as it flew up, just as if he had some exhortations to give to his fellows; and the latter, on hearing it, themselves set up a chirping and rose and flew up under the guidance of the one. Now Apollonius went on with his argument, for he knew what it was that made the sparrows take wing, but he did not explain the matter to the multitude who were listening to him; but when they all looked at the birds and some of them in their silliness thought it a miraculous occurrence, Apollonius interrupted his argument and said: "A boy has slipped who was carrying some barley in a bowl, and after carelessly gathering together what was fallen, he has gone off, leaving much of if scattered about it in yonder alley, and this sparrow, witnessing the occurrence has come here to acquaint his fellows with the good luck, and to invite them to come and eat it with him."

Most of his audience accordingly ran off to the spot, but Apollonius continued to those who remained with him the discourse he had proposed to himself on the topic of communism; and when they returned talking loudly and full of wonder, he continued thus: "You see how the sparrows care for one another and delight in communism, but we are far from approving of it, nay, should we happen to see anyone sharing his own in common with others, we set him down as a spendthrift and talk about his extravagance and so forth, while as for those who are supported by him, we call them parasites and flatterers. What then is left for us to do, except to shut ourselves up like birds that are being fed up and fattened, and gorge ourselves in the dark until we literally burst with fat?"

CHAPTER IV

A pestilence was creeping over Ephesus; but the disease had not yet reached its full violence, before Apollonius understood that it was approaching, and impressed with the danger he foretold it, and interspersed his discourses with such exclamations as "O earth, remain true to thyself!" and he added in a tone of menace such appeals as these:

"Do thou preserve these men here," and "Thou shalt not pass hither." But his hearers did not attend to these warnings and thought them mere rodomontade, all the more because they saw him constantly visiting all the temples in order to avert and deprecate the calamity. And since they conducted themselves so foolishly in respect of the scourge, he thought that it was not necessary to do anything more for them, but began a tour of the rest of Ionia, regulating their several affairs, and from time to time recommending in his discourses what was salutary for his audiences.

CHAPTER V

But when he came to Smyrna the Ionians went out to meet him, for they were just celebrating the pan-Ionian sacrifices. And he there read a decree of the Ionians, in which they besought him to take part in their solemn meeting; and in it he met with a name which had not at all an Ionian ring, for a certain Lucullus had signed the resolution. He accordingly sent a letter to their council expressing his astonishment at such an instance of barbarism; for he had, it seems, also found the name Fabricius and other such names in the decrees. The letter on this subject shows how sternly he reprimanded them.

CHAPTER VI

And on another day he presented himself before the meeting of the Ionians, and asked: "What is this cup?" And they answered: "It is the pan-Ionian cup." Whereupon he took a draught from it and poured a libation, saying: "O ye Gods, who are patrons of the Ionians, may ye grant to this fair colony to enjoy safety at sea, and that no disaster may wreak itself on them by land therefrom, and that Aegaeon, the author of earthquakes, may never shake down their cities." These words he uttered under divine impulse, because he foresaw, as I believe, the disasters which afterwards betook Smyrna and Miletus and Chios and Samos and several of the Iades.

CHAPTER VII

And remarking the zeal with which the people of Smyrna devoted themselves to all sorts of compositions, he encouraged them and increased their zeal, and urged them to take pride rather in themselves than in the beauty of their city; for although they had the most beautiful of cities under the sun, and although they had a friendly sea at their doors, which held the springs of the zephyr, nevertheless, it was more pleasing for the city to be crowned with men than with porticos and pictures, or even with gold in excess of what they needed. For, he said, public edifices remain where they are, and are nowhere seen except in that particular part of the earth where they exist, but good men are conspicuous everywhere, and everywhere they utter their thoughts; and so they can magnify the city more to which they belong, in proportion to the numbers in which they are able to visit any part of the earth."

And he said that cities which are beautiful in the same way as Smyrna was, resemble the statue of Zeus wrought in Olympia by Phidias; for there Zeus sits, just as it pleased the artist that he should, whereas men who visit all regions of the earth may be well compared with the Homeric Zeus, who is represented by Homer under many shapes, and is a more wonderful creation than the image made of ivory; for the latter is only to be seen upon earth, but the former is an ideal presence imagined everywhere in heaven.

CHAPTER VIII

And in his discussions, moreover, with the people of Smyrna he wisely taught them also how best to guarantee the security of those who live in the cities, for he saw that they were at issue with one another and did not agree in their ideals. He accordingly told them that for a city to be rightly conducted by its inhabitants, you need a mixture of concord with party spirit; and as this utterance seemed inadmissible and hardly logical, Apollonius realizing that most of them did not follow his argument, added: "White and black can never be one and the same, nor can bitter be wholesomely blended with sweet; but concord can be blended with party spirit to secure the safety of the cities. And let us consider my meaning to be somewhat as follows: Far be from your city the factiousness which leads men to draw swords and to stone one another; for in a city we need our children to be brought up properly, and we need laws, and we need inhabitants equally versed in discussion and in deeds. But mutual rivalry between men in behalf of the common weal, and with the object that one should give better advice than another, and that one should discharge better than another the duties of magistrate, and that one should discharge the office of an ambassador or of an aedile more brilliantly than his fellows—here," he said, "I think you have a worthy rivalry and a real contention among yourselves in behalf of the common weal. But that one person should practice one thing and another another with a view to benefiting the city seemed of old a foolish thing to the Lacedaemonians, because they only cultivated the arts of war, and because they all strengthened themselves for this end and interested themselves in nothing else; but to me it seems best that each man should do what he understands best and what he best can do. For that city will recline in peace, nay, will rather stand up erect, where one man is admired for his popular influence, and another for his wisdom, and another for his liberal expenditure on public objects, and another for his kindliness, and another for his severity and unbending sternness towards malefactors, and another because his hands are pure beyond suspicion."

CHAPTER IX

And as he was thus discoursing, he saw a ship with three masts leaving the harbor, of which the sailors were each discharging their particular duties in working it out to sea. Accordingly, calling the attention of his audience he said: "Now look at that ship's crew, how some of them being rowers have embarked in the tug-boats, while others are winding up and making fast the anchors, and others again are spreading the sails to the wind, and others are keeping an outlook at bow and stern. Now if a single member of this community abandoned any one of his particular tasks or went about his naval duties in an inexperienced manner, they would have a bad voyage and would themselves impersonate the storm; but if they vie with one another and are rivals only with the object of one showing himself as good a man as the other, then their ship will make the best of all havens, and all their voyage be one of fair weather and fair sailing, and the precaution they exercise about themselves will prove to be as valuable as if Poseidon our Lord of safety were watching over them."

CHAPTER X

With such harangues as these he knit together the people of Smyrna; but when the plague began to rage in Ephesus, and no remedy sufficed to check it, they sent a deputation to Apollonius, asking him to become physician of their infirmity; and he thought that he ought not to postpone his journey, but said: "Let us go." And forthwith he was in

Ephesus, performing the same feat, I believe, as Pythagoras, who was in Thurii and Metapontum at one and the same moment. He therefore called together the Ephesians, and said: "Take courage, for I will today put a stop to the course of the disease." And with these words he led the population entire to the theater, where the image of the Averting god has been set up. And there he saw what seemed an old mendicant artfully blinking his eyes as if blind, as he carried a wallet and a crust of bread in it; and he was clad in rags and was very squalid of countenance. Apollonius therefore ranged the Ephesians around him and said: "Pick up as many stones as you can and hurl them at this enemy of the gods." Now the Ephesians wondered what he meant, and were shocked at the idea of murdering a stranger so manifestly miserable; for he was begging and praying them to take mercy upon him. Nevertheless Apollonius insisted and egged on the Ephesians to launch themselves on him and not let him go. And as soon as some of them began to take shots and hit him with their stones, the beggar who had seemed to blink and be blind, gave them all a sudden glance and his eyes were full of fire. Then the Ephesians recognized that he was a demon, and they stoned him so thoroughly that their stones were heaped into a great cairn around him. After a little pause Apollonius bade them remove the stones and acquaint themselves with the wild animal they had slain. When therefore they had exposed the object which they thought they had thrown their missiles at, they found that he had disappeared and instead of him there was a hound who resembled in form and look a Molossian dog, but was in size the equal of the largest lion; there he lay before their eyes, pounded to a pulp by their stones and vomiting foam as mad dogs do. Accordingly the statue of the Averting god, Heracles, has been set up over the spot where the ghost was slain.

CHAPTER XI

Having purged the Ephesians of the plague, and having had enough of the people of Ionia, he started for Hellas. Having made his way then to Pergamun, and being pleased with the temple of Asclepius, he gave hints to the supplicants of the god, what to do in order to obtain favorable dreams; and having healed many of them he came to the land of Ilium. And when his mind was glutted with all the traditions of their past, he went to visit the tombs of the Achaeans, and he delivered himself of many speeches over them, and he offered many sacrifices of a bloodless and pure kind; and then he bade his companions go on board ship, for he himself, he said, must spend a night on the mound of Achilles. Now his companions tried to deter him—for in fact the sons of Dioscorus and the Phaedimi, and a whole company of such already followed in the train of Apollonius—alleging that Achilles was still dreadful as a phantom; for such was the conviction about him of the inhabitants of Ilium. "Nevertheless," said Apollonius, "I know Achilles well and that he thoroughly delights in company; for he heartily welcomed Nestor when he came from Pylos, because he always had something useful to tell him; and he used to honor Phoenix with the title of foster-father and companion and so forth, because Phoenix entertained him with his talk; and he looked most mildly upon Priam also, although he was his bitterest enemy, so soon as he heard him talk; and when in the course of a quarrel he had an interview with Odysseus, he made himself so gracious that Odysseus thought him more handsome than terrible.

For, I think that his shield and his plumes that wave so terribly, as they say, are a menace to the Trojans, because he can never forget what he suffered at their hands, when they played him false over the marriage. But I have nothing in common with Ilium, and I shall talk to him more pleasantly than his former companions; and if he slays me, as you say he will, why then I shall repose with Memnon and Cycnus, and perhaps Troy will bury me "in a hollow sepulcher" as they did Hector." Such were his words to his companions, half playful and half serious, as he went up alone to the barrow; but they went on board ship, for it was already evening.

CHAPTER XII

But Apollonius came about dawn to them and said: "Where is Antisthenes of Paros"? And this person had joined their society seven days before in Ilium. And when Antisthenes answered that he was there, he said: "Have you, O young man, any Trojan blood in your veins?" "Certainly I have," he said, "for I am a Trojan by ancestry." "And a descendant of Priam as well?" asked Apollonius.

"Why yes, by Zeus," answered the other, "and that is why I consider myself a good man and of good stock." "That explains then," said the sage, "why Achilles forbids me to associate with you; for after he bade me go as his deputy to the Thessalians in the matter of a complaint which he has against them, and I asked him whether there was anything else which I could do to please him, 'yes', he said, 'you must take care not to initiate the young man from Paros in your wisdom, for he is too much of a descendant of Priam, and the praise of Hector is never out of his mouth.'"

CHAPTER XIII

Accordingly, Antisthenes went off though against his will; and when the day broke and the wind off shore increased in strength, and the ship was ready to put to sea, it was invaded in spite of its small dimensions by a number of other people who were anxious to share the voyage with Apollonius; for it was already autumn and the sea was not much to be trusted. They all then regarded Apollonius as one who was master of the tempest and of fire and of perils of all sorts, and so wished to go on board with him. But as the company was many times too great for the ship, spying a larger ship—for there were many in the neighborhood of the tomb of Ajax—he said: "Let us go on board this, for it is a good thing to get home safely with as many as may be." He accordingly doubled the promontory of Troy, and then commanded the pilot to shape his course towards the country of the Aeolians, which lies over against Lesbos, and then to turn as close as he could to Methymna, and there to cast anchor. For there it was, he said, that Achilles declared Palamedes lay,, where also they would find his image a cubit high, representing however a man older than was ever Palamedes. And at the moment of disembarking from the ship, he said: "Let us show our respect, O ye Greeks, for so good a man to whom we owe all wisdom. For we shall anyhow prove ourselves better men than the Achaeans, if we pay tribute to the excellence of one whom they so unjustly slew." They then had hardly leapt of the ship, when he hit upon the tomb and found the statue buried beside it. And there were inscribed on the base of the statue the words: "To the divine Palamedes." He accordingly set it up again in its place, as I myself saw; and he raised a shrine around it of the size which the worshippers of the goddess of the crossways, called Enodia, use; for it was large enough for ten persons at once to sit and drink and keep good cheer in; and having done so he offered up the following prayer: "O Palamedes, do thou forget the wrath, wherewith thou wast wroth against the Achaeans, and grant that men may multiply in numbers and wisdom. Yea, O Palamedes, author of all eloquence, author the Muses, author of myself."

CHAPTER XIV

He also visited in passing the shrine of Orpheus when he had put in at Lesbos. And they tell that it was here that Orpheus once on a time loved to prophesy, before Apollo had turned his attention to him. For when the latter found that men no longer flocked to Gryneium for the sake of oracles nor to Clarus nor (to Delphi) where is the tripod of Apollo, and that Orpheus was the only oracle, his head having come from Thrace, he presented himself before the giver of oracles and said: "Cease to meddle with my affairs, for I have already put up long enough with your vaticinations."

CHAPTER XV

After this they continued their voyage along the sea of Euboea, which Homer considered to be one of the most dangerous and difficult to traverse. However the sea was smooth and was much better than you expected in that season; and their conversation turned upon the many and famous islands they were visiting, and upon shipbuilding and pilotage and other topics suitable to a voyage. But as Damis found fault with some of the things they said, and cut short many of their remarks, and would not allow some of their questions to be put, Apollonius realized that he was anxious to discuss some other topic and said: "What ails you, Damis, that you break in on the course of our questions in this way? For I am sure that it is not because you are seasick or in any way inconvenienced by the voyage, that you object to our conversation; for you see how smoothly our ship is wafted over her bosom by the submissive sea. Why then are you so uneasy?" "Because," replied the other, "when a great topic suggests itself, which we surely ought rather to be asking about, we are asking questions about these threadbare and antiquated subjects." "And what," said Apollonius, "may be this topic which makes you regard all others as superfluous?" "You have," he answered, "had an interview with Achilles, O Apollonius, and probably you have heard him speak at length of many things so far unknown to ourselves; and yet you tell us nothing about these, nor do you describe to us the figure of Achilles, but you fill you conversation with talk of the islands we are sailing round and of ship-building." "If you will not accuse me of bragging," said Apollonius, "you shall ear everything."

CHAPTER XVI

The rest of the company also besought him to tell them all about it, and as they were in a mood to listen to him, he said: "Well, it was not by digging a ditch like Odysseus, nor by tempting souls with the blood of sheep, that I obtained a conversation with Achilles; but I offered up the prayer which the Indians say they use in approaching their heroes. 'O Achilles,' I said, 'most of mankind declare that you are dead, but I cannot agree with them, nor can Pythagoras, my spiritual ancestor. If then we hold the truth, show to us your own form; for you would profit not a little by showing yourself to my eyes, if you should be able to use them to attest your existence.' Thereupon a slight earthquake shook the neighborhood of the barrow, and a youth issued forth five cubits high, wearing a cloak of Thessalian fashion; but in appearance he was by no means the braggart figure which some imagine Achilles to have been. Though he was stern to look upon, he had never lost his bright look; and it seems to me that his beauty has never received its meed of praise, even though Homer dwelt at length upon it; for it was really beyond the power of words, and it is easier for the singer to ruin his fame in this respect than to praise him as he deserved. At first sight he was of the size which I have mentioned, but he grew bigger, till he was twice as large and even more than that; at any rate he appeared to me to be twelve cubits high just at that moment when he reached his complete stature, and his beauty grew apace with his length. He told me then that he had never at any time shorn off his hair, bit preserved it to inviolate for the river Spercheus, for this was the river of his first intimacy; but on his cheeks you saw the first down.

And he addressed me and said: 'I am pleased to have met you, since I have long wanted a man like yourself. For the Thessalians for a long time past have failed to present their offerings to my tomb, and I do not yet wish to show my wrath against them; for if I did so, they would perish more thoroughly than ever the Hellenes did on this spot; accordingly I resort to gentle advice, and would warn them not to violate ancient custom, nor to prove themselves worse men than the Trojans here, who though they were robbed of so many of their heroes by myself, yet sacrifice publicly to me, and also give me the tithes of their fruits of season, and olive branch in hand ask for a truce from my hostility. But this I will not grant, for the perjuries which they committed against me will not suffer Ilium ever to resume its pristine beauty, nor to regain the prosperity which yet has favored many a city that was destroyed of old; nay, if they rebuild it, things shall go as hard with them as if their city had been captured only yesterday. In order then to save me from bringing the Thessalian polity then to the same condition, you must go as my envoy to their council in behalf of the object I have mentioned.' 'I will be your envoy,' I replied, 'for the object of my embassy were to save them from ruin. But, O Achilles, I would ask something of you.' 'I understand,' said he, 'for it is plain you are going to ask about the Trojan war. So ask me five questions about whatever you like, and that the Fates approve of.' I accordingly asked him firstly, if he had obtained burial in accordance with the story of the poets. 'I lie here,' he answered, 'as was most delightful to myself and Patroclus; for you know we met in mere youth, and a single golden jar holds the remains of both of us, as if we were one. But as for the dirges of the Muses and Nereids, which they say are sung over me, the Muses, I may tell you, never once came here at all, though the Nereids still resort to the spot.' Next I asked him, if Polyxena was really slaughtered over his tomb; and he replied that this was true, but that she was not slain by the Achaeans, but that she came of her own free will to the sepulcher, and that so high was the value she set on her passion for him and she for her, that she threw herself upon an upright sword. The third questions was this: 'Did Helen, O Achilles, really come to Troy or was it Homer that was pleased to make up the story?' 'For a long time,' he replied, 'we were deceived and tricked into sending envoys to the Trojans and fighting battles in her behalf, in the belief that she was in Ilium, whereas she really was living in Egypt and in the house of Proteus, whither she had been snatched away by Paris. But when we became convinced thereof, we continued to fight to win Troy itself, so as not to disgrace ourselves by retreat.' The fourth question which I ventured upon was this: 'I wonder,' I said, 'that Greece ever produced at any one time so many and such distinguished heroes as Homer says were gathered against Troy.' But Achilles answered: 'Why even the barbarians did not fall far short of us, so abundantly then did excellence flourish all over the earth.' And my fifth question was this: 'Why was it that Homer knew nothing about Palamedes, or if he knew him, then kept him out of your story?' 'If Palamedes,' he answered, 'never came to Troy, then Troy never existed either. But since this wisest and most warlike hero fell in obedience to Odysseus' whim, Homer does not introduce him into his poems, lest he should have to record the shame of Odysseus in his song.' And withal Achilles raised a wail over him as over one who was the greatest and most beautiful of men, the youngest and also the most warlike, one who in sobriety surpassed all others, and had often foregathered with the Muses. 'But you,' he added, 'O Apollonius, since sages have a tender regard for one another, you must care for his tomb and restore the image of Palamedes that has been so contemptuously cast aside; and it lies in Aeolis close to Methymna in Lesbos.' Wit these words and with the closing remarks concerning the youth from Paros, Achilles vanished with a flash of summer lightning, for indeed the cocks were already beginning their chant."

CHAPTER XVII

So much for the conversation on board; but having sailed into the Piraeus at the season of the mysteries, when the Athenians keep the most crowded of Hellenic festivals, he went post haste up from the ship into the city; but as he went forward, he fell in with quite a number of students of philosophy on their way down to Phaleron. Some of them were stripped and enjoying the heat, for in autumn the sun is hot upon the Athenians; and others were studying books, and some were rehearsing their speeches, and others were disputing. But no one passed him by, for they all guessed that it was Apollonius, and they turned and thronged around him and welcomed him warmly; and ten youths in a body met him and holding up their hands to the Acropolis, they cried: "By Athena yonder, we were on the point of going down to the Piraeus there to take ship to Ionia in order to visit you." And he welcomed them and said how much he congratulated them on their study of philosophy.

CHAPTER XVIII

It was then the day of the Epidaurian festival, at which it is still customary for the Athenians to hold the initiation at a second sacrifice after both proclamation and victims have been offered; and this custom was instituted in honor of Asclepius, because they still initiated him when on one occasion he arrived from Epidaurus too late for the mysteries. Now most people neglected the initiation and hung around Apollonius, and thought more of doing that than of being perfected in their religion before they went home; but Apollonius said that he would join them later on, and urged them to attend at once to the rites of the religion, for that he himself would be initiated. But the hierophant was not disposed to admit him to the rites, for he said that he would never initiate a wizard and charlatan, nor open the Eleusinian rite to a man who dabbled in impure rites. Thereupon Apollonius, fully equal to the occasion, said: "You have not yet mentioned the chief of my offense, which is that knowing, as I do, more about the initiatory rite than you do yourself, I have nevertheless come for initiation to you, as if you were wiser than I am." The bystanders applauded these words, and deemed that he had answered with vigor and like himself; and thereupon the hierophant, since he saw that his exclusion of Apollonius was not by any means popular with the crowd, changed his tone and said: "Be thou initiated, for thou seemest to be some wise man who has come here." But Apollonius replied: "I will be initiated at another time, and it is so and so," mentioning a name, "who will initiate me." Herein he showed his gift of prevision, for he glanced at the hierophant who succeeded the one he addressed, and presided over the temple four years later.

CHAPTER XIX

Many were the discourses which according to Damis the sage delivered at Athens; though he did not write down all of them, but only the more indispensable ones in which he handled great subjects. He took for the topic of his first discourse the matter of rite and ceremonies, and this because he saw that the Athenians were much addicted to sacrifices; and in it he explained how a religious man could best adapt his sacrifice, his libations, or prayers to any particular divinity, and at what hours of day and night he ought to offer them. And it is possible to obtain a book of Apollonius, in which he gives instructions in his own words. But Athens he discussed these topics with a view to improving his own wisdom and that of others in the first place, and in the second of convincing the hierophant of blasphemy and ignorance in the remarks he had made; for who could continue to regard as one impure in his religion a man who taught philosophically how the worship of the gods is to be conducted?

CHAPTER XX

Now while he was discussing the question of libations, there chanced to be present in his audience a young dandy who bore so evil a reputation for licentiousness that his conduct had long been the subject of coarse street-corner songs. His home was Corcyra, and he traced his pedigree to Alcinous the Phaeacian who entertained Odysseus. Apollonius then was talking about libations, and was urging them not to drink out of a particular cup, but to reserve it for the gods, without ever touching it or drinking out of it. But when he also urged them to have handles on the cup, and to pour the libation over the handle, because that is the part at which men are least likely to drink, the youth burst out into loud and coarse laughter, and quite drowned his voice. Then Apollonius looked up and said: "It is not yourself that perpetrates this insult, but the demon, who drives you without your knowing it." And in fact the youth was, without knowing it, possessed by a devil; for he would laugh at things that no one else laughed at, and then would fall to weeping for no reason at all, and he would talk and sing to himself. Now most people thought that it was boisterous humor of youth which led him into excesses; but he was really the mouthpiece of a devil, though it only seemed a drunken frolic in which on that occasion he was indulging. Now, when Apollonius gazed on him, the ghost in him began to utter cries of fear and rage, such as one hears from people who are being branded or racked; and the ghost swore that he would leave the you man alone and never take possession of any man again. But Apollonius addressed him with anger, as a master might a shifty, rascally, and shameless slave and so on, and he ordered him to quit the young man and show by a visible sign that he had done so. "I will throw down yonder statue," said the devil, and pointed to one of the images which were there in the king's portico, for there it was that the scene took place. But when the statue began by moving gently, and then fell down, it would defy anyone to describe the hubbub which arose thereat and the way they clapped their hand with wonder. But the young man rubbed his eyes as if he had just woke up, and he looked towards the rays of the sun, and assumed a modest aspect, as all had their attention concentrated on him; for he no longer showed himself licentious, nor did he stare madly about, but he had returned to his own self, as thoroughly as if he had been treated with drugs; and he gave up his dainty dress and summery garments and the rest of his sybaritic way of life, and he fell in love with the austerity of philosophers, and donned their cloak, and stripping off his old self modeled his life and future upon that of Apollonius.

CHAPTER XXI

And he is said to have rebuked the Athenians for their conduct of the festival of Dionysus, which they hold at the season of the month Anthesterion. For when he saw them flocking to the theater he imagined that the were going to listen to solos and compositions in the way of processional and rhythmic hymns, such as are sung in comedies and tragedies; but when he heard them dancing lascivious jigs to the rondos of a pipe, and in the midst of the sacred epic of Orpheus striking attitudes as the Hours, or as nymphs, or as bacchants, he set himself to rebuke their proceedings and said: "Stop dancing away the reputations of the victors of Salamis as well as of many other good men deported this life. For if indeed this were a Lacedaemonian form of dance, I would say, 'Bravo, soldiers; for you are training yourselves for war, and I will join in your dance'; but as it is a soft dance and one of effeminate tendency, what am I to say of your national trophies? Not as monuments of shame to the Medians or Persians, but to your own shame they will have been raised, should you degenerate so much from those who set them up. And what do you mean by your saffron robes and your purple and scarlet raiment? For surely the Acharnians never dressed themselves up in this way, nor ever the knights of Colonus rode in such garb. A woman commanded a ship from Caria and sailed against you with Xerxes, and about her there was nothing womanly, but she wore the garb and armor of a man; but you are softer than the women of Xerxes' day, and you are dressing yourselves up to your own despite, old and young and striplings alike, all those who of old flocked to the temple of Agraulus in order to swear to die in battle on behalf of the fatherland. And now it seems that the same people are ready to swear to become bacchants and don the thyrsus in behalf of their country; and no one bears a helmet, but "disguised as female harlequins," to use the phrase of Euripides, they shine in shame alone. Nay more, I hear that you turn yourselves into winds, and wave your skirts, and pretend that you are ships bellying their sails aloft. But surely you might at least have some respect for the winds that were your allies and once blew mightily to protect you, instead of turning Boreas who was your patron, and who of all the winds is the most masculine, into a woman; for Boreas would never have become the lover of Oreithya, if he had seen her executing, like you, a skirt dance."

CHAPTER XXII

He also corrected the following abuse at Athens. The Athenians ran in crowds to the theater beneath the Acropolis to witness human slaughter, and the passion for such sports was stronger there than it is in Corinth today; for they would buy for large sums adulterers and fornicators and burglars and cut-purses and kidnappers and such-like rabble, and then they took them and armed them and set them to fight with one another. Apollonius then attacked these practices, and when the Athenians invited him to attend their assembly, he refused to enter a place so impure and reeking with gore. And this he said in an epistle to them; he said that he was surprised "that the goddess had not already quitted the Acropolis, when you shed such blood under her eyes. For I suspect that presently, when you are conducting the pan-Athenaic procession, you will no longer be content with bull, but will be sacrificing hecatombs of men to the goddess. And thou, O Dionysus, dost thou after such bloodshed frequent their theater? And do the wise among the Athenians pour libations to thee there? Nay do thou depart, O Dionysus. Holier and purer is thy Cithaeron."

Such were the more serious of the subjects which I have found he treated of at that time in Athens in his philosophical discourses.

CHAPTER XXIII

And he also went as envoy to the Thessalians in behalf of Achilles at the time of the conferences held in Pylaea, at which the Thessalians transact the Amphictyonic business. And they were so frightened that they passed a resolution for the resumption of the ceremonies at the tomb. As for the monument of Leonidas the Spartan, he almost clasped it in his arms, so great was his admiration for the hero; and as he was coming to the mound where the Lacedaemonians are said to have been overwhelmed by the bolts which the enemy rained upon them, he heard his companions discussing with one another which was the loftiest hill in Hellas, this topic being suggested it seems by the sight of Oeta which rose before their eyes; so ascending the mound, he said: "I consider this the loftiest spot of all, for those who fell here in defense of freedom raised it to a level with Oeta and carried it to a height surpassing many mountains like Olympus. It is these men that I admire, and beyond any of them Megistias the Acarnanian; for he knew the death that they were about to die, and deliberately made up his mind to share in it with these heroes, fearing not so much death, as the prospect that he should miss death in such company."

CHAPTER XXIV

And he also visited all the Greek shrines, namely that of Dodona, and the Pythian temple, and the one at Abae, and he betook himself to those of Amphiaraus and of Trophonius, and he went up to the shrine of the Muses on Mount Helicon. And when he visited these temples and corrected the rites, the priests went in his company, and the votaries followed in his steps, and goblets were set up flowing with rational discourse and the thirsty quaffed their wine. And as the Olympic Games were coming on, and the people of Elis invited him to take part in the contest, he answered: "You seem to me to tarnish the glory of the Olympic Games, if you need to send special invitations to those who intend to visit you at their own promptings." And as he was at the Isthmus, when the sea was roaring around Lechaeum and hearing it, he said: "This neck of land shall be cut through, or rather it shall not be cut." And herein he uttered a prediction of the cutting of the Isthmus which was attempted soon afterwards, when Nero after seven years projected it. For the latter left his imperial palace and came to Hellas, with the intention of submitting himself to the heralds' commands, in the Olympic and Pythian festivals; and he also won the prize at the Isthmus, his victories being won in the contest of singing to the harp and in that of the heralds. And he also won the prize for the tragedians at Olympia. It is said that he then formed the novel project of cutting through the Isthmus, in order to make a canal of it for ships to sail through and not right round, uniting the Aegean with the Adriatic Sea. So instead of every ship having to round Cape Malea , most by passing through the canal so cut could abridge an otherwise circuitous voyage. But mark the upshot of the oracle of Apollonius. They began to dig the canal at Lechaeum, but they had not advanced more than about four stadia of continuous excavation, when Nero stopped the work of cutting it. Some say because Egyptian men of science explained him the nature of the seas, and declared that the sea above Lechaeum would flood and obliterate the island of Aegina, and others because he apprehended a revolution in the empire. Such then was the meaning of Apollonius' prediction that the Isthmus would be cut through and would not be cut through.

CHAPTER XXV

Now there was in Corinth at that time a man named Demetrius, who studied philosophy and had embraced in his system all the masculine vigor of the Cynics. Of him Favorinus in several of his works subsequently made the most generous mention, and his attitude towards Apollonius was exactly that which they say Antisthenes took up towards the system of Socrates: for he followed him and was anxious to be his disciple, and was devoted to his doctrines, and converted to the side of Apollonius the more esteemed of his own pupils. Among the latter was Menippus a Lycian of twenty-five years of age, well endowed with good judgment, and of a physique so beautifully proportioned that in mien he resembled a fine and gentlemanly athlete. Now this Menippus was supposed by most people to be loved by a foreign woman, who was good-looking and extremely dainty, and said that she was rich; although she was really, as it turned out, not one of these things, but was only so in semblance. For as he was walking all alone along the road towards Cenchraea, he met with an apparition, and it was a woman who clasped his hand and declared that she had been long in love with him, and that she was a Phoenician woman and lived in a suburb of Corinth, and she mentioned the name of the particular suburb, and said: "When you reach the place this evening, you will hear my voice as I sing to you, and you shall have wine such as you never before drank, and there will be no rival to disturb you; and we two beautiful beings will live together." The youth consented to this, for although he was in general a strenuous philosopher, he was nevertheless susceptible to the tender passion; and he visited her in the evening, and for the future constantly sought her company as his darling, for he did not yet realize that she was a mere apparition.

Then Apollonius looked over Menippus as a sculptor might do, and he sketched an outline of the youth and examined him, and having observed his foibles, he said: "You are a fine youth and are hunted by fine women, but in this case you are cherishing a serpent, and a serpent cherishes you." And when Menippus expressed his surprise, he added: "For this lady is of a kind you cannot marry. Why should you? Do you think that she loves you?" "Indeed I do," said the youth, "since she behaves to me as if she loves me." "And would you then marry her?" said Apollonius. "Why, yes, for it would be delightful to marry a woman who loves you." Thereupon Apollonius asked when the wedding was to be. "Perhaps tomorrow," said the other, "for it brooks no delay." Apollonius therefore waited for the occasion of the wedding breakfast, and then, presenting himself before the guests who had just arrived, he said: "Where is the dainty lady at whose instance ye are come?" "Here she is," replied Menippus, and at the same moment he rose slightly from his seat, blushing. "And to which of you belong the silver and gold and all the rest of the decorations of the banqueting hall?" "To the lady," replied the youth, "for this is all I have of my own," pointing to the philosopher's cloak which he wore.

And Apollonius said: "Have you heard of the gardens of Tantalus, how they exist and yet do not exist?" "Yes," they answered, "in the poems of Homer, for we certainly never went down to Hades." "As such," replied Apollonius, "you must regard this adornment, for it is not reality but the semblance of reality. And that you may realize the truth of what I say, this fine bride is one of the vampires, that is to say of those beings whom the many regard as lamias and hobgoblins. These beings fall in love, and they are devoted to the delights of Aphrodite, but especially to the flesh of human beings, and they decoy with such delights those whom they mean to devour in their feasts." And the lady said: "Cease your ill-omened talk and begone"; and she pretended to be disgusted at what she heard, and in fact she was inclined to rail at philosophers and say that they always talked nonsense. When, however, the goblets of gold and the show of silver were proved as light as air and all fluttered away out of their sight, while the wine-bearers and the cooks and all the retinue of servants vanished before the rebukes of Apollonius, the phantom pretended to weep, and prayed him not to torture her nor to compel her to confess what she really was. But Apollonius insisted and would not let her off, and then she admitted that she was a vampire, and was fattening up Menippus with pleasures before devouring his body, for it was her habit to feed upon young and beautiful bodies, because their blood is pure and strong. I have related at length, because it was necessary to do so, this the best-known story of Apollonius; for many people are aware of it and know that he incident occurred in the center of Hellas; but they have only heard in a general and vague manner that he once caught and overcame a lamia in Corinth, but they have never learned what she was about, nor that he did it to save Menippus, but I owe my own account to Damis and to the work which he wrote.

CHAPTER XXVI

It was at this time also that he had a difference with Bassus of Corinth; for the latter was regarded as a parricide and believed to be such. But he feigned a wisdom of his own, and no bridle could be set upon his tongue. However, Apollonius put a stop to his reviling himself, both by the letters which he sent him, and the harangues which he delivered against him. For everything which he said about his being a parricide was held to be true; for it was felt that such a man would never have condensed to mere personal abuse, not to have said what was not true.

CHAPTER XXVII

The career of our sage in Olympia was as follows: when Apollonius was on his way up to Olympia, some envoys of the Lacedaemonians met him and asked him to visit their city; there seemed, however, to be no appearance of Sparta about them, for they conducted themselves in a very effeminate manner and reeked of luxury. And seeing them to have smooth legs, and sleek hair, and that they did not even wear beards, nay were even dressed in soft raiment, he sent such a letter to the Ephors that the latter issued a public proclamation and forbade the use of pitch plasters in the baths[8], and drove out of the city the men who professed to rejuvenate dandies[9], and they restored the ancient régime in every respect. The consequence was that the wrestling grounds were filled once more with the youth, and the jousts and the common meals were restored, and Lacedaemon became once more like herself. And when he learned that they had set their house in order, he sent them an epistle from Olympia, briefer than any cipher dispatch of ancient Sparta; and it ran as follows:—

"Apollonius to the Ephors sends salutation.

"It is the duty of men not to fall into sin, but of noble men, to recognize that they are doing so."

---

[8] Adhesive plasters were used to remove superfluous hair from the body.
[9] Literally "hair-pluckers."

CHAPTER XXVIII

And looking at the statue set up at Olympia, he said: "Hail, O thou good Zeus, for thou art so good that thou dost impart thine own nature unto mankind." And he also gave them an account of the brazen statue of Milo and explained the attitude of this figure. For this Milo is seen standing on a disk with his two feet close together, and in his left hand he grasps a pomegranate, whole of his right hand the fingers are extended and pressed together as if to pass through a chink. Now among the people of Olympia and Arcadia the story told about this athlete is, that he was so inflexible that he could never be induced to leave the spot on which he stood; and they infer the grip of the clenched fingers from the way he grasps the pomegranate, and that they could never be separated from another, however much you struggled with any one of them, because the intervals between the extended fingers are very close; and they say that the fillet with which his head is bound is a symbol of temperance and sobriety. Apollonius while admitting that this account was wisely conceived, said that the truth was still wiser. "In order that you may know," said he, "the meaning of the statue of Milo, the people of Croton made this athlete a priest of Hera. As to the meaning then of this mitre, I need not explain it further than by reminding you that the hero was a priest. But the pomegranate is the only fruit which is grown in honor of Hera; and the disk beneath his feet means that the priest is standing on a small shield to offer his prayer to Hera; and this is also indicated by his right hand. As for the artist's rendering the fingers and feet, between which he has left no interval, that you may ascribe to the antique style of the sculpture."

CHAPTER XXIX

He was present at the rites, and he commended the solicitude with which the people of Elis administered them, and the good order with which they conducted them, as if they considered themselves to be as much on trial as the athletes who were contending for the prizes, anxious neither willing nor unwillingly to commit any error. And when his companions asked him what he thought of the Eleans in respect of their management of the Olympic games, he replied: "Whether they are wise, I do not know, but of their cleverness I am quite sure."

CHAPTER XXX

How great a dislike he entertained of people who imagine they can write, and how senseless he considered those to be who essay a literary task beyond their powers, we can learn from the following incident: A young man who thought he had talent met him in the precincts of the temple and said: "Pray honor me with your presence tomorrow, for I am going to recite something." When Apollonius asked him what he was going to recite, he replied: "I have composed a treatise upon Zeus." And as he said these words he showed, with no little pride at its stoutness, a book which he was carrying under his garments. "And," said Apollonius, "what are you going to praise about Zeus? Is it the Zeus of this fane, and are you going to say that there is nothing like him on the whole earth?" "Why that, of course," said the other, "and a great deal more that comes before that and also follows it. For I shall say how the seasons and how everything on earth and above the earth, and how the winds and all the stars belong to Zeus." And Apollonius said: "It seems to me that you are a past-master of encomium." "Yes," said the other, "and that is why I have composed an encomium of gout and of blindness and deafness." "And why not of dropsy too," said Apollonius; "for surely you won't rule out influenza from the sphere of your cleverness, since you are minded to praise such things? And while you are about it, you do as well to attend funerals and detail the praises of the various diseases of which the people died; for so you will somewhat soothe the regrets of the fathers and children and the near relations of the deceased." And as he saw that the effect of his words was to put a bridle on the young man's tongue, he added: "My dear author, which is the author of a panegyric likely best to praise, things which he knows or things which he does not?" "Things which he knows," said the youth. "For how can a man praise things which he does not know?" "I conclude then that you have already written a panegyric of your own father?" "I wanted to," said the other, "but as he appears to me rather a big man and a noble one, and the fairest of men I know, and a very clever housekeeper, and a paragon of wisdom all round, I gave up the attempt to compose a panegyric upon him, lest I should disgrace my father by a discourse which would not do him justice." Thereupon Apollonius was incensed, as he often was against trivial and vulgar people. "Then," said he, "you wretch, you are not sure that you can ever sufficiently praise your own father whom you know as well as you do yourself, and yet you set out in this light-hearted fashion to write an encomium of the father of men and of gods and of the creator of everything around us and above us; and you have no reverence for him whom you praise, nor have you the least idea that you are embarking on a subject which transcends the power of man."

CHAPTER XXXI

The conversations which Apollonius held in Olympia turned upon the most profitable topics, such as wisdom and courage and temperance, and in a word upon all the virtues. He discussed these from the platform of the temple, and he astonished everyone not only by the insight he showed but by his forms of expression. And the Lacedaemonians flocked round him and invited him to share their hospitality at their shrine of Zeus, and made him father of their youths at home, and legislator of their lives and the honor of their old men. Now there was a Corinthian who felt piqued at all this, and asked whether they were also going to celebrate a theophany for him. "Yes," said the other, "by Castor and Pollux, everything is ready anyhow." But Apollonius did not encourage them to pay him such honors, for he feared they would arouse envy. And when having crossed the mountain Taygetus, he saw a Lacedaemon hard at work before him and all the institutions of Lycurgus in full swing, he felt that it would be a real pleasure to converse with the authorities of the Lacedaemonians about things which they might ask his opinion upon; so they asked him when he arrived how the gods are to be revered, and he answered: "As your lords and masters." Secondly, they asked him: "And how the heroes?" "As fathers," he replied. And their third question was: "How are men to be revered?" And he answered: "Your question is not one which any Spartan should put." They asked him also what he thought of their laws, and he replied that they were most excellent teachers, adding that teachers will gain fame in proportion as their disciples are industrious. And when they asked him what advice he had to give them about courage, he answered: "Why what else, but that you should display it?"

CHAPTER XXXII

And about this time it happened that a certain youth of Lacedaemon was charged by his fellow citizens with violating the customs of his country. For though he was descended from Callicratidas who led the navy at the battle of Arginusae, yet he was devoted to seafaring and paid not attention to public affairs; but, instead of doing so, would sail off to Carthage or Sicily in the ships which he had had built. Apollonius then hearing that he was arraigned for this conduct, thought it a pity to desert the youth who had just fallen under the hand of justice, and said to him: "My excellent fellow, why do you go about so full of anxiety and with such a gloomy air?" "A public prosecution," said the other, "has been instituted against me, because I go in for seafaring and take no part in public affairs." "And was your father or your grandfather a mariner?" "Of course not," said the other; "they were all of them chiefs of the gymnasium and Ephors and public guardians; Callicratidas, however, my ancestor, was a real admiral of the fleet." "I suppose," said Apollonius, "you hardly mean him of Arginusae fame?" "Yes, that fell in the naval action leading his fleet." "Then," said Apollonius, "your ancestor's mode of death has not given you any prejudice against a seafaring life?" "No, by Zeus," said the other, "for it is not with a view to conducting battles by sea that I set sail." "Well, and can you mention any rabble of people more wretched and ill-starred than merchants and skippers? In the first place they roam from sea to sea, looking for some market that is badly stocked; and then they sell and are sold, associating with factors and brokers, and they subject their own heads to the most unholy rate of interest in their hurry to get back to the principal; and if they do well, their ship has a lucky voyage, and they tell you a long story of how they never wrecked it either willingly or unwillingly; but if their gains do not balance their debts, they jump into their long boats and dash their ships on to the rocks, and make no bones as sailors of robbing others of their substance, pretending in the most blasphemous manner that it is an act of God. And even if the seafaring crowd who go on voyages be not so bad as I make them out to be; yet is there any shame worse than this, for a man who is a citizen of Sparta and the child of forbears who of old lived in the heart of Sparta, to secrete himself in the hold of a ship, oblivious of Lycurgus and Iphitus, thinking of nought but of cargoes and petty bills of lading? For if he thinks of nothing else, he might at least bear in mind that Sparta herself, so long as she stuck to the land, enjoyed a fame reaching to heaven; but when she began to covet the sea, she sank down and down, and was blotted out at last, not only on the sea but on the land as well." The young man was so overcome by these arguments, that he bowed his head to the earth and wept, because he heard he was so degenerate from his fathers; and he sold the ships by which he lived. And when Apollonius saw that he was restored to his senses and inclined to embrace a career on land, he led him before the Ephors and obtained his acquittal.

CHAPTER XXXIII

Here is another incident that happened in Lacedaemon. A letter came from the Emperor heaping reproaches upon the public assembly of the Lacedaemonians, and declaring that in their license they abused liberty, and this letter had been addressed to them at the instance of the governor of Greece, who had maligned them. The Lacedaemonians then were at a loss what to do, and Sparta was divided against herself over the issue, whether in their reply to the letter they should try to appease the Emperor's wrath or take a lofty tone towards him. Under the circumstances they sought the counsel of Apollonius and asked him how to pitch the tone of their letter. And he, when he saw them to be divided on the point, came forward in their public assembly and delivered himself of the following short and concise speech: "Palamedes discovered writing not only in order that people might write, but also in order that they might know what they must not write." In this way accordingly he dissuaded the Lacedaemonians from showing themselves to be either too bold or cowardly.

CHAPTER XXXIV

He stayed in Sparta for some time after the Olympic Festival, until the winter was over; and at the beginning of the spring proceeded to Malea with the intention of setting out for Rome. But while he was still pondering this project, he had the following dream: It seemed as if a woman both very tall and venerable in years embraced him, and asked him to visit her before he set sail for Italy; and she said that she was the nurse of Zeus, and she wore a wreath that held everything that is on the earth or in the seas. He proceeded to ponder the meaning of the vision, and came to the conclusion that he ought first to sail to Crete, which we regard as the nurse of Zeus, because in that island Zeus was born; although the wreath might perhaps indicate some other island. Now there were several ships at Malea, making ready to set sail to Crete, so he embarked upon one sufficient for his association, which is the title he gave to his companions, and also his companions' servants, for he did not think it right to pass over the latter. And he bent his course for Cydonia, and sailed past that place to Knossus, where a labyrinth is shown, which, I believe, once on a time, contained the Minotaur. As his companions were anxious to see this he allowed them to do so, but refused himself to be a spectator of the injustice of Minos, and continued his course to Gortyna because he longed to visit Ida. He accordingly climbed up, and after visiting the sacred sites he passed on to the shrine of Lebena. And this is a shrine of Asclepius, and just as the whole of Asia flocks to Pergamon, so the whole of Crete flocked to this shrine; and many Libyans also cross the sea to visit it, for it faces towards the Libyan sea close to Phaestus, where the little rock keeps out a might sea. And they say that this shrine is named that of Lebena, because a promontory juts out from it which resembles a lion, for here, as often, a chance arrangement of the rocks suggests an animal form; and they tell a story about this promontory, how it was once one of the lion which were yoked in the chariot of Rhea. Here Apollonius was haranguing on one occasion about midday, and was addressing quite a number of people who were worshipping at the shrine, when an earthquake shook the whole of Crete at once, and a roar of thunder was heard to issue not from the clouds but from the earth, and the sea receded about seven stadia. And most of them were afraid that the sea by receding in this way would drag the temple after it, so that they would be carried away. But Apollonius said: "Be of good courage, for the sea has given birth and brought forth land." And they thought that he was alluding to the harmony of the elements, and was urging that the sea would never wreak any violence upon the land; but after a few days some travelers arrived from Cydoniatis and announced that on the very day on which this portent occurred and just at the same hour of midday, an island rose out of the sea in the firth between Thera and Crete. However, I must give up all prolixity and hurry on to relate the conversations which he held in Rome, subsequently to his stay in Crete.

CHAPTER XXXV

Nero was opposed to philosophy, because he suspected its devotees to be addicted to magic, and of being diviners in disguise; and at last the philosopher's mantle brought its wearers before the law courts, as if it were a mere cloak of the divining art. I will not mention other names, but Musonius of Babylon, a man only second to Apollonius, was thrown into prison for the crime of being a sage, and there lay in danger of death; and he would have died for all his gaoler cared, of it had not been for the strength of his constitution.

CHAPTER XXXVI

Such was the condition in which philosophy stood when Apollonius was approaching Rome; and at a distance of one hundred and twenty stadia from its walls he met Philolaus of Cittium in the neighborhood of the Grove of Aricia. Now Philolaus was a polished speaker, but too soft to bear any hardships. He had quitted Rome, and was virtually a fugitive, and any philosopher he met with he urged to take the same course. He accordingly addressed himself to Apollonius, and urged him to give way to circumstances, and not to proceed to Rome, where philosophy was in such bad odor; and he related to him what had taken place there, and as he did so he kept turning his head round, lest anybody should be listening behind him to what he said. "And you," he said, "after attaching this band of philosophers to yourself, a thing which will bring you into suspicion and odium, are on your way thither, knowing nothing of the officers set over the gates by Nero, who will arrest you and them before ever you enter or get inside." "And what," said Apollonius, "O Philolaus, are the occupations of the autocrat said to be?" "He drives a chariot," said the other, "in public; and he comes forward on the boards of the Roman theaters and sings songs, and he lives with gladiators, and hem himself fights as one and slays his man." Apollonius therefore replied and said: "Then, my dear fellow, do you think that there can be any better spectacle for men of education than to see an emperor thus demeaning himself? For if in Plato's opinion man is the sport of the gods, what a theme we have here provided for philosophers by an emperor who makes himself the sport of man and sets himself to delight the common herd with the spectacle of his own shame?" "Yes, by Zeus," said Philolaus, "if you could do it with impunity; but if you are going to be taken up and lose your life, and if Nero is going to devour you alive before you see anything of what he does, your interview with him will cost you dear, much dearer than it ever cost Ulysses to visit the Cyclops in his home; though he lost many of his comrades in his anxiety to see him, and because he yielded to the temptation of beholding so cruel a monster." But Apollonius said: "So you think that this ruler is less blinded than the Cyclops, if he commits such crimes?" And Philolaus answered: "Let him do what he likes, but do you at least save these your companions."

CHAPTER XXXVII

And these words he uttered in a loud voice and with an air of weeping; whereupon Damis conceived a fear lest the younger men of his party should be unmanned by the craven terrors of Philolaus. So he took aside Apollonius and said: "This hare, with all his panicky fears, will ruin these young men, and fill them with discouragement." But Apollonius said: "Well, of all the blessings which have been vouchsafed to me by the gods, often without my praying for them at all, this present one, I may say, is the greatest that I have ever enjoyed; for chance has thrown in my way a touchstone to test these young men, of a kind to prove most thoroughly which of them are philosophers, and which of them prefer some other line of conduct than that of philosopher." And in fact the knock-kneed among them were detected in no time, for under the influence of what Philolaus said, some of them declared that they were ill, others that they had no provisions for the journey, others that they were homesick, others that they had been deterred by dreams; and in the result thirty-four companions of Apollonius were willing to accompany him to Rome were reduced to eight. And all the rest ran away from Nero and philosophy, both at once, and took to their heels.

CHAPTER XXXVIII

He therefore assembled those who were left, among whom were Menippus, who had foregathered with the hobgoblin, and Dioscorides the Egyptian, and Damis, and said to them: "I shall not scold those who have abandoned us, but I shall rather praise you for being men like myself: nor shall I think a man a coward because he has disappeared out of dread of Nero, but anyone who rises superior to such fear I will hail as a philosopher, and I will teach him all I know. I think then that we ought first of all to pray to the gods who have suggested these different courses to you and to them; and then we ought to solicit their direction and guidance, for we have not any succor to rely upon apart from the gods. We must then march forward to the city which is the mistress of so much of the inhabited world; but how can anybody go forward thither, unless the gods are leading him? The more so, because a tyranny has been established in this city so harsh and cruel, that it does not suffer men to be wise. And let not anyone think it foolish so to venture along a path which many philosophers are fleeing from; for in the first place I do not esteem any human agency so formidable that a wise man can ever be terrified by it; and in the second place, I would not urge upon you the pursuit of bravery, unless it were attended with danger. Moreover, in traversing more of the earth than any man yet has visited, I have seen hosts of Arabian and Indian wild beasts; but as to this wild beast, which many call a tyrant, I know not either how many heads he has, nor whether he has crooked talons and jagged teeth. In any case, though this monster is said to be a social beast and to inhabit the heart of cities, yet he is also much wilder and fiercer in his disposition than animals of the mountain and forest, that whereas you can sometimes tame and alter the character of lions and leopards by flattering them, this one is only roused to greater cruelty than before by those who stroke him, so that he rends and devours all alike. And again there is no animal anyhow of which you can say that it ever devours its own mother, but Nero is gorged with such quarry. It is true, perhaps, that the same crime was committed in the case of Orestes and Alcmaeon, but they had some excuse for their deeds, in that the father of the one was murdered by his own wife, while the other's had been sold for a necklace; this man, however, has murdered the very mother to whom he owes his adoption by the aged emperor and his inheritance of the empire; for he shipwrecked and so slew her close to land in a vessel built for the express purpose of doing her to death. If, however, anyone is disposed to dread Nero for these reasons, and is led abruptly to forsake philosophy, conceiving that it is not safe for him to thwart his evil temper, let him know that the quality of inspiring fear really belongs to those who are devoted to temperance and wisdom, because they are sure of divine succor. But let him snap his fingers at the threats of the proud and insolent, as he would at those of drunken men; for we regard the latter surely as daft and silly, but not as formidable. Let us then go forward to Rome, if we are good men and true; for to Nero's proclamations in which he banishes philosophy, we may well oppose the verse of Sophocles:

"'For in no wise was it Zeus who made this proclamation unto me,'

nor the Muses either, nor Apollo the god of eloquence. But it may well be that Nero himself knows this iambic line, for he is, they say, addicted to tragedy."

This occasion reminds one of the saying of Homer, that when warriors are knit together with reason, they become as it were a single plume and helmet, and a single shield; and it seems to me that this very sentiment found its application in regard to these heroes; for they were welded together and encouraged by the words of Apollonius to die in behalf of their philosophy, and strengthened to show themselves superior to those who had run away.

CHAPTER XXXIX

They accordingly approached the gates of Rome, and the sentries asked them no questions, although they scanned their dress with some curiosity; for the fashion of it was that of religious ascetics, and did not in the least resemble that of beggars. And they put up at an inn close to the gate, and were taking their supper, for it was already eventide, when a drunken fellow with a far from harsh voice turned up as it were for a revel; and he was one it seems who was in the habit of going round about Rome singing Nero's songs and hired for the purpose, and anyone who neglected to listen to him or refused to pay him for his music, he had the right to arrest for violating Nero's majesty. And he carried a harp and all the outfit proper for a harpist, and he also had put away in a casket a second-hand string which others had fastened on their instruments and tuned up before him, and this he said he had purchased off Nero's own lyre for two minas, and that he would sell it to no one who was not a first-rate harpist and fit to contend for the prize at Delphi. He then struck up a prelude, according to his custom, and after performing a short hymn composed by Nero, he added various lays, some out of the story of Orestes, and some from the Antigone, and others from one or another of the tragedies composed by Nero, and he proceeded to drawl out the rondos which Nero was in the habit of murdering by his miserable writhings and modulations. As they listened with some indifference, he proceeded to accuse them of violating Nero's majesty and of being enemies of his divine voice; but they paid no attention to him. Then Menippus asked Apollonius how he appreciated these remarks, whereupon he said: "How do I appreciate them? Why, just a I did his songs. Let us, however, O Menippus, not take too much offence at his remarks, but let us give him something for his performance and dismiss him to sacrifice to the Muses of Nero."

CHAPTER XL

So ended the episode of this poor drunken fool. But at daybreak Telesinus, one of the consuls, called Apollonius to him, and said: "What is this dress which you wear?" And he answered: "A pure garment made from no dead matter." "And what is your wisdom?" "An inspiration," answered Apollonius, "which teaches men how to pray and sacrifice to the gods." "And is there anyone, my philosopher, who does not know that already?" "Many," said the sage, "and if there is here and there a man who understands these matters aright, he will be very much improved by hearing from a man who is wiser than himself that, what he knows, he knows for a certainty." When Telesinus heard this, for he was a man fairly disposed to worship and religion, he recognized the sage from the rumors which he had long before heard about him; and though he did not think he need openly ask him his name, in case he wished to conceal his identity from anyone, he nevertheless led him on to talk afresh about religion, for he was himself an apt reasoner, and feeling that he was addressing a sage, he asked: "What do you pray for when you approach the altars?" "I," said Apollonius, "for my part pray that justice may prevail, that the laws may not be broken, that the wise may continue to be poor, but that others may be rich, as long as they are so without fraud." "Then," said the other, "when you ask for so much, do you think you will get it?" "Yes, by Zeus," said Apollonius, "for I string together all my petitions in a single prayer, and when I reach the altars this is how I pray: 'O ye gods, bestow on me whatever is due.' If therefore I am of the number of worthy men, I shall obtain more than I have said; but if the gods rank me among the wicked, then they will send to me the opposite of what I ask; and I shall not blame the gods, because for my demerit I am judged worthy of evil." Telesinus then was greatly struck by these words, and wishing to show him a favor, he said: "You may visit all the temples, and written instructions shall be sent by me to the priests who minister in them to admit you and adopt your reforms." "And supposing you did not write," said Apollonius, "would they not admit me?" "No, by Zeus," said he, "for that is my own office and prerogative." "I am glad," said Apollonius, "that so generous a man as yourself holds such a high office, but I would like you to know this much too about me: I like to live in such temples as are not too closely shut up, and none of the gods object to my presence, for they invite me to share their habitation. So let this liberty too be accorded to me, inasmuch as even the barbarians always permitted it." And Telesinus said: "The barbarians have more to be proud of in this matter than the Romans, for I would that as much could be said of ourselves." Apollonius accordingly lived in the temples, though he changed them and passed from one to another; and when he was blamed for doing so, he said: "Neither do the gods live all their time in heaven, but they take journeys to Ethiopia, as also to Olympus and to Athos, and I think it is a pity that the gods should go roaming around all the nations of men, and yet that men should not be allowed to visit all the gods alike. What is more, though masters would incur no reproach for neglecting slaves, for whom they probably may feel a contempt because they are not good, yet the slaves who did not devote themselves wholly to their masters, would be destroyed by them as cursed wretches and chattels hateful to the gods."

CHAPTER XLI

The result of his discourses about religion was that the gods were worshipped with more zeal, and that men flocked to the temples where he was, in the belief that by doing so they would obtain an increase of divine blessings. And our sage's conversations were so far not objected to, because he held them in public and addressed himself to all men alike; for he did not hover about rich men's doors, nor hang about the mighty, though he welcomed them if they resorted to him, and he talked with them just as much as he did to the common people.

CHAPTER XLII

Now Demetrius being attracted to Apollonius, as I have said above in my account of the events at Corinth, betook himself subsequently to Rome, and proceeded to court Apollonius, at the same time that he launched out against Nero. In consequence our sage's profession was looked at askance, and he was thought to have set Demetrius on to proceed thus, and the suspicion was increased on the occasion of Nero's completion of the most magnificent gymnasium in Rome: for the auspicious day was being celebrated therein by Nero himself and the great Senate and all the knights of Rome, when Demetrius made his way into the gymnasium itself and delivered himself of a philippic against people who bathed, declaring that they enfeebled and polluted themselves; and he showed that such institutions were a useless expense. He was only saved from immediate death as the penalty of such language by the fact that Nero was in extra good voice when he sang on that day, and he sang in the tavern which adjoined the gymnasium, naked except for a girdle round his waste, like any low tapster. Demetrius, however, did not wholly escape the risk which he had courted by his language; for Tigellinus, to whom Nero had committed the power of life and death, proceeded to banish him from Rome, on the plea that he had ruined and overthrown the bath by the words he used; and he began to dog the steps of Apollonius secretly, in the hope that he would catch him out too in some compromising utterance.

CHAPTER XLIII

The latter, however, showed no disposition to ridicule the government, nor on the other hand did he display any of the anxiety usually felt by those who are on their guard against some danger. He merely continued to discuss in simple and adequate terms the topics laid before him; and Telesinus and others continued to study philosophy in his company, for although philosophy was just then in a perilous condition, they did not dream that they would imperil themselves with his studies. Yet he was suspected as I have said, and the suspicion was intensified by words he uttered in connection to a prodigy. For presently when there was an eclipse of the sun and a clap of thunder was heard, a thing that very rarely occurs at the moment of an eclipse, he glanced up to heaven and said: "There shall be some great event and there shall not be." Now at the time those who heard these words were unable to comprehend their meaning; but on the third day after the eclipse, everyone understood what was meant: for while Nero sat at meat a thunderbolt fell on the table, and clove asunder the cup that was in his hand and was close to his lips. And the fact that he so narrowly escaped being struck was intended by the words that a great event would happen and yet should not happen. Tigellinus when he heard this story began to dread Apollonius as one who was wise in supernatural matters; and though he felt that he had better not prefer any open charges against him, lest he should incur at his hands some mysterious disaster, nevertheless he used all the eyes with which the government sees, to watch Apollonius, whether he was talking or holding his tongue, or sitting down or walking about, and to mark what he ate, and in whose houses, and whether he offered sacrifice or not.

CHAPTER XLIV

Just then a distemper broke out in Rome, called by the physicians influenza; and it was attended, it seems, by coughings, and the voice of speakers was affected by it. Now the temples were full of people supplicating the gods, because Nero had a swollen throat, and his voice was hoarse. But Apollonius vehemently denounced the folly of the crowd, though without rebuking anyone in particular; nay, he even restrained Menippus, who was irritated by such goings on, and persuaded him to moderate his indignation, urging him to pardon the gods if they did show pleasure in the mimes of buffoons. This utterance was reported to Tigellinus, who immediately sent police to take him to prison, and summoned him to defend himself from the charge of impiety against Nero. And an accuser was retained against him who had already undone a great many people, and won a number of such Olympic victories. This accuser too held in his hands a scroll of paper on which the charge was written out, and he brandished it like a sword against the sage, and declared that it was so sharp that it would slay and ruin him. But when Tigellinus unrolled the scroll, and did not find upon it the trace of a single word or letter, and his eyes fell on a perfectly blank book, he came to the conclusion that he had to do with a demon; and this is said also subsequently to have been the feeling which Domitian afterwards entertained towards Apollonius. Tigellinus then took his victim apart into a secret tribunal, in which this class of magistrate tries in private the most important charges; and having ordered all to leave the court he plied him with questions, asking who he was. Apollonius gave his father's name and that of his country, and explained his motive in practicing wisdom, declaring that the sole use he had made of it was to gain knowledge of the gods and an understanding of human affairs, for that the difficulty of knowing another man exceeded that of knowing oneself. "And about the demons," said Tigellinus, "and the apparitions of specters, how, O Apollonius, do you exorcise them?" "In the same way," he answered, "as I should murderers and impious men." This was a sarcastic allusion to Tigellinus himself, for he taught and encouraged in Nero every excess of cruelty and wanton violence. "And," said the other, "could you prophesy, if I asked you to?" "How," said Apollonius, "can I, being no prophet?" "And yet," replied the other, "they say that it is you who predicted that some great event would come to pass and yet not come to pass." "Quite true," said Apollonius, "is what you heard; but you must not put this down to any prophetic gift, but rather to the wisdom which God reveals to wise men." "And," said the other, "why are you not afraid of Nero?" "Because," said Apollonius, "the same God who allows him to seem formidable, has also granted to me to feel no fear." "And what do you think," said the other, "about Nero?" And Apollonius answered: "Much better than you do; for you think it dignified for him to sing, but I think it dignified for him to keep silent." Tigellinus was astonished and said: "You may go, but you must give sureties for your person." And Apollonius answered: "And who can go surety for a body that no one can bind?" This answer struck Tigellinus as inspired and above the wit of man; and as he was careful not to fight with a god, he said: "You may go wherever you choose, for you are too powerful to be controlled by me."

CHAPTER XLV

Here too is a miracle which Apollonius worked: A girl had died just in the hour of her marriage, and the bridegroom was following her bier lamenting as was natural his marriage left unfulfilled, and the whole of Rome was mourning with him, for the maiden belonged to a consular family. Apollonius then witnessing their grief, said: "Put down the bier, for I will stay the tears that you are shedding for this maiden." And withal he asked what was her name. The crowd accordingly thought that he was about to deliver such an oration as is commonly delivered to grace the funeral as to stir up lamentation; but he did nothing of the kind, but merely touching her and whispering in secret some spell over her, at once woke up the maiden from her seeming death; and the girl spoke out loud, and returned to her father's house, just as Alcestis did when she was brought back to life by Heracles. And the relations of the maiden wanted to present him with the sum of 150,000 sesterces, but he said that he would freely present the money to the young lady by way of dowry. Now whether he detected some spark of life in her, which those who were nursing her had not noticed—for it is said that although it was raining at the time, a vapor went up from her face—or whether her life was really extinct, and he restored it by the warmth of his touch, is a mysterious problem which neither I myself nor those who were present could decide.

CHAPTER XLVI

About this time Musonius lay confined in the dungeons of Nero, a man who they say was unsurpassed in philosophic ability by anyone. Now they did not openly converse with one another, because Musonius declined to do so, in order that both their lives might not be endangered; but they carried on a correspondence through Menippus and Damis, who went to and fro the prison. Such of their letters as did not handle greater themes I will take no notice of, and only set before my reader the indispensable ones in which we get glimpses of lofty topics:

"Apollonius to Musonius the philosopher, greeting.

"I would fain came unto you, to share your conversation and lodgings, in the hope of being some use to you; unless indeed you are disinclined to believe that Heracles once released Theseus from hell; write what you would like me to do. Farewell."

"Musonius to Apollonius the philosopher, greeting.

"For your solicitude on my behalf, I shall never do anything but commend you: but he who has strength of mind to defend himself, and has proved that he has done no wrong, is a true man. Farewell."

"Apollonius to Musonius the philosopher sends greeting.

"Socrates of Athens, because he refused to be released by his own friends, went before the tribunal and was put to death. Farewell."

"Musonius to Apollonius the philosopher sends greeting.

"Socrates was put to death, because he would not take the trouble to defend himself; but I shall defend myself. Farewell."

CHAPTER XLVII

When Nero took his departure for Greece, after issuing a proclamation that no one should teach philosophy in public at Rome, Apollonius turned his steps to the Western regions of the earth, which they say are bounded by the Pillars, because he wished to visit and behold the ebb and flow of the ocean, and the city of Gadeira. For he had heard something of the love of wisdom entertained by the inhabitants of that country, and of how great an advance they had made in religion; and he was accompanied by all his pupils, who approved no less of the expedition than they did of the sage.

BOOK V

CHAPTER I

Now in regard to the Pillars which they say Heracles fixed in the ground as limits of the earth, I shall omit mere fables, and confine myself to recording what is worthy of our hearing and of our narrating. The extremes of Europe and Libya border on a strait sixty stadia wide, through which the ocean is admitted into the inner seas. The extremity of Libya, which bears the name Abinna, furnishes a haunt of lions, who hunt their prey along the brows of the mountains which are to be seen rising inland, and it marches with the Gaetuli and Tingae, both of them wild Libyan tribes; and it extends as you sail into the ocean as far as the mouth of the river Salex, some nine hundred stadia, and beyond that point a further distance which no one can compute, because when you have passed this river Libya is a desert which no longer supports a population. But the promontory of Europe, known as Calpis, stretches along the inlet of the ocean and tight hand side distance of six hundred stadia, and terminates in the ancient city of Gadeira.

CHAPTER II

Now I myself have seen among the Celts the ocean tides just as they are described; and after making various conjectures about why so vast a bulk of waters recedes and advances, I have come to the conclusion that Apollonius discerned the real truth. For in one of his letters to the Indians he says that the ocean is driven by submarine influences or spirits out of several chasms which the earth afford both underneath and around it, to advance outwards, and to recede again, whenever the influence or spirit, like the breath of our bodies, gives way and recedes. And this theory is confirmed by the course run by diseases in Gadeira; for at the time of high water the souls of the dying do not quit the bodies, and this would hardly happen, he says, unless the influence or spirit I have spoken of was also advancing towards the land. They also tell you of certain phenomena of the ocean in connection with the phases of the moon, according as it is born and reaches fulness and wanes. These phenomena I verified, for the ocean exactly keeps pace with the size of the moon, decreasing and increasing with her.

CHAPTER III

And whereas the day succeeds the night and night succeeds the day in the land of the Celts by a very slow diminution of the darkness and of the light respectively, as in this country, in the neighborhood of Gadeira on the contrary and of the Pillars, it is said that the change bursts upon the eyes all at once, like a flash of lightning. And they also say that the Islands of the Blessed are to be fixed by the limits of Libya where they rise towards the uninhabited promontory.

CHAPTER IV

Now the city of Gadeira is situated at the extreme end of Europe, and its inhabitants are excessively given to religion; so much so that they have set up an altar to old age, and unlike any other race they sing hymns in honor of death; and altars are found there set up to poverty, and to art, and to Heracles of Egypt, and there are others in honor of Heracles the Theban. For they say that the latter advanced against the neighboring town of Erythea, on which occasion he took captive Geryon and his cows; the other, they say, in his devotion to wisdom measured the whole earth up to its limits. They say moreover that there is a Hellenic culture at Gadeira, and that they educate themselves in our own fashion; anyhow, that they are fonder of the Athenians than of any other Hellenes, and they offer sacrifice to Menestheus the Athenian, and from admiration of Themistocles the naval commander, and to honor him for his wisdom and bravery, they have set up a brazen statue of him in thoughtful attitude and, as it were, pondering an oracle.

CHAPTER V

They say that they saw trees here such as are not found elsewhere upon the earth; and that these were called the trees of Geryon. There were two of them, and they grew upon the mound raised over Geryon: they were a cross between the pitch tree and the pine, and formed a third species; and blood dripped from their bark, just as gold does from the Heliad poplar. Now the island on which the shrine is built is of exactly the same size as the temple, and there is not a rough stone to be found in it, for the whole of it has been given the form of a polished turning-post. In the shrine they say there is maintained a cult both of one and the other Heracles, though there are no images of them; altars however there are, namely, to the Egyptian Heracles two of bronze and perfectly plain, to the Theban, one of stone; on the latter they say are engraved in relief hydras and the mares of Diomedes and the twelve labors of Heracles. And as to the golden olive of Pygmalion, it too is preserved in the temple of Heracles, and it excited their admiration by the clever way in which the branch work was imitated; and they were still more astonished at its fruit, for this teemed with emeralds. And they say that the girdle of Teucer of Telamon was also exhibited there of gold, but how he ever sailed as far as the ocean, or why he did so, neither Damis by his own admission could understand nor ascertain from the people of the place. But he says that the pillars in the temple were made of gold and silver smelted together so as to be of one color, and they were over a cubit high, of square form, resembling anvils; and their capitals were inscribed with letters which were neither Egyptian nor Indian nor of any kind which he could decipher. But Apollonius, since the priests would tell him nothing, remarked: "Heracles of Egypt does not permit me not to tell all I know. These pillars are ties between earth and ocean, and they were inscribed by Heracles in the house of the Fates, to prevent any discord arising between the elements, and to save their mutual affection for one another from violation."

CHAPTER VI

They tell also of how they sailed up the river Baetis, which throws no little light upon the nature of the ocean. For whenever it is high tide, the river in its course remounts towards its sources, because apparently a current of air drives it away from the sea. And the mainland of Baetica, after which the river is called, is the best by their account of any continent; for it is well furnished with cities and pastures, and the river is brought by canals through all the towns, and it is very highly cultivated with all sorts of crops; and it enjoys a climate similar to that of Attica in the autumn season when the mysteries are celebrated.

CHAPTER VII

The conversations which Apollonius held about things which met his eyes were, according to Damis, many in number, but the following he said deserve to be recorded. On one occasion they were sitting in the temple of Heracles and Menippus gave a laugh, for it happened that Nero had just come to his mind, "And what," he said, "are we to think of this splendid fellow? In which of the contests has he won wreaths of late? Don't you think that self-respecting Hellenes must shake with laughter when they are on their way to the festivals?" And Apollonius replied: "As I have heard from Telesinus, the worthy Nero is afraid of the whips of the Eleans; for when his flatterers urged him to win at Olympia and to proclaim Rome as the victor, he answered: 'Yes, if the Eleans will only not depreciate me, for they are said to use whips and to look down upon me.' And many worse bits of nonsense than this forecast fell from his lips. I however admit that Nero will conquer at Olympia, for who is bold enough to enter the lists against him? But I deny that he will win at the Olympic festival, because they are not keeping it at the right season. For custom requires that this should have been held last year, but Nero has ordered the Eleans to put it off until his own visit, in order that they may sacrifice to him rather than to Zeus. And it is said that he has announced a tragedy and a performance on the harp for people who have neither a theater nor a stage for such entertainments, but only the stadium which nature has provided, and races which are all run by athletes stripped of their clothes. He however is going to take the prize for performances which he ought to have hidden in the dark, for he has thrown off the robes of Augustus and Julius and has dressed himself up in the garb of an Amoebeus or a Terpnus. What can you say of such a record? And then he betrays such a meticulous care in playing the part of Creon and Oedipus, that he is afraid of falling into some error, of coming in by the wrong door, or of wearing the wrong dress, of using the wrong scepter; but he has so entirely forgotten his own dignity and that of the Romans, that instead of carrying on the work of making laws, he has taken to singing, and strolls like a player outside the gates within which the Emperor ought to take his seat on his throne, deciding the fate of land and sea. There are, O Menippus, several troupes in which has inscribed himself as an actor. What next? Supposing any one of these actors quitted the theater after playing Oenomaus or Cresphontes, so full of his part as to want to rule others, and imagine himself to be a tyrant, what would you say of him? Surely you would recommend a dose of hellebore and the taking of drugs of a kind that clear the intellect? Well, here is the man himself who wields absolute power, throwing in his lot with actors and artists, cultivating a soft voice and trembling before the people of Elis or of Delphi; or if he does not tremble, yet misrepresenting his art so thoroughly as [not] to anticipate he will be whipped by the people over whom he has been set to rule. What will you say of the unhappy people who have to live under such a scum? And in what light do you think the Hellenes regard him? Is it as a Xerxes burning their houses down or as a Nero singing songs? Think of the supplies they have to collect for his songs, and how they are thrust out of their houses and forbidden to own a decent bit of furniture or slave. Think of how Nero picks out of every other house women and children, to gratify his infamous desires, and of the horrors they will suffer over them, of the crop of prosecutions which will be brought, and without dwelling upon the rest, just fix your attention upon those which will arise out of his theatrical and singing ambitions. This is what you hear: 'You did not come to listen to Nero,' or: 'You were present, but you listened to him without enthusiasm, 'You laughed,' or 'You did not clap your hands, 'or 'You have not offered a sacrifice in behalf of his voice not prayed that it may be more splendid than ever at the Pythian festival.' You can imagine that the Greeks will endure whole Iliads of woe at these spectacles. For I have long ago learned by the revelation of heaven that the Isthmus will be cut through and will not be cut through, and just now, they say, it is being cut." Here Damis took him up and said: "As for myself, O Apollonius, I think this scheme of cutting through the Isthmus excels all other undertakings of Nero, for you yourself see how magnificent a project it is." "I admit," he said, "that it is, O Damis; but it will go against him that he never could complete it, that just as he never finished his songs, so he never finished his digging. When I review the career of Xerxes, I am disposed to praise him not because he bridged the Hellespont, but because he got across it; but as for Nero, I perceive that he will neither sail his ships through the Isthmus, nor ever come to an end of his digging; and I believe, unless truth has wholly departed from among men, that he has retired from Hellas in a fit of panic."

CHAPTER VIII

At this time a swift runner arrived at Gadeira, and ordered them to offer sacrifices for the good tidings, and to sing hymns in honor of Nero who had thrice won the prize at Olympia. In the city of Gadeira indeed they understood the meaning of the victory, and that there had been some famous contest in Arcadia; for, as I said before, the people of Gadeira affect Hellenic civilization. But the cities in the neighborhood of Gadeira neither knew what the Olympic Festival was, nor what a contest nor an arena meant; nor did they understand what they were sacrificing for, but they indulged in the most ridiculous suppositions, and imagined that it was a victory in war that Nero had won and that he had taken captive some men called Olympians; for they had never been spectators either of a tragedy or of a harp-playing performance.

CHAPTER IX

Damis indeed speaks of the singular effect which a tragic actor produced upon the minds of the inhabitants of Ipola, which is a city of Baetica, and I think the story is worthy of being reproduced by me. The cities were multiplying their sacrifices in honor of the Emperor's victories, for those at the Pythian festival were already anounced, when an actor of tragedy, who was one of those that had not ventured to contend for the prize against Nero, was on a strolling tour round the cities of the west, and by his histrionic talent he had won no small fame among the less barbarous of the populations, for two reasons, firstly because he found himself among people who had never before heard a tragedy, and secondly because he pretended exactly to reproduce the melodies of Nero. But when he appeared at Ipola, they showed some fear of him before he ever opened his lips upon the stage, and they shrank in dismay at his appearance when they saw him striding across the stage, with his mouth all agape, mounted on buskins extra high, and clad in the most wonderful garments; but when he lifted up his voice and bellowed out loud, most of them took to their heels, as if they had a demon yelling at them. Such and so old-fashioned are the manners of the barbarians of that country.

CHAPTER X

The governor of Baetica was very anxious to have a conversation with Apollonius, and though the latter said that his conversation must seem tedious to any but philosophers, the other insisted in his demand. And as he was said to be a worthy person and detested the mimes of Nero, Apollonius wrote to him a letter asking him to come to Gadeira; and he, divesting himself of all the pomp of authority, came with a few of his most intimate friends. They greeted one another, and no one knows what they said to one another in an interview from which they excluded the rest of the company; but Damis hazards the opinion that they formed a plot against Nero. For after three days spent in private conversations, the governor went away, after embracing Apollonius, while the latter said: "Farewell, and do not forget Vindex." Now what was the meaning of this? When Nero was singing in Achaea, Vindex is said to have stirred up against him the nations of the West, and he was a man quite capable of cutting out the strings which Nero so ignorantly twanged. For he addressed a speech, inspired by the loftiest sentiments which a man can feel against a tyrant, to the troops which he commanded, and he declared in it that Nero was anything rather than a harpist, and a harpist rather than a sovereign. And he taxed him with madness and avarice and cruelty and wantonness of every kind, though he omitted to tax him with the cruelest of crimes; for he said that he had quite rightly put to death his mother, because she had borne such a monster. Apollonius, forecasting how all this must be, had accordingly brought into line with Vindex the governor of a neighboring province, and so all but took up arms himself in behalf of Rome.

CHAPTER XI

But as matters in the west were in such an inflamed condition, Apollonius and his friends returned thence towards Libya and the Tyrrhenian land; and, partly on foot and partly by sea, they made their way to Sicily, where they stopped at Lilybaeum. Then they coasted along to Messina and to the Straits, where the junction of the Tyrrhenian Sea with the Adriatic gives rise to the dangers of the Charybdis. Here they say they heard that Nero had taken to flight, tough Vindex was dead; and that various claimants were snatching at the throne, some from Rome itself, and others from various countries. Now when his companions asked him what would be the issue of these events, and who would gain possession of the throne, he answered: "Many Thebans will have it." For he compared the pretenders, namely, Vitellius and Galba and Otho, in view of the short lease of power which they enjoyed, to Thebans, for it was only during a very short time that they held dominion over the Hellenic world.

CHAPTER XII

That he was enabled to make such forecasts by some divine impulse, and that it is no sound inference to infer, as some people do, that our hero was a wizard, is clear from what I have already said. But let us consider these facts also: wizards, whom for my part I reckon to be the most unfortunate of mankind, claim to alter the course of destiny, by having recourse either to the torture of lost spirits or to barbaric sacrifices, or to certain incantations or anointings; and many of them when accused of such practices have admitted that they were adepts in such practices. But Apollonius submitted himself to the decrees of the Fates, and only foretold that things must come to pass; and his foreknowledge was gained not by wizardry, but from what the gods revealed to him. And when among the Indians he beheld their tripods and their dumb waiters and other automata, which I described as entering the room on their own accord, he did not ask how they were contrived, nor did he ask to be informed; he only praised them, but did not aspire to imitate them.

CHAPTER XIII

Now when they reached Syracuse a woman of a leading family was brought to bed of such a monster as never any woman had delivered of before: for her child had three heads, and each head had a neck of its own, but below them was a single body. Of the vulgar and stupid interpretations of this prodigy, one was that it signified the impending ruin of Sicily—for it has three headlands—unless the inhabitants composed their feuds and could live together in peace; for as a matter of fact several of the cities were at variance both with themselves and with one another, and such a thing as orderly life was unknown in the island. Another explanation was that Typhon, a many-headed monster, was threatening Sicily with his violence. But Apollonius said: "Go, O Damis, and look if the child is really made up as they say." For the thing was exposed to public view for the miracle-mongers to exercise their ingenuity upon it. When Damis reported that it was a three-headed creature and of the male sex, Apollonius got together his companions and said: "It signifies three emperors of Romans, whom yesterday I called Thebans; and not one of them shall enjoy complete dominion, but two of them shall perish after holding sway in Rome itself, and the third after doing so in the countries bordering upon Rome; and they shall shuffle off their masks more quickly than if they were tragic actors playing the part of tyrant." And the truth of his statement was almost immediately revealed; for Galba died in Rome itself, just after he grasped the crown; and Vitellius died after only dreaming of the crown; and Otho died among the Gauls of the west, and was not even accorded a public funeral, but lies buried like any private person. And Fate's episode was past and over within a single year.

CHAPTER XIV

Next they came to Catana, where is Mount Etna; and they say that they heard from the inhabitants of the city a story about Typho being bound on the spot and about fire rising from him, and this fire sends up the smoke[10] of Etna; but they themselves came to more plausible conclusions and more in keeping with philosophy. And they say that Apollonius began the discussion by asking his companions: "Is there such a thing as mythology?" "Yes, by Zeus," answered Menippus, "and I mean by it that which furnishes poets with their themes." "What then do you think of Aesop?" "He is a mythologist and writer of fables and no more." "And which set of myths show any wisdom?" "Those of the poets," he answered, "because they are represented in the poems as having taken place." "And what then do you think of the stories of Aesop?" "Frogs," he answered, "and donkeys and nonsense only fit to be swallowed by old women and children." "And yet for my own part," said Apollonius, "I find them more conducive to wisdom than the others. For those others, of which all poetry is so fond, and which deal with heroes, positively destroy the souls of their hearers, because the poet relates stories of outlandish passion and of incestuous marriages, and repeats calumnies against the gods, of how they ate their own children, and committed crimes of meanness, and quarreled with one another; and the affectation and pretense of reality leads passionate and jealous people and miserlike and ambitious persons to imitate the stories. Aesop on the other hand had in the first place the wisdom never to identify himself with those who put such stories into verse, but took a line of his own; and in the second, like those who dine well off the plainest dishes, he made use of humble incidents to teach great truths, and after serving up a story he adds to it the advice to do a thing or not to do it. Then, too, he was really more attached to truth than the poets are; for the latter do violence to their own stories in order to make them probable; but he by announcing a story which everyone knows not to be true, told the truth by the very fact that he did not claim to be relating real events. And the poet, after telling his story, leaves a healthy-minded reader cudgeling his brains to know whether it really happened; whereas one who, like Aesop, tells a story which is false and does not pretend to be anything else, merely investing it with a good moral, shows that he

---

[10] There is a pun in the Greek between Typhô = Typhon and typho = to smoke.

has made use of the falsehood merely for its utility to his audience. And there is another charm about him, namely, that he puts animals in a pleasing light and makes them interesting to mankind. For after being brought up from childhood with these stories, and after being as it were nursed by them from babyhood, we acquire certain opinions of the several animals and think of some of them as royal animals, of others as silly, of others as witty, and others as innocent. And whereas the poet, after telling us that there are 'many forms of heavenly visitation'[11] or something of the kind, dismisses his chorus and departs, Aesop adds an oracle to his story, and dismisses his hearers just as they reach the conclusion he wished to lead the up to.

CHAPTER XV

And as for myself, O Menippus, my mother taught me a story about the wisdom of Aesop when I was a mere child, and told me that he was once a shepherd, and was tending his flocks hard by a temple of Hermes, and that he was a passionate lover of wisdom and prayed to Hermes that he might receive it. Many other people, she said, also resorted to the temple of Hermes asking for the same gift, and one of them would hang on the altar gold, another silver, another a herald's wand of ivory, and others other rich presents of the kind. Now Aesop, she said, was not in a position to own any of these things; but he saved up what he had, and poured a libation of as much milk as a sheep would give at one milking in honor of Hermes, and brought a honeycomb and laid it on the altar, big enough to fill the hand, and he thought too of regaling the god with myrtle berries, or perhaps by laying just a few roses or violets at the altar. 'For,' said he, 'would you, O Hermes, have me weave crowns for you and neglect my sheep?' Now when on the appointed day they arrived for the distribution of the gifts of wisdom, Hermes as the god of wisdom and eloquence and also of gain and profit, said to him who, as you may well suppose, had made the biggest offering: 'Here is philosophy for you'; and to him who had made the next handsomest present, he said: 'Do you take your place among the orators'; and to others he said: 'You shall have the gift of astronomy or you shall be a musician, or you shall be an epic poet and write in heroic metre, or you shall be a writer of iambics.' Now although he was a most wise and accomplished god he exhausted, not

---

[11] Eurip. *Alcestis*, last line.

meaning to do so, all the various departments of wisdom, and then found that he had quite forgotten Aesop. Thereupon he remembered the Hours, by whom he himself had been nurtured on the peaks of Olympus, and bethought him of how once, when he was still in swaddling clothes, they had told him a story about the cow, which had a conversation with the man about herself and about the earth, and so set him aflame for the cows of Apollo. Accordingly he forthwith bestowed upon Aesop the art of fable called mythology, for that was all that was left in the house of wisdom, and said: "Do you keep what was the first thing I learnt myself." Aesop then acquired the various forms of his art from that source, and the issue was such as we have seen in the matter of mythology.

CHAPTER XVI

Perhaps I have done a foolish thing," went on Apollonius, "for it was my intention to recall you to more scientific and truer explanations than the poetical myths given by the vulgar of Etna; and I have let myself be drawn into a eulogy of myths. However, the digression has not been without a charm of its own, for the myth which we repudiate is not one of Aesop's stories, but belongs to the class of dramatic stories which fill the mouths of our poets. For they say that a certain Typho or Enceladus lies bound under the mountain, and in his death agony breathes out this fire that we see. Now I admit that giants have existed, and that gigantic bodies are revealed all over earth when tombs are broken open; nevertheless I deny that they ever came into conflict with the gods; at the most they violated their temples and statues, and to suppose that they scaled the heaven and chased away the gods therefrom—this it is madness to relate and madness to believe. Nor can I any more respect that other story, though it is more reverent in its tone, to the effect that Hephaestus attends to his forge in Etna, and that there is there an anvil on which he smites with his hammer; for there are many other mountains all over the earth that are on fire, and yet we should never be done with it if we assigned to them giants and gods like Hephaestus.

CHAPTER XVII

"What then is the explanation of such mountains? It is this: the earth by affording a mixture of asphalt and sulphur, begins to smoke of its own nature, but it does not yet belch out fire; if however it be cavernous and hollow and there be spirit or force circulating underneath it, it at once lifts up into the air as it were a beacon-fire; this flame gathers force, and gets hold of all around, and then like water it streams of the mountains and flows into the plains, and the mass of fire reaches the sea, forming mouths, out of which it issues, like the mouths of rivers. And as for the place of the Pious Ones, around whom the fire flowed, we will allow that such exists even here; but at the same time let us not forget that the whole earth affords secure ground for the doers of holiness, and that the sea is safely traversed not only by people in ships but even by people attempting to swim." For in this way he continually ended up his discourses with useful and pious exhortations.

CHAPTER XVIII

He stayed in Sicily and taught philosophy there as long as he had sufficient interest in doing so, and then repaired to Greece about the rising of Arcturus. After a pleasant sail he arrived at Leucas, where he said: "Let us get out of this ship, for it is better not to continue in it our voyage to Achaea." No one took any notice of the utterance except those who knew the sage well, but he himself together with those who desired to make the voyage with him embarked on a Leucadian ship, and reached the port of Lechaeum; meanwhile the Syracusan ship sank as it entered the Crisaean Gulf.

CHAPTER XIX

At Athens he was initiated by the same hierophant of whom he had delivered a prophecy to his predecessor; here he met Demetrius the philosopher, for after the episode of Nero's bath and of his speech about it, Demetrius continued to live at Athens, with such noble courage that he did not quit Athens even during the period when Nero was outraging Greece over the games. Demetrius said that he had fallen in with Musonius at the Isthmus, where he was fettered and under orders to dig; and that he addressed to him such consolations as he could, but Musonius took his spade and stoutly dug it into the earth, and then looking up, said: "You are distressed, Demetrius, to see me digging through the Isthmus for Greece; but if you saw me playing the harp like Nero, what would you feel then?" But I must pass over the sayings of Musonius, though they were many and remarkable, else I shall seem to take liberties with the man, who uttered them carelessly.

CHAPTER XX

Apollonius spent the winter in various Hellenic temples, and towards spring he embarked on the road for Egypt, after administering many rebukes indeed, yet giving much good counsel to the cities, many of which won his approval, for he never refused praise when anything was done in a right and sensible way. When he descended to the Piraeus, he found a ship riding there with its sails set, just about to start for Ionia; but the owner would not allow him to embark, for he wished to go on a private cruise. Apollonius asked him what his freight consisted of. "Of gods," he replied, "whose images I am exporting to Ionia, some made of gold and stone, and others of ivory and gold." "And are you going to dedicate them or what?" "I am going to sell them," he replied, "to those who desire to dedicate them." "Then you are afraid, my most excellent man, lest we should steal your images on board ship?" "I am not afraid of that," he answered, "but I do not think it proper that they should have to share the voyage with so many people and be defiled by such bad company as you get on board ship." "And may I remind you, most worthy man," answered Apollonius, "for you appear to me to be an Athenian, that on the ships which your countrymen employed against the barbarians, although they were full of a disorderly naval crowd, the gods embarked along with them, yet had no suspicion of being polluted thereby; you however in your gross ignorance drive men who are lovers of wisdom out of your ship, in whose company as in that of none others the gods delight, and this although you are trafficking in the gods? But the image-makers of old behaved not in this way, nor did they go round the cities selling their gods. All they did was to export their own hands and their tools for working stone and ivory; others provided the raw materials, while they plied their handicraft in the temples themselves; but you are leading the gods into harbors and market places just as if they were wares[12] of the Hyrcanians and of the Scythians —far be it from me to name these— and so you think you are doing no impiety? It is true that there are babbling buffoons who hang upon their persons images of Demeter or Dionysus, and pretend that they are nurtured by the gods they carry;

---

[12] Probably temple slaves or prostitutes.

but as for feeding on the gods themselves as you do, without ever being surfeited on this diet, that is a horrible commerce and one, I should say, savoring of lunacy, even if you have no misgivings of your own about the consequences." And having administered this rebuke he took his passage on another ship.

CHAPTER XXI

And when he had sailed as far as Chios, without even setting foot on the shore, he leapt across into another ship hard by, which was advertised to go to Rhodes; and without a word his companions jumped after him, for it was an essential part of their philosophic discipline to imitate his every word and action. With a favorable wind Apollonius made the passage and held the following conversation in Rhodes. As he approached the statue of the Colossus, Damis asked him, if he thought anything could be greater than that; and he replied, "Yes, a man who loves wisdom in a sound and innocent spirit." At that time Canus was living in Rhodes, who was esteemed to be the best of all pipe-players of his age. He therefore called him and said: "What is the business of a pipe-player?" "To do," replied the other, "everything which his audience wants him to." "Well, but many," replied Apollonius, "in the audience want to be rich rather than to hear a pipe played; I gather then that what you find them desiring this, namely to be rich, you turn them into rich men." "Not at all," replied the other, "though I would like to do so." "Well, then, perhaps you make the young people in your audience good-looking? For all who are still enjoying youth wish to be handsome." "Nor that either," replied the other, "although I can play many an air of Aphrodite on my instrument." "What then is it," said Apollonius, "which you think your audience want?" "Why, what else," replied Canus, "except that the mourner may have his sorrow lulled to sleep by the pipe, and that they that rejoice may have their cheerfulness enhanced, and the lover may wax warmer in his passion, and that the lover of sacrifice may become more inspired and full of sacred song?" "This then," he said, "O Canus, "would you allow to be the effect of the pipe itself, because it is constructed of gold or brass and of the shin of a stag, or perhaps of the shin of a donkey, or is it something else which has these effects?" "It is something else," he replied, "O Apollonius; for the music and the modes and the blending of strains and the easy variations of the pipe and the characters of the harmonies, it is all this that composes the souls of listeners and brings them to such a state of contentment as they want." "I understand," he replied, "O Canus, what it is that your art performs; for you cultivate and exhibit to those who come to learn of you the changefulness of your music and the variety of its modes. But as for myself, I think that your pipe wants other resources in addition to those you have mentioned, namely reserves of breath, and a right use of the lips, and manual skill on the part of the player; and facility of breath consists in its being clear and distinct, unmarred by any husky click in the throat, for that would rob the sound of its musical character. And facility with the lips consists in their taking in the reed of the pipe and blowing without blowing out the cheeks; and manual skill I consider very important, for the wrist must not weary from being bent, nor must the fingers be slow in fluttering over the notes, and manual skill is especially shown in the swift transition from mode to mode. If then you have all these facilities, you may play with confidence, O Canus, for the Muse Euterpe will be with you."

CHAPTER XXII

It happened that a young man was building a house in Rhodes who was a nouveau riche without any education, and he collected in his house rare pictures and gems from different countries. Apollonius then asked him how much money he had spent upon teachers and education. "Not a farthing," he replied. "And how much upon your house?" "Twelve talents," he replied, "and I mean to spend as much again upon it." "And what," said the other, "is the good of your house to you?" "Why, as a residence, it is splendidly suited to my bodily training, for there are colonnades in it and groves, and I shall seldom need to walk out into the market place, but people will come in and talk to me with all the more pleasure, just as if they were visiting a temple." "And," said Apollonius, "are men to be valued more for themselves or for their belongings?" "For their wealth," said the other, "for wealth has the most influence." "And," said Apollonius, "my good youth, which is the best able to keep his money, an educated person or an uneducated?" And as the other made no answer, he added: "My good boy, it seems to me that it is not you that own the house, but the house rather that owns you. As for myself I would far rather enter a temple, no matter how small, and behold in it a statue of ivory and gold, than behold one of pottery and bad workmanship in a vastly larger one."

CHAPTER XXIII

And meeting a young man who was young and fat and prided himself upon eating more than anybody else, he remarked: "Then you, it seems are the glutton." "Yes, and I sacrifice to the gods out of gratitude for the same." "And what pleasure," said Apollonius, "do you get by gorging yourself in this way?" "Why, everyone admires me and stares at me; for you have probably heard of Heracles, how people took as much pains to celebrate what he ate as what labors he performed." "Yes, for he was Heracles," said Apollonius; "but as for yourself, you scum, what good points are there about you? There is nothing left for you but to burst, if you want to be stared at."

CHAPTER XXIV

Such were his experiences in Rhodes, and others ensued in Alexandria, so soon as his voyage ended there. Even before he arrived Alexandria was in love with him, and its inhabitants longed to see Apollonius with the unique devotion of one friend for another; and as the people of Upper Egypt are intensely religious they too prayed him to visit their several societies. For owing to the fact that so many come hither and mix with us from Egypt, while an equal number pass hence to visit Egypt, Apollonius was already celebrated among them and the ears of the Egyptians were literally pricked up to hear him. It is no exaggeration to say that, as he advanced from the ship into the city, they gazed upon him as if he was a god, and made way for him in the alleys, as they would for priests carrying the sacraments. As he was being thus escorted with more pomp than if he had been a governor of the country, he met twelve men who were being led to execution on the charge of being bandits, he looked at them and said: "They are not all guilty, for this one," and he gave his name, "has been falsely accused and will escape." And to the executioners by whom they were being led, he said: "I order you to relax your pace and bring them to the ditch a little more leisurely, and to put this one to death last of all, for he is guiltless of the charge; but you would anyhow act with more piety, if you spared them for a brief portion of the day, since it were better not to slay them at all." And withal he dwelt upon this theme at what was for him unusual length. And the reason for his doing so was immediately shown; for when eight of them had had their heads cut off, a man on horseback rode up to the ditch, and shouted: "Spare Pharion;

for," he added, "he is no robber, but he gave false evidence against himself from fear of being racked, and others of them in their examination under torture have acknowledged that he is guiltless." I need not describe the exultation of Egypt, nor how the people, who were anyhow ready to admire him, applauded him for this action.

CHAPTER XXV

And when he had gone up into the temple, he was struck by the orderliness of its arrangements, and thought the reason given for everything thoroughly religious and wisely framed. But as for the blood of bulls and the sacrifices of geese and other animals, he disapproved of them nor would he bring them to repasts of the gods. And when a priest asked him what induced him not to sacrifice like the rest: "Nay, you," he replied," should rather answer me what induces you to sacrifice in this way." The priest replied: "And. who is so clever that he can make corrections in the rites of the Egyptians?" "Anyone," he answered, "with a little wisdom, if only he comes from India." "And," he added, "I will roast a bull to ashes this very day, and you shall hold communion with us in the smoke it makes; for you cannot complain, if you only get the same portion which is thought enough of a repast for the gods." And as his image[13] was being melted in the fire he said: "Look at the sacrifice." "What sacrifice," said the Egyptian, "for I do not see anything there." And Apollonius said: "The Iamidae and the Telliadae and the Clytiadae and the oracle of the black-footed ones, have they talked a lot of nonsense, most excellent priest, when they went on at such length about fire, and pretended to gather so many oracles from it? For as to the fire from pine wood and from the cedar, do you think it is really fraught with prophecy and capable of revealing anything, and yet not esteem a fire lit from the richest and purest gum to be much preferable? If then you had really any acquaintance with the lore of fire worship, you would see that many things are revealed in the disc of the sun at the moment of its rising."

CHAPTER XXVI

With these words he rebuked and silenced the Egyptian, showing that he was ignorant of religion. But because the Alexandrians are

---

[13] A frankincense model of a bull.

devoted to horses, and flock into the racecourse to see the spectacle, and murder one another in their partisanship, he therefore administered a grave rebuke to them over these matters, and entering the temple, he said: "How long will you persist in meeting your deaths, not in behalf of your families or of your shrines, but because you are determined to pollute the sacred precincts by entering them reeking with gore and to slaughter one another within the walls? And Troy it seems was ravaged and destroyed by a single horse, which the Achaeans of that day had contrived; but your chariots and horses are yoked to your own despite and leave you no chance of living in submission to the reins of law. You are being destroyed therefore not by the sons of Atreus nor by the sons of Ajax, but by one another, a thing that the Trojans would not have done even when they were drunk. At Olympia, however, where there are prizes for wrestling and boxing and for the mixes athletic contests, no one is slain in behalf of the athletes, though it were quite excusable if one should show an excess of zeal in the rivalry of human beings like himself. But here I see you rushing at one another with drawn swords, and ready to hurl stones, all over a horse race. I would like to call down fire upon a city as this, where amidst the groans and insulting shouts 'of the destroyers and the destroyers the earth runs with blood.' Can you not feel reference for the Nile, the common mixing bowl of Egypt? But why mention the Nile to men whose gauges measure a rising tide of blood rather than of water?" And many other rebukes of the same kind he addressed to him, as Damis informs us.

CHAPTER XXVII

Vespasian was harboring thoughts of seizing the absolute power, and was at this time in the countries bordering upon Egypt; and when he advanced as far as Egypt, people like Dion and Euphrates, of whom I shall have something to say lower down, urged that a welcome should be given to him. For the first autocrat, by whom the Roman state was organized, was succeeded for the space of fifty years by tyrants so harsh and cruel, that not even Claudius, who reigned thirteen years in the interval between them, could be regarded as a good ruler, and that, although he was fifty years of age when he succeeded to the throne, an age when a man's judgment is most likely to be sane, and though he had the reputation of being fond of culture of all kinds; nevertheless he too in spite of his advanced age committed many youthful follies, and gave up the empire to be devoured, as sheep devour a pasture, by silly women, who murdered him, because he was so indolent that, though he knew beforehand what was in store for him, he would not be on his guard even against what he foresaw. Apollonius no less than Euphrates and Dion rejoiced in the new turn of events; but he did not make use of them as a theme in his public utterances, because he considered such an argument too much in the style of a rhetor. When the autocrat approached the city, the priests met him before the gates, together with the magistrates of Egypt and the representatives of the different provinces into which Egypt is divided. The philosophers also were present and all their schools. Apollonius however did not put himself forward in this way, but remained conversing in the temple. The autocrat delivered himself of noble and gentle sentiments, and after making a short speech, said: "Is the man of Tyana living here?" "Yes," they replied, "and he has much improved us thereby." "Can he then be induced to give us an interview?" said the emperor. "For I am very much in want of him." "He will meet you," said Dion, "at the temple, for he admitted as much to me when I was on my way here." "Let us go on," said the king, "at once to offer our prayers to the gods, and to meet so noble a man." This is how the story grew up, that it was during his conduct of the siege of Jerusalem that the idea of making himself emperor suggested itself to him; and that he sent for Apollonius to ask his advice on the point; but that the latter declined to enter a country which its inhabitants polluted both by what they did and by what they suffered, which was the reason why Vespasian came in person to Egypt, as well because he now had possession of the throne, as in order to hold with our sage the conversations which I shall relate.

CHAPTER XXVIII

For after he had sacrificed, and before he gave official audiences to the cities, he addressed himself to Apollonius, and as if making prayer he said to him: "Do thou make me king." And he answered: "I have done so already, for I have already offered a prayer for a king who should be just and noble and temperate, endowed with the wisdom of grey hairs, and the father of legitimate sons; and surely in my prayer I was asking from the gods for none other but thyself." The emperor was delighted with this answer, for the crowd too in the temple shouted their agreement with it. "What then," said the emperor, "did you think of the reign of Nero?" And Apollonius answered: "Nero perhaps understood how to tune a lyre, but he disgraced the empire both by letting the strings go too slack and by drawing them too tight." "Then," said the other, "you would like a ruler to observe the mean?" "Not I," said Apollonius, "but God himself, who has defined equity as consisting in the mean. And these gentlemen here, they too are good advisers in this matter," he added, pointing to Dion and Euphrates, for the latter had not yet quarreled with him. Thereupon the king held up his hand and said: "O Zeus, may I hold sway over wise men, and wise men hold sway over me." And turning himself round towards the Egyptians he said: "You shall draw as liberally upon me as you do upon the Nile."

CHAPTER XXIX

The result as that the Egyptians regained their prosperity, for they were already exhausted by the oppressions they suffered; but as he went down from the temple he grasped the hand of Apollonius, and taking him with him into the palace, said: "Perhaps some will think me young and foolish because I assume the reins of kingship nigh on the sixtieth year of my life. I will then communicate to you my reasons for doing so, in order that you may justify my actions to others. For I was never the slave of wealth that I know of, even in my youth; and in the matter of the magistracies and honors in the gift of the Roman sovereign, I bore myself with so much soberness and moderation as to avoid being thought either overbearing or, on the other hand, craven and cowardly. Nor did I cherish any but loyal feelings towards Nero; but, inasmuch as he had received the crown, if not in strict accordance with the law, at any rate from an autocrat, I submitted to him for the sake of Claudius, who made me consul and sharer of his counsels. And, by Athena, I never saw Nero demeaning himself without shedding tears, when I thought of Claudius, and contrasted with him the wretch who had inherited the greatest of his possessions. And now when I see that even the disappearance from the scene of Nero has brought no change for the better in the fortunes of humanity, and that the throne has fallen into such dishonor as to be assigned to Vitellius, I boldly advance to take it myself; firstly, because I wish to endear myself to men and win their esteem, and secondly, because the man I have to contend with is a mere drunkard. For Vitellius uses more ointment in his bath than I do water, and I believe that if you ran a sword into him, more ointment would issue from the wound than blood; and his continuous bouts of drinking have made him mad, and one who were he dicing would be full of apprehension lest the pieces should play him false, is yet hazarding the empire in play; and though he is the slave of mistresses, he nevertheless insults married women, and says that he likes to spice his amours with a little danger. His worst excesses I will not mention for I would rather not allude to such matters in your presence. May I then never submit tamely, while the Romans are ruled by such a man as he; let me rather ask the gods to guide me so that I may be true to myself. And this, Apollonius, is why I, as it were, make fast my cable to yourself, for they say that you have the amplest insight into the will of the gods, and why I ask you to share with me in my anxieties and aid me in my plans on which rests the safety of sea and land; to the end that, supposing the goodwill of heaven show itself on my side, I may fulfill my task; but if heaven opposes and favors neither myself nor the Romans, that I may not trouble the gods against their wills."

CHAPTER XXX

Apollonius clinched his words with an appeal to heaven: "O Zeus," said he, "of the Capitol, for thou art he whom I know to be the arbiter of the present issue, do thou preserve thyself for this man and this man for thyself. For this man who stands before thee is destined to raise afresh unto thee the temple which only yesterday the hands of malefactors set on fire." And on the emperor expressing astonishment at his words: "The facts themselves," he said, "will reveal, so do thou ask nothing of me; but continue and complete that which thou hast so rightly purposed." Now it happened that just then as a matter of fact that in Rome Domitian, the son of Vespasian, was matched with Vitellius in the struggle to gain the empire for his father, and was besieged in the Capitol, with the result that although he escaped the fury of the besiegers, the temple was burnt down; and all this was revealed to Apollonius more quickly than if it had taken place in Egypt. When they had held their conversation, he left the emperor's presence, saying that it was not permitted him by the religion of the Indians to proceed at midday in any other way than the Indians do themselves; at the same time the emperor brightened up, and with fresh enthusiasm, instead of allowing matters to slip through his hands, persevered in his policy, convinced by Apollonius' words that his future was stable and assured to him by heaven.

CHAPTER XXXI

Next day at dawn Apollonius came to the palace and asked the guards what the emperor was doing; from whom learning that he had long risen and was engaged in his correspondence, he went off and remarked to Damis: "This man shall be sovereign." About sunrise he returned to find Dion and Euphrates already at the door, in return to whose eager inquiries concerning the interview, he repated the defense of his policy which he had heard from the emperor, though at the same time he let no word escape him of his own opinions. But on being summoned to enter in advance of them, he said: "O King, Euphrates and Dion, long your acquaintances, are at your door, being highly anxious for your welfare. I pray you, call them in also to join in our conversation, for they are both of them wise men." "I throw my doors open," he replied, "to wise men; but to you I purpose to open my breast as well."

CHAPTER XXXII

When they had been called in, he continued: "In defense of my own plans, I said, gentlemen, what I had to say, yesterday to Apollonius our esteemed friend." "We have heard that defense," said Dion, "and it was most reasonable." "Well, today," he went on, "my dear Dion, let us concert some wise conclusions in support of the counsels adopted by me, of a kind to ensure my general policy being honorable and salutary to mankind. For I cannot forget how Tiberius was the first to degrade the government into an inhuman and cruel system, of how he was followed by Gaius, who filled with Bacchic frenzy, dressed in Lydian fashion, won sham fights and by his disgraceful revels violated all Roman institutions. There followed the worthy Claudius, and I remember that he was so much the thrall of women as to lose all sense of sovereignty, nay even of self-preservation; for they say he was murdered by them. Nero I hardly need assail, for Apollonius in brief and terse remarks has exposed the faults of over-indulgence and undue severity by which he disgraced his reign. Nor need I dwell on the system of Galba, who was slain in the middle of the Forum in the act of adopting those strumpet sons of his Otho and Piso. As for Vitellius, we had rather Nero should come to life again than surrender the empire to him, the most dissolute of all. Perceiving then, my friends, that the throne has fallen into hatred and contempt by reason of the tyrants I have enumerated, I would fain have you advise me how best I can restore it, so that it should not remain what it has become, namely, a stumbling block to mankind." Apollonius replied as follows: "There was a first-rate pipe-player, it is said, who used to send his pupils to much worse players than himself, that they might learn how not to pipe. As then you, my sovereign, have learned from these your good-for-nothing predecessors, how not to rule, let us, then, now turn our attention to the problem, how a sovereign ought to rule."

CHAPTER XXXIII

While Apollonius spoke, Euphrates concealed the jealousy he already felt of one whose utterances clearly interested the emperor hardly less than those of an oracular shrine interest those who repair to it for guidance. But now at last his feelings overcame him, and, raising his voice above its usual pitch, he cried: "We must not flatter men's impulses, nor allow ourselves to be carried away against our better judgment by men of unbridled ambition; but we should rather, if we are enamored of wisdom, recall them to the sober facts of life. Here is a policy about the very expediency of which we should first calmly deliberate, and yet you would have us prescribe a way of executing it, before you know if the measures under discussion are desirable. For myself, I quite approve of the deposition of Vitellius, whom I know to be a ruffian drunk with every sort of profligacy; nevertheless, although I know you to be a worthy man and of pre-eminent nobility of character, I deny that you ought to undertake the correction of Vitellius without first establishing an ideal for yourself. I need not instruct you in the excesses chargeable to monarchy as such, for you have yourself described them; but this I would have you recognize, that whereas youth leaping into the tyrant's saddle does but obey its own instincts—for playing the tyrant comes natural to young men as wine or women, and we cannot reproach a young man merely for making himself a tyrant, unless in pursuit of his role he shows himself a murderer, a ruffian, or a debauchee—on the other hand when an old man makes himself a tyrant, the first thing we blame in him is that he ever nursed such an ambition. It is no use his showing himself an example of humanity and moderation, for of these qualities we shall give the credit not to himself, but to his age and mature training. And men will believe that he nursed the ambition long before, when he was still a stripling, only that he failed to realize it; and such failures are partly attributed to ill luck, partly to pusillanimity. I mean that he will be thought to have renounced his dream of becoming a tyrant, because he distrusted his own star, or that he stood aside and made way for another who entertained the same ambition and whose superior manliness was dreaded. As for the count of ill luck, I may dismiss it; but as for that of cowardice, how can you avoid it? How escape the reproach of having been afraid of Nero, the most cowardly and supine of rulers? Look at the revolt against him planned by Vindex, you surely were the man of the hour, its natural leader, not he! For you had an army at your back, and the forces you were leading against the Jews, would they not have been more suitably employed in chastising Nero? For the Jews have long been in revolt not only against the Romans, but against humanity; and a race that has made its own a life apart and irreconcilable, that cannot share with the rest of mankind in the pleasures of the table nor join in their libations or prayers or sacrifices, are separated from ourselves by a greater gulf than divides us from Susa or Bactra or the more distant Indies. What sense then or reason was there in chastising them for revolting from us, whom we had better have never annexed? As for Nero, who would not have prayed with his own hand to slay a man well-nigh drunk with human blood, singing as he sat amidst the hecatombs of his victims? I confess that I ever pricked up my ears when any messenger from yonder brought tidings of yourself, and told us how in one hand battle you had slain thirty thousand Jews and in the next fifty thousand. In such cases I would take the courier aside and ask him: 'But what of the great man? Will he not rise to higher things than this?' Since then you have discovered in Vitellius an image and ape of Nero, and are turning your arms against him, persist in the policy you have embraced, for it too is a noble one, only let its sequel be noble too. You know how dear to the Romans are the popular institutions, and how nearly all their conquests were won under a free polity. Put then an end to monarchy, of which you have repeated to us so evil a record; and bestow upon Romans a popular government, and on yourself the glory of inaugurating for them a reign of liberty."[14]

CHAPTER XXXIV

Throughout Euphrates' long speech, Apollonius noticed that Dion shared his sentiments, for he manifested his approval both by his

---

[14] Cp. Tacitus, Hist. i. 16: dignus eram a quo respublica inciperet.

gestures and the applause with which he hailed his words; so he asked him he could not add some remarks of his own to what he had just heard. "By heaven, I can," answered Dion, "and I should agree in part and in part disagree with his remarks; for I think I have myself told you that you would have been much better employed deposing Nero than setting Jewry to rights. But your anxiety appeared to be never to have him deposed, for anyone who composed the disorder of his affairs merely strengthened the fellow against all the victims in his power. I approve however of the campaign against Vitellius; for I consider it a greater achievement to prevent a tyranny from ever growing up, than to put an end to it when it is established. And while I welcome the idea of democracy—for though this form of polity is inferior to an aristocracy, nevertheless moderate men will prefer it to tyrannies and oligarchies—I fear lest the servility to which these successive tyrannies have reduced the Romans will render any change difficult to effect; I doubt if they are able to comport themselves as free men or even to lift their eyes to a democracy, any more than people who have been kept in the dark are able to look on a sudden blaze of light. I conclude that Vitellius ought to be driven from power, and would fain see this effected as quickly and as well as can be; I think however that though you should be prepared for war, yet you yourself instead of declaring war against him, ought rather to threaten him with condign punishment, in case you capture him, as I believe you will easily do, then I would fain see you give the people of Rome the right to choose their own polity, and, if they choose a democracy, allow it them. For this will bring you greater glory than many tyrannies and many victories at Olympia. Your name will be inscribed all over the city, and brazen statues will be erected everywhere; and you will furnish us with a theme for harangues in which neither Harmodius nor Aristogeiton will bear comparison with you. If however they accept monarchy, whom can they all possibly decree the throne except yourself? For what you already possess, and are about to resign into the hands of the public, they will surely rather confer on yourself than on another."

CHAPTER XXXV

There followed a spell of silence during which the emperor's countenance betrayed contending emotions; for though he was an absolute ruler both in title and fact, it looked as if they were trying to divert him from his resolution to remain such; and accordingly

Apollonius remarked: "It seems to me you are mistaken in trying to cancel a monarchical policy when it is already a foregone conclusion; and that you indulge a garrulity as childish as it is in such a crisis idle. Were it I that had stepped into such a position of influence as he has, and were I, when taking counsel about what good I could do to the world, treated to such advice as you now give, your arguments would carry some force, for philosophic aphorisms might amend the philosophically-minded of your listeners; but as it is a consul and a man accustomed to rule, whom you pretend to advise, one moreover over whom ruin impends if he fall from power, need we carp, if instead of rejecting the gifts of fortune, he welcomes them when they come, and only deliberates how to make a discreet use of what is his own? Let us take a similar case. Suppose we saw an athlete well endowed with courage and stature, and by his well-knit frame marked out as a winner in the Olympic contest, suppose we approached him when he was already on his way thither from Arcadia, and, while encouraging him to face his rivals, yet insisted that, in the event of his winning the prize, he must not allow himself to be proclaimed the victor, nor consent to wear the wreath of wild olive—should we not be set down as imbeciles, mocking at another's labors? Similarly when we regard the eminent man before us, and think of the enormous army at his disposal, of the glint of their brazen arms, of his clouds of cavalry, of his own personal qualities, of his generosity, self-restraint, of his fitness to attain his object—ought we not to send him forward on the path that leads to his goal, with favoring encouragement, and with more auspicious pledges for his future than these you have recorded? For there is another thing you have forgotten, that he is the father of two sons who are already in the command of armies, and whose deepest enmity he will incur if he does not bequeath the empire to them. Is he not confronted by the alternative of embroiling himself in hostilities with his own family? If however he accepts the throne, he will have the devoted service of his own children, they will lean on him and he on them, using them as his bodyguard, and, by Zeus, as a bodyguard not hired by money, nor levied by force nor feigning loyalty with their faces only, but attached to him by bonds of natural instinct and true affection.

"For myself I care little about constitutions, seeing that my life is governed by the Gods; but I do not like to see the human flock perish for want of a shepherd at once just and moderate. For just as a single man pre-eminent in virtue transforms a democracy into the guise of a government of a single man who is the best; so the government of one man, of it provides all round for the welfare of the community, is popular government. You did not, we are told, help to depose Nero. And did you, Euphrates, or you, Dion? Did I myself? However, no one finds fault with us for that, nor regards us as cowardly, because, after philosophers have destroyed a thousand tyrannies, we have missed the glory of string a blow for liberty. Not but that, as regards myself, I did take the field against Nero, and besides frequent aspersions in my lectures assailed his cut-throat Tigellinus to his face; and the aid I rendered to Vindex in the western half of the empire was, I hardly need say, in the nature of a redoubt raised against Nero. But I should not on that account claim for myself the honor of having pulled down that tyrant, any more than I should regard yourselves as falling short of the philosopher's ideal of courage and constancy, because you did nothing of the sort. For a man then of philosophic habit it is enough that he should say what he really thinks; but he will, I imagine, take care not to talk like a fool or a madman. For a consul, on the other hand, who designs to depose a tyrant, the first requisite is plenty of deliberation, with a view to conceal his plans till they are ripe for action; and the second is a suitable pretense to save him from the reproach of breaking his oath. For before he dreams of resorting to arms against the man who appointed him general and whose welfare he swore to safeguard in the council-chamber and on the field, he must surely in self-defense furnish heaven with proof that he perjures himself in the cause of religion. He will also need many friends, if he is not to approach the enterprise unfenced and unfortified, and also all the money he can get so as to be able to win over the men in power, the more so as he attacks a man who commands the resources of the entire earth. All this demands no end of care, no end of time. And you may take all this as you like, for we are not called upon to sit in judgment on ambitions which he may possibly have entertained, but in which fortune resolved to second him, ere ever he came to fight for them. What answer, however, will you make to the following proposition? Here is one who yesterday assumed the throne, who accepted the crown offered by the cities here in the temples around us, whose rescripts are as brilliant as they are ungrudging: do you bid him issue a proclamation today to the effect that for the future he retires into private life, and only assumed the reigns of government in an access of madness? As, if he carries through the policy on which he is resolved, he will confirm the loyalty of the guards relying on whom he first entertained it; so, if he falters and departs from it, he will find an enemy in everyone whom from that moment he must mistrust."

CHAPTER XXXVI

The emperor listened gladly to the above and remarked: "If you were the tenant of my breast, you could not more accurately report my inmost thoughts. 'tis yourself then I will follow, for every word which falls from your lips I regard as inspired; therefore instruct me, I pray, in all the duties of a good king." Apollonius answered: "You ask of me a lore which cannot be imparted by any teacher; for kingship is at once the greatest of human attainments, and not to be taught. However, I will mention you all the things which, if you do them, you will in my opinion do wisely. Look not on that which is laid by as wealth—for how is it better than so much sand drifted no matter whence—nor on what flows into your coffers from populations racked by the tax-gatherer, for gold lacks luster and is mere dross, if it be wrung from men's tears; you will make better use of your wealth than every sovereign did if you employ it in succoring the poor, at the same time that you render their wealth secure for the rich. Tremble before the very absoluteness of your prerogative, for so you will exercise it with the greater moderation. Mow not down the loftier stalks which overtop the rest, for this maxim of Aristotle's is unjust; but try rather to pluck disaffection out of men's hearts, as you would tares out of your cornfields; and inspire awe of yourself in revolutionists less by actual punishment than by showing them that they will not go unpunished. Let the law govern you as well as them, O king; for you will be all the wiser as a legislator for so holding the laws in respect. Reverence the gods more than ever before, for you have received great blessings at their hands and have still great ones to pray for. In what appertains to your prerogative, act as a sovereign; in what to your own person, as a private citizen. About dice and drink and dissipation and the necessity of abhorring these vices, why need I tender you any advice, who, they say, never approved of them even in youth. You have, my sovereign, two sons, both, they say, of generous disposition. Let them before all obey your authority, for their faults will be charged to your account. Let your disciplining of them even proceed the to length of threatening not to bequeath them your throne, unless they remain good men and honest; otherwise they will be prone to regard it not as a reward of excellence so much as a mere heritage. As for the pleasures which have made of Rome their home and residence—and they are many—I would advise you, my sovereign, to use much discretion in suppressing them; for it is not easy to convert an entire people on a sudden to wisdom and temperance; but you must feel your way and instill order and rhythm in their characters step by step, partly by open, partly by secret correction. Let us put an end to pride and luxury on the part of the freedmen and slaves whom your high position assigns to you, by accustoming them to think all the more humbly of themselves, because their master is so powerful. There remains only one topic to address you on; it concerns the governors sent out to rule the provinces. Of those you will yourself select, I need say nothing, for I am sure you will assign commands by merit; I only refer to those who will acquire them by lot. In their case too, I maintain, those only should be sent out to the various provinces so obtained who are in sympathy, so far as the system of appointing by lot allows of it, with the populations they will rule. I mean, that over Hellenes should be set men who can speak Greek, and Romans over those who speak that language or dialects allied to it. I will tell you what made me think of this. During the period in which I lived in the Peloponnese Hellas was governed by a man who knew as little of the Hellenes and their tongue as they understood of his. What was the result? He was in his mistakes as much sinned against as sinner, for his assessors and those who shared with him judicial authority trafficked in justice, and abused his authority as if he had been not their governor but their slave. This, my sovereign, is all that occurs to me today; but if anything else should come into my mind, we can hold another interview. So now apply yourself to the duties of your throne, lest your subjects accuse you of indolence."

CHAPTER XXXVII

Euphrates declared his assent to all these conclusions, "For," said he, "what can I gain by continuing to oppose such teaching? But, O my sovereign, as henceforth we must address you, I have only one thing left to say, and that is that while you approve and countenance that philosophy which accords with nature, you should have nothing to do with that which affects a secret intercourse with the gods, for we are easily puffed up by the many absurdities this lying philosophy falsely ascribes to providence." The above remark was aimed at Apollonius, who, however, without paying any attention to it, departed with his companions as soon as he had ended his discourses. And Euphrates would have taken further liberties with his character, only the emperor noticed it and put him aside by saying: "Call in those who have business with the government, and let my council resume its usual form."

Thus Euphrates failed to see that he only prejudiced himself, and gained with the emperor the reputation of being a jealous and insolent fellow, who aired these sentiments in favor of democracy, not because he really entertained them, but only by way of contradicting the opinions Apollonius held in regard to the empire. Notwithstanding, the emperor did not cast him off or shew any resentment at his opinions. As for Dion, he did not cease to be fond of him, though he regretted his seconding the opinions of Euphrates. For Dion was a delightful conversationalist and always declined to quarrel. He moreover imparted to his discourses that sort of charm which exhales from the perfumes at a sacrifice; and he had also, better than any living man, the talent of extempore oratory. Apollonius the emperor nor merely loved for his own sake, but was ever ready to listen to his accounts of antiquity, to his descriptions of the Indian Phraotes, and to his graphic stories of the rivers of India, and of the animals that inhabit it; above all to the forecasts and revelations imparted to him by the gods concerning the future of the empire. On quitting Egypt, after settling and rejuvenating the country, he invited Apollonius to share his voyage; but the latter declined, on the ground that he had not yet visited or conversed with the naked sages of that land, whose wisdom he was very anxious to compare with that of India. "Nor," he added, "have I drunk of the sources of the Nile." The emperor understood that he was about to set out for Ethiopia and said: "Will you not bear me in mind?" "I will indeed," replied the sage, "if you continue to be a good sovereign and mindful of yourself."

CHAPTER XXXVIII

Thereafter the emperor offered his sacrifice in the temple and publicly promised him presents. But Apollonius, as if he had a favor to ask, said: "And what presents, O king, will you give me?" "Ten," he replied, "now; and when you come to Rome everything I have." And Apollonius answered: "Then I must husband your riches as if they were my own, and squander in the present what is hereafter to be reserved to me in its entirety. But I pray you, O king, to attend rather to these gentlemen here, for they look as if they wanted something." And suiting his words, he pointed to Euphrates and his friends. The emperor accordingly pressed them to ask boldly what they desired, whereupon

Dion with a blush said: "Reconcile me, O king, with Apollonius my teacher for that I lately ventured to oppose him in argument; for never till now have I ventured to contradict him." The emperor, approving, said: "As long ago as yesterday I asked for this favor, and it is already granted. But do you ask for some gift." "Lasthenes," replied Dion, "of Apamea, a Bithynian city, who was my companion in philosophy, fell in love with the uniform and took to a soldier's life. Now, he says, he longs afresh to wear the sage's cloak, so would you let him out from the service, for that is the extent of his own request; and you will confer on me the privilege of turning him into a saint, and on him the liberty of living as he wishes to." "Let him be released," said the emperor, "but I confer on him the rights of a veteran, since he is equally fond of wisdom and of yourself." Next the emperor turned to Euphrates, who had drawn up a letter embodying his requests, and held it out in expectation that his sovereign would peruse it in private. But the latter was determined to expose him to criticism, so he read it out loud before everyone; and it was found to contain various petitions, some for himself, some for others; and of the presents asked some consisted of cash down and others of credit notes. Whereupon Apollonius with a laugh remarked: "Then your intention of asking a monarch for all this did not prevent you from giving him that good advice in favor of democracy."

CHAPTER XXXIX

Such I find was the occasion of the quarrel between Apollonius and Euphrates; and after the emperor had departed they openly attacked one another, Euphrates in his anger resorting to coarse insults, which his antagonist met in a philosophical spirit, only refuting him. His accusations, I may remark, of Euphrates to the effect that his conduct violated the decencies of philosophical life, can be learned from the epistles Apollonius addressed to him, for they are not a few. For myself I herewith dismiss this gentleman; for it is not part of my scheme to say ill of him, but only to furnish with a life of Apollonius those who were as yet ignorant. As to the tale of the stick, which he is said to have brandished against Apollonius when he was discoursing, though without applying it—most people attribute his having so refrained to the skill at single-stick of the man he was about to strike; but I prefer to set it down to the good sense of the would-be striker, and to think that it was that which enabled him to overcome an angry impulse which had all but overmastered him.

CHAPTER XL

Dion's philosophy struck Apollonius as being too rhetorical and overmuch adapted to please and flatter, an that is why he addressed to him by way of correction the words: "You should use a pipe and a lyre, if you want to tickle men's senses, not a speech." And in many passages of his letters to Dion he censures his use of words to captivate the crowd.

CHAPTER XLI

I must also explain how it came about that he never approached the emperor again, nor visited him after their encounter in Egypt, although the latter invited him and wrote often to him in that sense. The fact is, Nero restored the liberties of Hellas with a wisdom and moderation quite alien to his character; and the cities regained their Doric and Attic characteristics, and a general rejuvenescence accompanied the institution among them of a peace and harmony such as not even ancient Hellas ever enjoyed. Vespasian, however, on his arrival in the country took away her liberty, alleging their factiousness with other pretexts hardly justifying such extreme severity.

This policy seemed not only to those who suffered by it, but to Apollonius as well, of a harshness quite out of keeping with a royal temper and character, and accordingly he addressed the following letters to the Emperor:

"Apollonius to the Emperor Vespasian, Greeting:

"You have, they say, enslaved Hellas, and you imagine you have excelled Xerxes. You are mistaken. You have only fallen below Nero. For the latter held our liberties in his hand and respected them. Farewell."

"To the same.

"You have taken such a dislike to the Hellenes, that you have enslaved them although they were free. What do you want with my company? Farewell."

"To the same.

"Nero freed the Hellenes in play, but you have imprisoned them in all seriousness. Farewell."

Such were the grounds of Apollonius' taking a dislike to Vespasian. However, when he heard of the excellence of his subsequent acts of government he made no attempt to conceal his satisfaction, but looked at it in the light of a benefaction conferred on himself.

CHAPTER XLII

The following incident also of Apollonius' stay in Egypt was thought remarkable. There was a man led a tame lion about by a string, as if it had been a dog; and the animal not only fawned upon him, but on anyone who approached it. It went collecting alms all around the towns, and was admitted even in the temples, being a pure animal; for it never licked up the blood of the victims, nor pounced on them when they were being flayed and cut up, but lived upon honeycakes and bread and dried fruits and cooked meat; and you also came on it drinking wine without losing its character. One day it came up to Apollonius when he was sitting in the temple, and whined and fawned at his knees, and begged of him more earnestly than it had ever done of anybody. The bystanders imagined it wanted some solid reward, but Apollonius exclaimed: "This lion is begging me to make you understand that a human soil is within him, the soul namely of Amasis, the king of Egypt in the province of Sais." And when the lion heard that, he gave a piteous and plaintive roar, and crouching down began to lament, shedding tears. Thereupon Apollonius stroked him, and said: "I think the lion ought to be sent to Leontopolis and dedicated to the temple there, for I consider it wrong that a king who has been changed into the most kingly of beasts should go begging, like any human mendicant." In consequence the priests met and offered sacrifice to Amasis; and having decorated the animal with a collar and ribbons, they conveyed him up country into Egypt with pipings, hymns and songs composed in his honor.

CHAPTER XLIII

Having had enough of Alexandria the sage set out for Egypt an Ethiopia to visit the naked sages. Menippus then, as he was by now a qualified disputant and remarkably outspoken, he left behind to watch Euphrates: and perceiving that Dioscorides had not a strong enough propensity for foreign travel, he deprecated his undertaking the journey. The rest of his company he mustered, for though some had left him at

Aricia, many others had subsequently joined him, and he explained to them about his impending journey and began as follows:—

"I must needs preface in Olympic wise my address to you, my brave friends; and the following is an Olympic exordium. When the Olympic games are coming on, the people of Elis train the athletes for thirty days in their own country. Likewise, when the Pythian games approach, the natives of Delphi; and when the Isthmian, the Corinthians assemble them and say: 'Go now into the arena and prove yourselves men worthy of victory.' The Eleans however on their way to Olympia address the athletes thus: 'If ye have labored so hard as to be entitled to go to Olympia and have banished all sloth and cowardice from your lives, then march boldly on; but as for those who have not so trained themselves, let them depart whithersoever they like'."

The companions of the sage understood his meaning, and about of twenty of them remained with Menippus; but the rest, ten in number, I believe, offered prayer to the gods, and having sacrificed such an offering as men offer when they embark for a voyage, they departed straight for the pyramids, mounted on camels and keeping the Nile on their right hand. In several places they took boats across the river in order to visit every sight on it; for there was not a city, fane or sacred site in Egypt, that they passed by without discussion. For at each they either learned or taught some holy story, so that any ship on which Apollonius embarked resembled the sacred galley of a religious legation.

PHILOSTRATUS

THE LIFE OF APOLLONIUS OF TYANA

THE EPISTLES OF APOLLONIUS AND THE TREATISE OF EUSEBIUS

WITH AN ENGLISH TRANSLATION

BY F.C. CONYBEARE, M.A.

LATE FELLOW AND PRELECTOR OF UNIVERSITY COLLEGE, OXFORD

IN TWO VOLUMES

II

CHAPTER I

ETHIOPIA covers the western wing of the entire earth under the sun, just as India does the eastern wing; and at Meroe it adjoins Egypt, and, after skirting a part of Libya Incognita, it ends at the sea which the poets call by the name of the Ocean, that being the name they applied to the mass of water which surrounds the earth. This country supplies Egypt with the river Nile, which takes its rise at the cataracts (*Catadupi*), and brings down from Ethiopia all Egypt, the soil of which in flood-time it inundates. Now in size this country is not worthy of comparison with India, not for that matter is any of the continents that are famous among men; and even if you put together all Egypt with Ethiopia, and we may regard the river as so combining the two, we should not compare the two together with India, so vast is the standard of comparison. However their respective rivers, the Indus and the Nile, resemble one another, if we consider their creatures. For they both spread their moisture over the land in the summer season, when the earth most wants it, and unlike all other rivers they produced the crocodile and the river-horse; and the religious rites celebrated over them correspond with one another, for many of the religious invocations of the Indians are repeated in the case of the Nile. We have a proof of the similarity of the two countries in the spices which are found in them, also in the fact that the lion and the elephant are captured and confined in both the one and the other. They are also the haunts of animals not found elsewhere, and of black men -a feature not found in other continents- and we meet in them with races of pigmies and of people who bark in various ways instead of talking, and other wonders of the kind. And the griffins of the Indians and the ants of the Ethiopians, though they are dissimilar in form, yet, from what we hear, play similar parts; for in each country they are the guardians of gold, and devoted to the gold reefs of the two countries. But we will not pursue these subjects; for we must resume the course of our history and follow in the sage's footsteps.

CHAPTER II

FOR when he arrived at the confines of Ethiopia and Egypt, and the name of the place is Sycaminus, he came across a quantity of uncoined gold and linen and an elephant and various roots and myrrh and spices, which are all lying without anyone to watch them at the crossways. I will explain the meaning of this, for the same custom still survives among ourselves. It was a market place to which the Ethiopians bring all the products of their country; and the Egyptians in their turn take them all away and bring to the same spot their own wares of equal value, so bartering what they have got for what they have not. Now the inhabitants of the marches are not yet fully black but are half-breeds in matter of color, for they are partly not so black as the Ethiopians, yet partly more so than the Egyptians. Apollonius, accordingly, when he realized the character of the market, remarked: "Contrast our good Hellenes: they pretend they cannot live unless one penny begets another and unless they can force up the price of their goods by chaffering or holding them back; and one pretends that he has got a daughter whom it is time to marry, and another that he has got a son who has just reached manhood, and a third that he has to pay his subscription to his club, and a fourth that he is having a house built for him, and a fifth that he would be ashamed of being thought a worse man of business than his father was before him. What a splendid thing then it would be, if wealth were held in less honor and equality flourished a little more and 'if the black iron were left to rust in the ground,' for all men would agree with one another, and the whole earth would be like one brotherhood."

CHAPTER III

With such conversations, the occasions providing as usual the topics he talked about, he turned his steps towards Memnon; an Egyptian showed them the way, of whom Damis gives the following account: Timasion was the name of this stripling, who was just emerging from boyhood, and was now in the prime of life and strength. He had a stepmother who had fallen in love with him; and when he rejected her overtures, she set upon him and by way of spiting him had poisoned his father's mind against him, condescending to a lower intrigue than ever Phaedra had done, for she accused him of being effeminate, and of finding his pleasure in pederasts rather than in women. He had accordingly abandoned Naucratis, for it was there that all this happened, and was living in the neighborhood of Memphis; and he had acquired and manned a boat of his own and was plying as a waterman on the Nile. He then, was going down the river when he saw Apollonius sailing up it; and he concluded that the crew consisted of wise men, because he judged them by the cloaks they wore and the books they were hard at work studying. So he asked them whether they would allow one who was so passionately fond of wisdom as himself to share their voyage; and Apollonius said: "This youth is wise, my friends, so let him be granted his request." And he further related the story about his stepmother to those of his companions who were nearest to him in a low tone while the stripling was still sailing towards them. But when the ships were alongside of one another, Timasion stepped out of his boat, and after addressing a word or two to his pilot, about the cargo in his own boat, he greeted the company. Apollonius then ordered him to sit down under his eyes, and said: "You stripling of Egypt, for you seem to be one of the natives, tell me what you have done of evil or what of good; for in the one case you shall be forgiven by me, in consideration of your youth; but in the other you shall reap my commendation and become a fellow-student of philosophy with me and with these gentlemen." Then noticing that Timasion blushed and checked his impulse to speak, and hesitated whether to say or not what he had been going to say, he pressed his question and repeated it, just as if he had no foreknowledge of the youth at his command. Then Timasion plucked up courage and said: "O Heavens, how shall I describe myself? for I am not a bad boy, and yet I do not know whether I ought to be considered a good one, for there is no particular merit in having abstained from wrong." But Apollonius cried: "Bravo, my boy, you answer me just as if you were a sage from India; for this was just the sentiment of the divine Iarchas. But tell me how you came to form these opinions, and how long ago; for it strikes me that you have been on your guard against some sin." The youth then began to tell them of his stepmother's infatuation for himself, and of how he had rejected her advances; and when he did so, there was a shout in recognition of the divine inspiration under which Apollonius had foretold these details. Timasion, however, caught them up and said: "Most excellent people, what is the matter with you? for my story is one which calls as little for your admiration, I think, as for your ridicule." But Damis said: "It was not that we were admiring, but something else which you don't know about yet. As for you, my boy, we praise you because you think that you did nothing very remarkable." And Apollonius said: "Do you sacrifice to Aphrodite, my boy?" And Timasion answered: "Yes, by Zeus, every day; for I consider that this goddess has great influence in human and divine affairs." Thereat Apollonius was delighted beyond measure, and cried: "Let us, gentlemen, vote a crown to him for his continence rather than to Hippolytus the son of Theseus, for the latter insulted

Aphrodite; and that perhaps is why he never fell a victim to the tender passion, and why love never ran riot in his soul; but he was allotted an austere and unbending nature. But our friend here admits that he is devoted to the goddess, and yet did not respond to his stepmother's guilty overtures, but went away in terror of the goddess herself, in case he were not on his guard against another's evil passions; and the mere aversion to any one of the gods, such as Hippolytus entertained in regard to Aphrodite, I do not class as a form of sobriety; for it is a much greater proof of wisdom and sobriety to speak well of the gods, especially at Athens, where altars are set up in honor even of unknown gods." So great was the interest which he took in Timasion. Nevertheless he called him Hippolytus for the eyes with which he looked at his stepmother. It seemed also that he was a young man who was particular about his person and enhanced its charms by attention to athletic exercises.

CHAPTER IV

Under his guidance, they say, they went on to the sacred enclosure of Memnon, of whom Damis gives the following account. He says that he was the son of the Dawn, and that he did not meet his death in Troy, where indeed he never went; but that he died in Ethiopia after ruling the land for five generations. But his countrymen being the longest lived of men, still mourn him as a mere youth and deplore his untimely death. But the place in which his statue is set up resembles, they tell us, an ancient market-place, such as remain in cities that were long ago inhabited, and where we come on broken stumps and fragments of columns, and find traces of walls as well as seats and jambs of doors, and images of Hermes, some destroyed by the hand of man, others by that of time. Now this statue, says Damis, was turned towards the sunrise, and was that of a youth still unbearded; and it was made of a black stone, and the two feet were joined together after the style in which statues were made in the time of Daedalus; and the arms of the figure were perpendicular to the seat pressing upon it, for though the figure was still sitting it was represented in the very act of rising up. We hear much of this attitude of the statue, and of the expression of its eyes, and of how the lips seem about to speak; but they say that they had no opportunity of admiring these effects until they saw them realized; for when the sun's rays fell upon the statue, and this happened exactly at dawn, they could not restrain their admiration; for the lips spoke immediately the sun's ray touched them, and the eyes seemed to stand out and gleam against the light as do those of men who love to bask in the sun. Then they say they understood that the figure was of one in the act of rising and making obeisance to the sun, in the way those do who worship the powers above standing erect. They accordingly offered a sacrifice to the Sun of Ethiopia and to Memnon of the Dawn, for this the priests recommended them to do, explaining that one name was derived from the words signifying "to burn and be warm"[15] and the other from his mother. Having done this they set out upon camels for the home of the naked philosophers.

CHAPTER V

On the way they met a man wearing the garb of the inhabitants of Memphis, but who was wandering about rather than wending his steps to a fixed point; so Damis asked him who he was and why he was roving about like that. But Timasion said: "You had better ask me, and not him; for he will never tell you what is the matter with him, because he is ashamed of the plight in which he finds himself; but as for me, I know the poor man and pity him, and I will tell you all about him. For he has slain unwittingly a certain inhabitant of Memphis, and the laws of Memphis prescribe that a person exiled for an involuntary offense of this kind,—and the penalty is exile,—should remain with the naked philosophers until he has washed away the guilt of bloodshed, and then he may return home as soon as he is pure, though he must first go to the tomb of the slain man and sacrifice there some trifling victim. Now until he has been received by the naked philosophers, so long he must roam about these marches, until they take pity upon him as if he were a suppliant." Apollonius therefore put the question to Timasion: "What do the naked philosophers think of this particular exile?" And he answered: "I do not know anything more than that this is the seventh month that he has remained here as a suppliant, and that he has not yet obtained redemption." Said Apollonius: "You don't call men wise, who refuse to purify him, and are not aware that Philiscus whom he slew was a descendant of Thamus the Egyptian, who long ago laid waste the

---

[15] *Aithô* = I burn; *Aithiôps* = an Aethiop.

country of these naked philosophers." Thereat Timasion said in surprise: "What do you mean?" " I mean," said the other, "my good youth, what was actually the fact; for this Thamus once on a time was intriguing against the inhabitants of Memphis, and these philosophers detected his plot and prevented him; and he having failed in his enterprise retaliated by laying waste all the land upon which they live, for by his brigandage he tyrannized the country round Memphis. I perceive that Philiscus whom this man slew was the thirteenth in descent from this Thamus, and was obviously an object of execration to those whose country the latter so thoroughly ravaged at the time in question. Where then is their wisdom? Here is a man that they ought to crown, even if he had slain the other intentionally; and yet they refuse to purge him of a murder which he committed involuntarily on their behalf.". The youth then was astounded and said: "Stranger, who are you?" And Apollonius replied: "He whom you shall find among these naked philosophers. But as it is not allowed me by my religion to address one who is stained with blood, I would ask you, my good boy, to encourage him, and tell him that he will at once be purged of guilt, if he will come to the place where I am lodging." And when the man in question came, Apollonius went through the rites over him which Empedocles and Pythagoras prescribe for the purification of such offenses, and told him to return home, for that he was now pure of guilt.

CHAPTER VI

Thence they rode out at sunrise, and arrived before midday at the academy of the naked sages, who dwell, they relate, upon a moderate-sized hill a little way from the bank of the Nile; and in point of wisdom they fall short of the Indians rather more than they excel the Egyptians. And they wear next to no clothes in the same way as people do at Athens in the heat of summer. And in their district there are few trees, and a certain grove of no great size to which they resort when they meet for the transaction of common affairs; but they do not build their shrines in one and the same place, as Indian shrines are built, but one is in one part of the hill and another in another, all worthy of observation, according to the accounts of the Egyptians. The Nile is the chief object of their worship, for they regard this river as land and water at once. They have no need, however, of hut or dwelling, because they live in the open air directly under the heaven itself, but they have built an hospice to accommodate strangers, and it is a portico of no great size, about equal in length to those of Elis, beneath which the athletes await the sound of the midday trumpet.

CHAPTER VII

At this place Damis records an action of Euphrates, which if we do not regard it as juvenile, was anyhow unworthy of the dignity of a philosopher. Euphrates had heard Apollonius often say that he wished to compare the wisdom of India with that of Egypt, so he sent up to the naked sages one Thrasybulus, a native of Naucratis, to take away our sage's character. Thrasybulus at the same time that he pretended to have come there in order to enjoy their society, told them that the sage of Tyana would presently arrive, and that they would have no little trouble with him, because he esteemed himself more highly than the sages of India did themselves, though he extolled the latter whenever he opened his mouth; and he added that Apollonius had contrived a thousand pitfalls for them, and that he would not allow any sort of influence either to the sun, or to the sky, or to the earth, but pretended to move and juggle and rearrange these forces for whatever end he chose.

CHAPTER VIII

Having concocted these stories the man of Naucratis went away; and they, imagining they were true, did not indeed decline to meet Apollonius when he arrived, but pretended that they were occupied with important business and were so intent upon it, that they could only arrange an interview with him if they had time, and if they were informed first of what he wanted and of what attracted him thither. And a messenger from the bade them stay and lodge in the portico, but Apollonius remarked: "We do not want to hear about a house for ourselves, for the climate here is such that anyone can live naked,"—an unkind reference this to them, as it implied that they went without clothes not to show their endurance, but because it was too to wear any. And he added: "I am not surprised indeed at their nor yet knowing what I want, and what I am come here for, though the Indians never asked me these questions."

CHAPTER IX

Accordingly Apollonius lay down under one of the trees, and let his companions who were there with him ask whatever question they pleased. Damis took Timasion apart and asked him the question in private: "About these naked sages, my good fellow, as you have lived with them, and in all probability know, tell me what their wisdom comes to?" "It is," answered the other, "manifold an profound." "And yet," said Damis, "their demeanor towards us does not evince any wisdom, my fine fellow; for when they refuse to converse about wisdom with so great a man as our master, and assume all sorts of airs against him, what can I say of them except that they are too vain and proud." "Pride and vanity!" said the other, "I have already come among them twice, and I never saw any such thing about them; for they were always very modest and courteous towards those who came to visit them. At any rate a little time ago, perhaps a matter of fifty days, one Thrasybulus was staying here who achieved nothing remarkable in philosophy, and they received him with open arms merely because he said he was a disciple of Euphrates." Then Damis cried: "What's that you say, my boy? Then you saw Thrasybulus of Naucratis in this academy of theirs?" "Yes, and what's more," answered the other, "I conveyed him hence, when he went down the river, in my own boat." "Now I have it, by Athena," cried Damis, in a loud tone of indignation. "I warrant he has played us some dirty trick." Timasion then replied: "Your master, when I asked him yesterday who he was, would not answer me at once, but kept his name a secret; but do you, unless this is a mystery, tell me who he is, for then I could probably help you to find what you seek." And when he heard from Damis, that it was the sage of Tyana, "You have put the matter," he said, "in a nutshell. For Thrasybulus, as he descended the Nile with me, in answer to my question what he had gone up there for, explained to me that his love for wisdom was not genuine, and said that he had filled these naked sages with suspicion of Apollonius, to the end that whenever he came here they might flout him; and what his quarrel is with him I know not, but anyhow, it is, I think, worthy of a woman or of a vulgar person to backbite him as he has done. But I will address myself to these people and ascertain their real disposition; for they are friendly to me." And about eventide Timasion returned, though without telling Apollonius any more than that he had interchanged words with them; however he told Damis in private that they meant to come the next morning primed with all that they had heard from Thrasybulus.

CHAPTER X

They spent that evening conversing about trifles which are not worth recording, and then they lay down to sleep on the spot where they had supped; but at daybreak Apollonius, after adoring the sun according to his custom, had set himself to meditate upon some problem, when Nilus, who was the youngest of the naked philosophers, running up to him, exclaimed: "We are coming to you." "Quite right," said Apollonius, "for to get to you I have made this long journey from the sea all the way here." And with these words he followed Nilus. So after exchanging greetings with the sages, and they met him close to the portico. "Where," said Apollonius, "shall we hold our interview?" "Here," said Thespesion, pointing to the grove. Now Thespesion was the eldest of the sect, and led them in procession; and they followed him with an orderly and leisurely step, just as the jury of the athletic sports at Olympia follow the eldest of their number. And when they had sat down, which they did anyhow, and without the observing their previous order, they all fixed their eyes on Thespesion as the one who should regale them with a discourse, which he proceeded as follows: "They say, Apollonius, that you have visited the Pythian and Olympian festivals; for this was reported of you here by Stratocles of Pharos, who says he met you there. Now those who come to the Pythian festival are, they say, escorted with the sound of pipe and song and lyre, and are honored with shows of comedies and tragedies; and then last of all they are presented with an exhibition of games and races run by naked athletes. At the Olympic festival, however, these superfluities are omitted as inappropriate and unworthy of the place; and those who go to the festival are only provided with the show of naked athletes originally instituted by Heracles. You may see the same contrast between the wisdom of the Indians and our own. For they, like those who invite others to the Pythian festival, appeal to the crowd with all sorts of charms and wizardry; but we, like the athletes of Olympia, go naked. Here earth strews for us no couches, nor does it yield us milk or wine as if we were bacchants, nor does the air uplift us and sustain us aloft. But the earth beneath us is our only couch, and we live by partaking of its natural fruits, which we would have it yield to us gladly and without being tortured against its will. But you shall see that we are not unable to work tricks if we like. Heigh! you tree yonder," he cried, pointing to an elm tree, the third in the row from that under which they were talking, "just salute the wise Apollonius, will you?" And forthwith the tree saluted him, as it was bidden to do, in accents which were articulate and like those of a woman. Now he wrought this sign to discredit the Indians, and in the belief that by doing so he would wean Apollonius of his excessive estimate of their powers; for he was always recounting to everybody what the Indians said and did.

Then the Egyptian added these precepts: he said that it is sufficient for the sage to abstain from eating all flesh of living animals, and from the roving desires which mount up in the soul through the eyes, and from envy which ends by teaching injustice to hand and will, and that truth stands not in need of miracle-mongering and sinister arts. "For look," he said, "at the Apollo of Delphi, who keeps the center of Hellas for the utterance of his oracles. There then, as you probably know yourself, a person who desires a response, puts his question briefly, and Apollo tells what he knows without any miraculous display. And yet it would be just as easy for him to convulse the whole mountain of Parnassus, and to alter the springs of the Castalian fountain so that it should run with wine, and to check the river Cephisus and stay its stream; but he reveals the bare truth without any of this show of ostentation. Nor must we suppose that it is by his will, that so much gold and showy offerings enter his treasury, nor that he would care for his temple even if it were made twice as large as it already is. For once on a time this god Apollo dwelt in quite a humble habitation; and a little hut was constructed for him to which the bees are said to have contributed their honeycomb and wax, and the birds their feathers. For simplicity is the teacher of wisdom and the teacher of truth; and you must embrace it, if you would have men think you really wise, and forget all your legendary tales that you have acquired among the Indians. For what need is there to beat the drum over such simple matters as: 'Do this, or do not do it,' or 'I know it, or I do not know it,' or 'It is this and not that'? What do you want with thunder, nay, I would say, What do you want to be thunder-struck for?

You have seen in picture-books the representation of Heracles by Prodicus; in it Heracles is represented as a youth, who has not yet chosen the life he will lead; and vice and virtue stand in each side of him plucking his garments and trying to draw him to themselves. Vice is adorned with gold and necklaces and with purple raiment, and her cheeks are painted and her hair delicately plaited and her eyes underlined with henna; and she also wears golden slippers, for she is pictured strutting about in these; but virtue in the picture resembles a woman worn out with toil, with a pinched look; and she has chosen for her adornment rough squalor, and she goes without shoes and in the plainest of raiment, and she would have appeared naked if she had not too much regard for her feminine decency. Now figure yourself, Apollonius, as standing between Indian wisdom on one side, and our humble wisdom on the other; imagine that you hear the one telling you how she will strew flowers under you when you lie down to sleep, yes, and by Heaven, how she will regale you upon milk and nourish you on honey-comb, and how she will supply you with nectar and wings, whenever you want them; and how she will wheel in tripods, whenever you drink, and golden thrones; and you shall have no hard work to do, but everything will be flung unsought into your lap. But the other discipline insists that you must lie on the bare ground in squalor, and be seen to toil naked like ourselves; and that you must not find dear or sweet anything which you have not won by hard work; and that you must not be boastful, not hunt after vanities and pursue pride; and that you must be on your guard against all dreams and visions which lift you off the earth. If then you really make the choice of Heracles, and steel your will resolutely, neither to dishonor truth, nor to decline the simplicity of nature, then you may say that you have overcome many lions and have cut off the heads of many hydras and of monsters like Geryon and Nessus, and have accomplished all his other labors, but if you embrace the life of a strolling juggler, you will flatter men's eyes and ears, but they will think you no wiser than anybody else, and you will become the vanquished of any naked philosopher of Egypt."

CHAPTER XI

When he ended, all turned their eyes upon Apollonius; his own followers knowing well that he would reply, while Thespesion's friends wondered what he could say in answer. But he, after praising the fluency and vigor of the Egyptian, merely said: "Have you anything more to say?" "No, by Zeus," said the other, "for I have said all I have to say." Then he asked afresh: "And has not any one of the rest of the Egyptians anything to say?" "I am their spokesman," answered his antagonist, "and you have heard them all." Apollonius accordingly paused for a minute and then, fixing his eyes, as it were, on the discourse he had heard, he spoke as follows: "You have very well described and in a sound philosophic spirit the choice which Prodicus declares Heracles to have made as a young man; but, ye wise men of the Egyptians, it does not apply in the least to myself. For I am not come here to ask your advice about how to live, insomuch as I long ago made choice of the life which seemed best to myself; and as I am older than any of you, except Thespesion, I myself am better qualified, now I have got here, to advise you how to choose wisdom, if I did not find that you had already made the choice. Being, however, as old as I am, and so far advanced in wisdom as I am, I shall not hesitate as it were to make you the auditors of my life and motives, and teach you that I rightly chose this life of mine, than which no better one has ever suggested itself to me. For I discerned a certain sublimity in the discipline of Pythagoras, and how a certain secret wisdom enabled him to know, not only who he was himself, but also who he had been; and I saw that he approached the altars in purity, and suffered not his belly to be polluted by partaking of the flesh of animals and that he kept his body pure of all garments woven of dead animal refuse; and that he was the first of mankind to restrain his tongue, inventing a discipline of silence described in the proverbial phrase, "An ox sits upon it." I also saw that his philosophical system was in other respects oracular and true. So I ran to embrace his teachings, not choosing one form of wisdom rather than another of two presented me, as you, my excellent Thespesion, advise me to do. For philosophy marshaled before me her various points of view, investing them with the adornment proper to each and she commanded me to look upon them and make a sound choice. Now they were all possessed of an august and divine beauty; and some of them were of such dazzling brightness that you might well have closed your eyes. However I fixed my eyes firmly upon all of them, for they themselves encouraged me to do so by moving towards me, and telling me beforehand how much they would give me. Well, one of them professed that she would shower upon me a swarm of pleasures without any toil on my part and another that she would give me rest after toil; and a third that she would mingle mirth and merriment in my toil; and everywhere I had glimpses of pleasures and of unrestrained indulgence in the pleasures of the table; and it seemed that I had only to stretch out my hand to be rich, and that I needed not to set any bridle upon my eyes, but love and loose desire and such-like feelings were freely allowed me. One of them, however, boasted that she would restrain me from such things, but she was bold and abusive and in an unabashed manner elbowed all others aside; and I beheld the ineffable form of wisdom which long ago conquered the soul of Pythagoras; and she stood, I may tell you, not among the many, but kept herself apart and in silence; and when she saw that I ranged not myself with the rest, though as yet I knew not what were her wares, she said: 'Young man, I am unpleasing and a lady full of sorrows; for, if anyone betakes himself to my abode, he must of his own choice put away all dishes which contain the flesh of living animals, and he must forget wine, nor make muddy therewith the cup of wisdom which is set in the souls of those that drink no wine; nor shall blanket keep him warm, nor wool shorn from a living animal. But I allow him shoes of bark, and he must sleep anywhere and anyhow, and if I find my votaries yielding to sensual pleasures, I have precipices to which justice that waits upon wisdom carries them and pushes them over; and I am so harsh to those who make choice of my discipline that I have bits ready to restrain their tongues. But learn from me what rewards you shall reap by enduring all this: Temperance and justice unsought and at once, and the faculty to regard no man with envy, and to be dreaded by tyrants rather than cringe to them, and to have your humble offerings appear sweeter to the gods than the offerings of those who pour out before them the blood of bulls. And when you are pure I will grant you the faculty of foreknowledge, and I will so fill your eyes with light, that you shall distinguish a god, and recognize a hero, and detect and put to shame the shadowy phantoms which disguise themselves in the form of men.' This was the life I chose, ye wise of the Egyptians; it was a sound choice and in the spirit of Pythagoras, and in making it I neither deceived myself, nor was deceived; for I have become all that a philosopher should become, and all that she promised to bestow upon the philosopher, that is mine. For I have studied profoundly the problem of the rise of the art and whence it draws its first principles; and I have realized that it belongs to men of transcendent religious gifts, who have thoroughly investigated the nature of the soul, the well-springs of whose existence lie back in the immortal and in the unbegotten.

Now I agree that this doctrine was wholly alien to the Athenians; for when Plato in their city lifted up his voice and discoursed upon the soul, full of inspiration and wisdom, they caviled against him and adopted opinions of the soul opposed thereto and altogether false. And one may well ask whether there is any city, or any race of men, where not one more and another less, but wherein men of all ages alike, will enunciate the same doctrine of the soul. And I myself, because my youth and inexperience so inclined me, began by looking up to yourselves, because you had the reputation of an extraordinary knowledge of most things; but when I explained my views to my own teacher, he interrupted me, and said as follows: 'Supposing you were in a passionate mood and being of an impressionable age were inclined to form a friendship; and suppose you met a handsome youth and admired his looks, and you asked whose son he was, and suppose he were the son of a knight or a general, and that his grand-parents had been furnishers of a chorus—if then you dubbed him the child of some skipper or policeman, do you suppose that you would thereby be the more likely to captivate his affections, and that you would not rather make yourself odious to him by refusing to call him by his father's name, and giving him instead that of some ignoble and spurious parent? If then you were enamored of the wisdom which the Indians discovered, would you call it not by the name which its natural parents bore, but by the name of its adoptive sires; and so confer upon the Egyptians a greater boon, than if that were to happen over again which their own poets relate, namely if the Nile on reaching its full were found to be with honey blent?' It was this which turned my steps to the Indians rather than to yourselves; for I reflected that they were more subtle in their understanding, because such men as they live in contact with a purer daylight, and entertain truer opinions of nature and of the gods, because they are near unto the latter, and live on the edge and confines of that thermal essence which quickens all unto life. And when I came among them, their message made the same impression upon me as the talent of Aeschylus is said to have made upon the Athenians. For he was a poet of tragedy, and finding the art to be rude and inchoate and as yet not in the least elaborated, he went to work, and curtailed the prolixity of the chorus[16], and invented dialogues for the actors, discarding the long monodies of the earlier time; and he hit upon a plan of killing people behind the stage instead of their being slain before the eyes of the audience. Well, if we cannot deny his talent in making all these improvements, we must nevertheless admit that they might have suggested themselves equally well to an inferior dramatist. But his talent was twofold. On the one hand as a poet he set himself to make his diction worthy of tragedy, on the other hand as a manager, to adapt his stage to sublime, rather than to humble and groveling themes. Accordingly he devised masks which represented the forms of the heroes, and he mounted his actors on buskins so that their gait might

---

[16] or "reduced in size the unduly large choruses."

correspond to the characters they played; and he was the first to devise stage dresses, which might convey an adequate impression to the audience of the heroes and heroines they saw. For all these reasons the Athenians accounted him to be the father of tragedy; and even after his death they continued to invite him to represent his plays at the Dionysiac festival, for in accordance with public decree the plays of Aeschylus continued to be put upon the stage and win the prize anew. And yet the gratification of a well-staged tragedy is insignificant, for its pleasures last a brief day, as brief as is the season of the Dionysiac festival; but the gratification of a philosophic system devised to meet the requirements of a Pythagoras, and also breathing the inspiration in which Pythagoras was anticipated by the Indians, lasts not for a brief time, but for an endless and incalculable period. It is then not unreasonable on my part, I think, to have devoted myself to a philosophy so highly elaborated, and to one which, to use a metaphor from the stage, the Indians mount, as it deserves to be mounted, upon a lofty and divine mechanism, and then wheel it forth upon the stage. And that I was right to admire them, and that I am right in considering them to be wise and blessed, it is now time to convince you. I beheld men dwelling upon the earth, and yet not upon it, I beheld them fortified without fortifications, I beheld them possessed of nothing, and yet possessed of all things. You will say that I have taken to riddles, but the wisdom of Pythagoras allows of this; for he taught us to speak in riddles, when he discovered that the word is the teacher of silence. And there was a time when you yourselves took counsel with Pythagoras, and were advocates of this same wisdom; that was in the time when you could say nothing too good of the Indian philosophy, for to begin with and of old you were Indians. Subsequently because your soil was wrath with you, you came hither; and then ashamed of the reasons owing to which you quitted it, you tried to get men to regard you as anything rather than Ethiopians who had come from India hither, and you took every pains to efface your past. This is why you stripped yourselves of the apparel in which you came thence, as if you were anxious to doff along with it your Ethiopian nationality. This is why you have resolved to worship the gods in the Egyptian rather than in your own fashion, and why you have set yourselves to disseminate unflattering stories of the Indians, as if in maligning them you did not foul your own nest. And in this respect you have not yet altered your tone for the better; for only today you have given here an exhibition of your propensities for abuse and satire, pretending that the Indians are no better employed than in startling people and in pandering to their eyes and ears. And because as yet you are ignorant of my wisdom, you show yourself indifferent to the fame which crowns it. Well, in defense of myself I do not mean to say anything, for I am content to be what the Indians think me; but I will not allow them to be attacked. And if you are so sound and sane as to possess any tincture of the wisdom of the man of Himera, who composed in honor of Helen a poem which contradicted a former one and called it a palinode, it is high time for you also to use the words he used and say: 'This discourse of ours is not true,' so changing your opinion and adopting one better than you at present entertain about these people. But if you have not the wit to recant, you must at least spare men to whom the gods vouchsafe, as worthy of them, their own prerogatives, and whose possessions they do not disdain for themselves.

"You have also, Thespesion, made some remarks about the simplicity and freedom from pomp which characterizes the Pythian oracle; and by way of example you instanced the temple composed of wax and feathers; but I do not myself find that even this was devoid of pomp, for we have the line

'O bird bring hither your wings, and bees your wax.'

Such language betokens a carefully prepared home and the form of house. And the god I believe regarded even this as too humble and below the dignity of wisdom, and therefore desired to have another and yet another temple, big ones these and a hundred feet in breadth; and from one of them it is said that golden figures of the wryneck were hung up which possessed in a manner the charm of the Sirens; and the god collected the most precious of the offerings into the Pythian temple for ornament; nor did he reject works of statuary, when their authors brought him to his temple colossal figures of gods and men, and also of horses, oxen and other animals; nor did he refuse the gift of Glaucus brought thither of a stand for a goblet, nor the picture of the taking of the citadel of Ilium which Polygnotus painted there. For I imagine he did not consider that the gold of Lydia really beautified the Pythian fane, but he admitted it on behalf of the Hellenes themselves, by way of pointing out to them, I believe, the immense riches of the barbarians, and inducing them to covet that rather than continue to ravage one another's lands. And he accordingly adopted the Greek fashion of art which suited his particular wisdom, and adorned his shrine therewith. And I believe that it was by way of adornment that he also puts his oracles in metrical form. For if he did not wish to make a show in this matter, he would surely make his responses in such forms as the following: 'Do this, or do not do that'; and 'go, or do not go,' or 'choose allies, or do not choose them.' For here are short formulas, or as you call it naked ones. But in order to display his mastery of the grand style, and in order to please those who came to consult his oracle, he adopted the poetical form; and he does not allow that anything exists which he does not know, but claims to have counted the sands of the sea and to know their number, and also to have fathomed the depths of the sea.

"But I suppose you will call it miracle-monging, that Apollo dictates his oracles with such proud dignity and elation of spirit? But if you will not be annoyed, Thespesion, at what I say, there are certain old women who go about with sieves in their hands to shepherds, sometimes to cow-herds, pretending to heal their flocks, when they are sick, by divination, as they call it, and they claim to be called wise women, yea wiser than those who are unfeignedly prophets. It seems to me that you are in the same case, when I contrast your wisdom with that of the Indians; for they are divine, and have trimmed and adorned their science after the matter of the Pythian oracle; but you—however I will say no more, for modesty in speech is as dear to me as it is dear to the Indians, and I would be glad to have it at once to attend upon and to guide my tongue, seeking to compass what is in my power when I am praising those to whom I am so devoted, but leaving alone what is too high for me to attain unto, without bespattering it with petty disapproval. But you no doubt delight in the story which you have read in Homer about the Cyclopes, how their land, all unsown and unploughed, nourished the most fearless and lawless of beings; and if it is some Edoni or Lydians who are conducting bacchic revels, you are quite ready to believe that the earth will supply them with fountains of milk and wine, and give them to drink thereof; but you would deny to these Indians, lovers of all wisdom as enthusiastic as ever bacchants were, the unsought bounties which earth offers them. Moreover tripods, gifted with will of their own, attend the banquets of the gods also; and Ares, ignorant and hostile as he was to Hephaestus, yet never accused him merely for making them; nor is it conceivable that the gods ever listened to such an indictment as this: 'You commit an injustice, O Hephaestus, in adorning the banquet of the gods, and encompassing it with miracles.' Nor was Hephaestus ever sued for constructing handmaids of gold, nor accused of debasing the metals because he made the gold to breath. For ever art is interested to adorn, and the very existence of the arts was a discovery made in behalf of ornament. Moreover a man who goes without shoes and wears a philosopher's cloak and hangs a wallet on his back is a creature of ornament; nay, more even the nakedness which you affect, in spite of its rough and plain appearance, has for its object ornament and decoration, and it is not even exempt from the proverbial "pride of your own sort to match"[17]. We must judge by their own standard the religion of the Sun and the national rites of the Indians and any cult in which that god delights; for the subterranean gods will always prefer deep trenches and ceremonies conducted in the hollows of the earth, but the air is the chariot of the sun; and those who would sing his praise in a fitting manner must rise from the earth and soar aloft with god; and this everyone would like to do, but the Indians alone are able to do it."

Damis says that he breathed afresh when he heard this address; for that the Egyptians were so impressed by Apollonius' words, that Thespesion, in spite of the blackness of his complexion, visibly blushed, while the rest of them seemed in some way stunned by the vigorous and fluent discourse which they listened to; but the youngest of them, whose name was Nilus, leapt up from the ground, he says, in admiration, and passing over to Apollonius shook hands with him, and besought him to tell him about the interviews which he had had with the Indians. And Apollonius, he says, replied: "I should not grudge you anything, for you are ready to listen, as I see, and are ready to welcome wisdom of every kind; but I should not care to pour out the teachings I gathered there upon Thespesion or on anyone else who regards the lore of the Indians as so much nonsense." Whereupon Thespesion said: "But if you were a merchant or a seafarer, and you brought to us some cargo or other from over there, would you claim, merely because it came from India, to dispose of it untested and unexamined, refusing us either the liberty of looking at it or tasting it?" But Apollonius repled as follows: "I should furnish it to those who asked for it; but if the moment my ship had reached the harbor, someone came down the beach and began to run down my cargo and abuse myself, and say that I came from a country which produces nothing worth having, and if he reproached me for sailing with a cargo of shoddy goods, and tried to persuade the rest to think like himself, do you suppose that one would, after entering such a harbor, cast anchor or make his cables fast, and not rather hoist his sails and put to sea afresh, entrusting his goods more

---

[17] See Plato's retort in Diogenes Laertius, 6. 26.

gladly to the winds than to such undiscerning and inhospitable people?" "Well, I anyhow," said Nilus, "lay hold on your cables, and entreat you, my skipper, to let me share your goods that you bring hither; and I would gladly embark with you in your ship as a super-cargo and a clerk to check your merchandise."

CHAPTER XIII

Thespesion, however, was anxious to put a stop to such propositions, so he said: "I am glad, Apollonius, that you are annoyed at what we said to you; for you can the more readily condone our annoyance at the misrepresentation you made of our local wisdom, long before you had gained any experience of its quality." Apollonius was for a moment astonished at these words, for he had heard nothing as yet of the intrigues of Thrasybulus and Euphrates; but as was his wont, he guessed the truth and said: "The Indians, O Thespesion, would never have behaved as you have, nor have given ear to these insinuation dropped by Euphrates, for they have a gift of prescience. Now I never have had any quarrel of my own with Euphrates; I only tried to wean him of his passion for money and cure his propensity to value everything by what he could make out of it; but I found that my advice was not congenial to him, nor in his case practicable; nay he merely takes it as a tacit reproach, and never loses any opportunity of intriguing against me. But since you have found his attacks upon my character so plausible, I may as well tell you that it is you, rather than myself, that he has calumniated. For though, as is clear to me, the victims of calumny incur considerable dangers, since they are, I suppose, sure to be disliked without having done any wrong, yet neither are those who incline to listen to the calumnies free from danger; for in the first place they will be convicted of paying respect to lies and giving them as much attention as they would to the truth, and secondly they are convicted of levity and credulity, faults which it is disgraceful even for a stripling to fall into. And they will be thought envious, because they allow envy to teach them to listen to unjust tittle-tattle; and they expose themselves all the more to calumny, because they think it true of others. For man is by nature inclined to commit a fault which he does not discredit when he hears it related to others. Heaven forbid that a man of these inclinations should become a tyrant, or even president of a popular state; for in his hands even a democracy would become a tyranny; nor let him be made a judge, for surely he will not ever discern the truth. Nor let him be captain of a ship, for the crew would mutiny, nor general of an army, for that would bring luck to the adversary; nor let one of his disposition attempt philosophy, for he would not consider the truth in forming his opinions. But Euphrates has deprived you of even the quality of wisdom; for how can those on whom he has imposed with his falsehoods claim wisdom for themselves? have they not deserted from it to take sides with one who has persuaded them of improbabilities?" Here Thespesion tried to calm him, and remarked: "Enough of Euphrates and of his small-minded affairs; for we are quite ready even to reconcile you with him, since we consider it the proper work of a sage to be umpire in the disputes of other sages." "But," said Apollonius, "who shall reconcile me with you? For the victim of lies must surely be driven into hostility by the falsehood." ... "Be it so," said Apollonius, "and let us hold a conversation, for that will be the best way of reconciling us."

CHAPTER XIV

And Nilus, as he was passionately anxious to listen to Apollonius, said: "And what's more, it behoves you to begin the conversation, and to tell us all about the journey which you made to the people of India, and about the conversations which you held there, I have no doubt, on the most brilliant topics." "And I too," said Thespesion, "long to hear about the wisdom of Phraotes, for you are said to have brought from India some examples of his arguments." Apollonius accordingly began by telling them about the events which occurred in Babylon, and told them everything, and they gladly listened to him, spellbound by his words. But when it was midday, they broke of the conversations, for at this time of day the naked sages, like others, attend to the ceremonies of religion.

CHAPTER XV

Apollonius and his comrades were about to dine, when Nilus presented himself with vegetables and bread and dried fruits, some of which he carried himself, while his friends carried the rest; and very politely he said: "The sages send these gifts of hospitality, not only to yourselves but to me; for I mean to share in your repast, not uninvited, as they say, but inviting myself." "It is a delightful gift of hospitality," said Apollonius, "which you bring to us, O youth, in the shape of yourself and your disposition, for you are evidently a philosopher without guile, and an enthusiastic lover of the doctrines of the Indians and of Pythagoras. So lie down here and eat with us." "I will do so," said the other, "but your dishes will not be ample enough to satisfy me." "It seems to me," said the other, "that you are a gourmand and an appalling eater." "None like me," said the other, "for although you have set before me so ample and so brilliant a repast, I am not sated; and after a little time I am come back again to eat afresh. What then can you call me but an insatiable cormorant?" "Eat your fill," said Apollonius, "and as for topics of conversation, some you must yourself supply, and I will give you others."

CHAPTER XVI

So when they had dined, "I," said Nilus, "until now have been camping together with the naked sages, and joined my forces with them as with certain light armed troops or slingers. But now I intend to put on my heavy armor, and it is your shield that shall adorn me." "But," said Apollonius, "I think, my good Egyptian, that you will incur the censure of Thespesion and his society for two reasons; firstly, that after no further examination and testing of ourselves you have left them, and secondly that you give the preference to our manners and discipline with more precipitancy than is admissible where a man is making choice of how he shall live." "I agree with you," said the young man, "but if I am to blame for making this choice, I might also be to blame if I did not make it; and anyhow they will be most open to rebuke, if they make the same choice as myself. For it will be more justly reprehensible in them, as they are both older and wiser than myself, not to have made the choice long ago which I make now; for with all their advantages they will have failed to choose what in practice would so much redound to their advantage." "A very generous sentiment indeed, my good youth, is this which you have expressed," said Apollonius; "but beware lest the mere fact of their being so wise and aged should give them an appearance, at any rate, of being right in choosing as they have done, and of having good reason for rejecting my doctrine; and lest you should seem to take up a very bold position in setting them to rights rather than in following them." But the Egyptian turned short round upon Apollonius and countering his opinion said: "So far as it was right for a young man to agree with his elders, I have been careful to do so; for so long as I thought that these gentlemen were possessed of a wisdom which belonged to no other set of men, I attached myself to them; and the motive which actuated me to do so was the following: My father once made a voyage on his own initiative to the Red Sea, for he was, I may tell you, captain of the ship which the Egyptians send to the Indies. And after he had had intercourse with the Indians of the seaboard, he brought home stories of the wise men of that region, closely similar to those which you have told us. And his account which I heard was somewhat as follows, namely that the Indians are the wisest of mankind, but that the Ethiopians are colonists sent from India, who follow their forefathers in matters of wisdom, and fix their eyes on the institutions of their home. Well, I, having reached my teens, surrendered my patrimony to those who wanted it more than myself, and frequented the society of these naked sages, naked myself as they, in the hope of picking up the teaching of the Indians, or at any rate teaching allied to theirs. And they certainly appeared to me to be wise, though not after the manner of India; but when I asked them point blank why they did not teach the philosophy of India, they plunged into abuse of the natives of that country very much as you have heard them do in their speeches this very day. Now I was still young, as you see, so they made me a member of their society, because I imagine they were afraid I might hastily quit them and undertake a voyage to the Red Sea, as my father did before me. And I should certainly have done so, yes, by Heaven, I would have pushed on until I reached the hill of the sages, unless someone of the gods had sent you hither to help me and enabled me without either making any voyage over the Red Sea or adventuring to the inhabitants of the Gulf, to taste the wisdom of India. It is not today therefore for the first time that I shall make my choice, but I made it long ago, though I did not obtain what I hoped to obtain. For what is there to wonder at if a man who has missed what he was looking for, returns to the search? And if I should convert my friends yonder to this point of view, and persuade them to adopt the convictions which I have adopted myself, should I, tell me, be guilty of any hardihood? For you must not reject the claim that youth makes, that in some way it assimilates an idea more easily than old age; and anyone who counsels another to adopt the wisdom and teaching which he himself has chosen, anyhow escapes the imputation of trying to persuade others of things he does not believe himself. And anyone who takes the blessings bestowed upon him by fortune into a corner and there enjoys them by himself, violates their character as blessings, for he prevents their sweetness from being enjoyed by as many as possible."

CHAPTER XVII

When Nilus had finished these arguments, and juvenile enough they were, Apollonius took him up and said: "If you were in love with my wisdom, had you not better, before I begin, discuss with me the question of my reward?" "Let us discuss it," answered Nilus, "and do you ask whatever you like." "I ask you," he said, "to be content with the choice you have made, and not to annoy the naked sages by giving them advice which they will not take." "I consent," he said, "and let this be agreed upon as your reward." This then was the substance of their conversation, and when Nilus at its close asked him how long a time he would stay among the nakes sages he replied: "So long as the quality of their wisdom justifies anyone in remaining in their company; and after that I shall take my way to the cataracts, in order to see the springs of the Nile, for it will be delightful not only to behold the sources of the Nile, but also to listen to the roar of its waterfalls."

CHAPTER XVIII

After they had held this discussion and listened to some recollections of India, they lay down to sleep upon the grass; but at daybreak, having offered their accustomed prayers, they followed Nilus, who led them into the presence of Thespesion. They accordingly greeted one another, and sitting down together in the grove they began a conversation in which Apollonius led as follows: "How important it is," said he, "not to conceal wisdom, is proved by our conversation of yesterday; for because the Indians taught me as much of their wisdom as I thought it proper for me to know, I not only remember my teachers, but I go about instilling into others what I heard from them. And you too will be richly rewarded by me, if you send me away with a knowledge of your wisdom as well; for I shall not cease to go about and repeat your teachings to the Greeks, while to the Indians I shall write them."

CHAPTER XVIII

"Ask," they said, "for you know question comes first and argument follows on it." "It is about the gods that I would like to ask you a question first, namely, what induced you to impart, as your tradition, to the people of this country forms of the gods that are absurd and grotesque in all but a few cases? In a few cases, do I say? I would rather say that in very few are the gods' images fashioned in a wise and god-like manner, for the mass of your shrines seem to have been erected in honor rather of irrational and ignoble animals than of gods." Thespesion, resenting these remarks, said: "And your own images in Greece, how are they fashioned?" "In the way," he replied, "in which it is best and most reverent to construct images of the gods." "I suppose you allude," said the other, "to the statue of Zeus in Olympia, and to the image of Athena and to that of the Cnidian goddess and to that of the Argive goddess and to other images equally beautiful and full of charm?" "Not only to these," replied Apollonius, "but without exception I maintain, that whereas in other lands statuary has scrupulously observed decency and fitness, you rather make ridicule of the gods than really believe in them." "Your artists, then, like Phidias," said the other, "and like Praxiteles, went up, I suppose, to heaven and took a copy of the forms of the gods, and then reproduced these by their art or was there any other influence which presided over and guided their molding?" "There was," said Apollonius, "and an influence pregnant with wisdom and genius." "What was that?" said the other, "for I do not think you can adduce any except imitation." "Imagination," said Apollonius, "wrought these works, a wiser and subtler artist by far than imitation; for imitation can only create as its handiwork what it has seen, but imagination equally what it has not seen; for it will conceive of its ideal with reference to the reality, and imitation is often baffled by terror, but imagination by nothing; for it marches undismayed to the goal which it has itself laid down. When you entertain a notion of Zeus you must, I suppose, envisage him along with heaven and seasons and stars, as Phidias in his day endeavoured to do, and if you would fashion an image of Athena you must imagine in your mind armies and cunning, and handicrafts, and how she leapt out of Zeus himself. But if you make a hawk or an owl or a wolf or a dog, and put it in your temples instead of Hermes or Athena or Apollo, your animals and your birds may be esteemed and of much price as likenesses, but the gods will be very much lowered in their dignity." "I think," said the other, "that you criticize our religion very superficially; for if the Egyptians have any wisdom, they show it by their deep respect and reverence in the representation of the gods, and by the circumstance that they fashion their forms as symbols of a profound inner meaning, so as to enhance their solemnity and august character." Apollonius thereon merely laughed and said: "My good friends, you have indeed greatly profited by the wisdom of Egypt and Ethiopia, if your dog and your ibis and your goat seem particularly august and god-like, for this is what I learn from Thespesion the sage. But what is there that is august or awe-inspiring in these images? Is it not likely that perjurers and temple-thieves and all the rabble of low jesters will despise such holy objects rather than dread them; and if they are to be held for the hidden meanings which they convey, surely the gods in Egypt would have met with much greater reverence, if no images of them had ever been set up at all, and if you had planned your theology along other lines wiser and more mysterious. For I imagine you might have built temples for them, and have fixed the altars and laid down rules about what to sacrifice and what not, and when and on what scale, and with what liturgies and rites, without introducing any image at all, but leaving it to those who frequented the temples to imagine the images of the gods; for the mind can more or less delineate and figure them to itself better than can any artist; but you have denied to the gods the privilege of beauty both of the outer eye and of an inner suggestion." Thespesion replied and said: "There was a certain Athenian, called Socrates, a foolish old man like ourselves, who thought that the dog and the goose and the plane tree were gods and used to swear by them." "He was not foolish," said Apollonius, "but a divine and unfeignedly wise man; for he did not swear by these objects on the understanding that they were gods, but to save himself from swearing by the gods."

CHAPTER XX

Thereupon Thespesion as if anxious to drop the subject, put some questions to Apollonius, about the scourging in Sparta, and asked if the Lacedaemonians were smitten with rods in public. "Yes," answered the other, "as hard, O Thespesion, as men can smite them; and it is especially men of noble birth among them that are so treated." "Then what do they do to menials," he asked, "when they do wrong?" "They do not kill them nowadays," said Apollonius, "as Lycurgus formerly allowed, but the same whip is used to them too." "And what judgment does Hellas pass upon the matter?" "They flock," he answered, "to see the spectacle with pleasure and utmost enthusiasm, as if to the festival of Hyacinthus, or to that of the naked boys." "Then these excellent Hellenes are not ashamed, either to behold those publicly whipped who erewhile governed them or to reflect that they were governed by men who are whipped by men who are whipped before the eyes of all? And how is it that you did not reform this abuse? For they say that you interested yourself in the affairs of the Lacedaemonians, as of other people." "So far as anything could be reformed, I gave them my advice, and they readily adopted it; for they are the freest of the Hellenes; but at the same time they will only listen to one who gives them good advice. Now the custom of scourging is a ceremony in honor of the Scythian Artemis, so they say, and was prescribed by oracles, and to oppose the regulations of the gods is in my opinion utter madness." "'Tis a poor wisdom, Apollonius," he replied, "which you attribute to the gods of the Hellenes, if they countenance scourging as a part of the discipline of freedom." "It's not the scourging," he said, "but the sprinkling of the altar with human blood that is important, for the Scythians too held the altar to be worthy thereof; but the Lacedaemonians modified the ceremony of sacrifice because of its implacable cruelty, and turned it into a contest of endurance, undergone without any loss of life, and yet securing to the goddess as first fruits an offering of their own blood." "Why then," said the other, "do they not sacrifice strangers right out to Artemis, as the Scythians formerly considered right to do?" "Because," he answered, "it is not congenial to any of the Greeks to adopt in full rigor the manners and customs of barbarians." "And yet," said the other, "it seems to me that it would be more humane to sacrifice one or two of them than to enforce as they do a policy of exclusion against all foreigners."

"Let us not assail," said the other, "O Thespesion, the law-giver Lycurgus; but we must understand him, and then we shall see that his prohibition to strangers to settle in Sparta and live there was not inspired on his part by mere boorish exclusiveness, but by a desire to keep the institutions of Sparta in their original purity by preventing outsiders from mingling in her life." "Well," said the other, "I should allow the men of Sparta to be what they claim to be, if they had ever lived with strangers, and yet had faithfully adhered to their home principles; for it was not by keeping true to themselves in the absence of strangers, but by doing so in spite of their presence, that they needed to show their superiority. But they, although they enforced his policy of excluding strangers, corrupted their institutions, and were found doing exactly the same as did those of the Greeks whom they most detested. Anyhow, their subsequent naval program and policy of imposing tribute was modelled entirely upon that of Athens, and they themselves ended by committing acts which they had themselves regarded as a just *casus belli* against the Athenians, whom they had no sooner beaten in the field than they humbly adopted, as if they were the beaten party, their pet institution. And the very fact that the goddess was introduced from Taurus and Scythia was the action of men who embraced alien customs. But if an oracle prescribed this, what want was there of the scourge? What need to feign an endurance fit for slaves? Had they wanted to prove the disdain that Lacedaemonians felt for death, they had I think done better to sacrifice a youth of Sparta with his own consent upon the altar. For this would have been a real proof of the superior courage of the Spartans, and would have disinclined Hellas from ranging herself in the opposite camp to them. But you will say that they had to save their young men for the battlefield; well, in that case the law which prevails among the Scythians, and sentences all men of sixty years of age to death, would have been more suitably introduced and followed among the Lacedaemonians then among the Scythians, supposing that they embrace death in its grim reality and not as a mere parade. These remarks of mine are directed not so much against the Lacedaemonians, as against yourself, O Apollonius. For if ancient institutions, whose hoary age defies our understanding of their origins, are to be examined in an unsympathetic spirit, and the reason why they are pleasing to heaven subjected to cold criticism, such a line of speculation will produce a crop of odd conclusions; for we could attack the mystery rite of Eleusis in the same way and ask, why it is this and not that; and the same with the rites of the Samothracians, for in their ritual they avoid one thing and insist on another; and the same with the Dionysiac ceremonies and the phallic symbol, and the figure erected in Cyllene, and before we know where we are we shall be picking holes in everything. Let us choose, therefore, any other topic you like, but respect the sentiment of Pythagoras, which is also our own; for it is better, if we can't hold our tongues about everything, at any rate to preserve silence about such matters as these." Apollonius replied and said, "If, O Thespesion, you had wished to discuss the topic seriously, you would have found that the Lacedaemonians have many excellent arguments to advance in favor of their institutions, proving that they are sound and superior to those of other Hellenes; but since you are so averse to continue the discussion, and even regard it as impious to talk about such things, let us proceed to another subject, of great importance, as I am convinced, for it is about justice that I shall now put a question."

CHAPTER XXI

"Let us," said Thespesion, tackle the subject; for it is one very suitable to men, whether they are wise or not wise. But lest we should drag in the opinions of Indians, and so confuse our discussion, and go off without having formed any conclusions, do you first impart to us the views held by the Indians concerning justice, for you probably examined their views on the spot; and if their opinion is proved to be correct we will adopt it; but if we have something wiser to put in its place, you must adopt our view, for that too is plain justice." Said Apollonius: "Your plan is excellent and most satisfactory to me; so do listen to the conversation which I held there. For I related to them how I had once been captain of a large ship, in the period when my soul was in command of another body, and how I thought myself extremely just because, when robbers offered me a reward, if I would betray my ship by running it into roads where they were going to lie in wait for it, in order to seize its cargo, I agreed and made the promise, just to save them from attacking us, but intending to slip by them and get beyond the place agreed upon." "And," said Thespesion, "did the Indians agree that this was justice?" "No, they laughed at the idea," he said, "for they said that justice was something more than not being unjust." "It was very sensible," said the other, "of the Indians to reject such a view; for good sense is something more than not entertaining nonsense, just as courage is something more than not running away from the ranks; and so temperance is something more than the avoidance of adultery, and no one reserves his praise for a man who has simply shown himself to be not bad. For because a thing, no matter what, is equidistant between praise and punishment, it is not on that account to be reckoned offhand to be virtue" "How then. O Thespesion," said Apollonius, "are we to crown the just man and for what actions?" "Could you have discussed justice more completely and more opportunely," said the other, "than when the sovereign of so large and flourishing a country intervened in your philosophic discussion of the art of kingship, a thing intimately connected with justice?" "If it had been Phraotes," said Apollonius, "who turned up on that occasion, you might rightly blame me for not gravely discussing the subject of justice in his presence. But you from the account which I gave of him yesterday that the man is a drunkard and an enemy of all philosophy. What need therefore was there to inflict on him the trouble? Why should we try to win credit for ourselves in the presence of a sybarite who thinks of nothing but his own pleasures? But inasmuch as it is incumbent upon wise men like ourselves to explore and trace out justice, more so than on kings and generals, let us proceed to examine the absolutely just man. For though I thought myself just in the affair of the ship, and thought others just too because they do not practice injustice, you deny that this in itself constitutes them just or worthy of honor." "And rightly so," said the other, " for whoever heard of a decree drafted by Athenians or Lacedaemonians in favor of crowning so and so, because he is not a libertine, or of granting the freedom of the city to so and so, because the temples have not been robbed by him? Who then is the just man and what are is actions? For neither did I ever hear of anyone being crowned merely for his justice, nor of a decree being proposed over a just man to the effect that so and so shall be crowned, because such and such actions of his show him to be just. For anyone who considers the fate of Palamedes in Troy or Socrates in Athens, will discover that even justice is not sure of success among men, for assuredly these men suffered most unjustly being themselves most just. Still they at least were put to death on the score of acts of injustice imputed on them, and the verdict was a distortion of the truth; whereas in the case of Aristides the son of Lysimachus, it was very justice that was the undoing of him, for he in spite of his integrity was banished merely because of his reputation for this very virtue. And I am sure that justice will appear in a very ridiculous light; for having been appointed by Zeus and by the Fates to prevent men being unjust to one another, she has never been able to defend herself against injustice.

And the history of Aristides is sufficient to me to show the difference between one who is nor unjust and one who is really just. For, tell me, is not this the same Aristides of whom your Hellenic compatriots when they come here tell us that he undertook a voyage to the islands to fix the tribute of the allies, and after settling it on a fair basis, returned again to his country still wearing the same cloak in which he left it?" "It is he," answered Apollonius, "who made the love of poverty once to flourish." "Now," said the other, "let us suppose that there were at Athens two public orators passing an encomium upon Aristides, just after he had returned from the allies; one of the proposes that he shall be crowned, because he has come back again without enriching himself or amassing any fortune, but the poorest of the Athenians, poorer than he was before; and the other orator, we will suppose, drafts his motion somewhat as follows: 'Whereas Aristides has fixed the tribute of the allies according to their ability to pay, and not in excess of the resources of their respective countries; and whereas he has endeavored to keep them loyal to the Athenians, and to see that they shall feel it no grievance to pay upon this scale, it is hereby resolved to crown him for justice.' Do you not suppose that Aristides himself would have opposed the first of these resolutions, as an indignity to his entire life, seeing that it only honored him for not doing injustice; whereas, he might perhaps have supported the other resolution as a fair attempt to express his intentions and policy? For I imagine it was with an eye to the interest of Athenians and subject states alike, that he took care to fix the tribute on a fair and moderate basis, and in fact his wisdom in this matter was conclusively proved after his death. For when the Athenians exceeded his valuations and imposed heavier tributes upon the islands, their naval supremacy at once went to pieces, though it more than anything else had made them formidable; on the other hand the prowess of the Lacedaemonians passed on to the sea itself; and nothing was left of Athenian supremacy, for the whole of the subject states rushed into revolution and made good their escape. It follows then, O Apollonius, that rightly judged, it is not the man who abstains from injustice that is just, but the man who himself does what is just, and also influences others not to be unjust; and from such justice as his there will spring up a crop of other virtues, especially those of the law-court and of the legislative chamber. For such a man as he will make a much fairer judge than people who take their oaths upon the dissected parts of victims, and his legislation will be similar to that of Solon and of Lycurgus; for assuredly these great legislators were inspired by justice to undertake their work."

CHAPTER XXII

Such, according to Damis, was the discussion held by them with regard to the just man, and Apollonius, he says, assented to their argument, for he always agreed with what was reasonably put. They also had a philosophic talk about the soul, proving its immortality, and about nature, along much the same lines which Plato follows in his Timaeus; and after some further remarks and discussions of the laws of the Hellenes, Apollonius said: "For myself I have come all this way to see yourselves and visit the springs of the Nile; for a person who only comes as far as Egypt may be excused if he ignores the latter, but if he advances as far as Ethiopia, as I have done, he will be rightly reproached if he neglects to visit them, and to draw as it were from their well-springs some arguments of his own." "Farewell then," said the other, "and pray to the springs for whatever you desire, for they are divine. But I imagine you will take as your guide Timasion, who formerly lived at Naucratis, but is now of Memphis; for he is well acquainted with the springs of the Nile and he is not so impure as to stand in need of further lustrations. But as for you, O Nilus, we would like to have a talk to you by ourselves." The meaning of this sally was clear enough to Apollonius, for he well understood their annoyance at Nilus' preference for himself; but to give them an opportunity of speaking him apart, he left them to prepare and pack up for his journey, for he meant to start at daybreak. And after a little time Nilus returned, but did not tell them anything of what they had said to him, though he laughed a good deal to himself. And no one asked him what he was laughing about, but they respected his secret.

CHAPTER XXIII

They then took their supper and after a discussion of certain trifles they laid them down to sleep where they were; but at daybreak they said goodbye to the naked sages, and started off along the road which leads to the mountains, keeping the Nile on their right hand, and they saw the following spectacles deserving of notice. The Catadupi [the first cataract] are mountains formed of good soil, about the same size as the hill of the Lydians called Tmolus; and from them the Nile flows rapidly down, washing with it the soil of which it creates Egypt; but the roar of the stream, as it breaks down in a cataract from the mountains and hurls itself into the Nile, is terrible and intolerable to the ears, and many of those have approached it too close have returned with the loss of their hearing.

CHAPTER XXIV

Apollonius, however, and his party pushed on till they saw some round-shaped hills covered with trees, the leaves and bark and gum of which the Ethiopians regard as of great value; and they also saw lions close to the path, and leopards and other such wild animals; but they were not attracted by any of them, for they fled from them in haste as if they were scared at the sight of men. And they also saw stags and gazelles, and ostriches an asses, the latter in great numbers, and also many wild bulls and ox-goats, the former of these two animals being a mixture of the stag and the ox, that latter of the creatures from which its name is taken. They found moreover on the road the bones and half-eaten carcases of these; for the lions, when they have gorged themselves with fresh prey, care little for what is left over of it, because, I think, they feel sure of catching fresh quarry whenever they want it.

CHAPTER XXV

It is here that the nomad Ethiopians live in a sort of colony upon wagons, and not far from them the elephant-hunters, who cut up these animals and sell the flesh, and are accordingly called by a name which signifies the selling of elephants. And the Nasamones and the man-eaters and the pigmies and the shadow-footed people are also tribes of Ethiopia, and they extend as far as the Ethiopian ocean, which no mariners ever enter except castaways who do so against their will.

CHAPTER XXVI

As our company were discussing these animals and talking learnedly about the food which nature supplies in their different cases, they heard a sound as of thunder; not a crashing sound, but of thunder as it is when it is still hollow and concealed in the cloud. And Timasion said: "A cataract is at hand, gentlemen, the last for those who are descending the river, but the first to meet you on your way up." And after they had advanced about ten stades, he says that they saw a river discharging itself from the hill-side as big as the Marsyas and the Meander at their first confluence; and he says that after they had put up a prayer to the Nile, they went on till they no longer saw any animals at all; for the latter are naturally afraid of noise, and therefore live by calm waters rather than by those which rush headlong with a noise. And after fifteen stades they heard another cataract which this time was horrible and unbearable to the senses, for it was twice as loud as the first one and it fell from much higher mountains. And Damis relates that his own ears and those of one of his companions were so stunned by the noise, that he himself turned back and besought Apollonius not to go further; however he, along with Timasion and Nilus, boldly pressed on to the third cataract, of which he made the following report on their return. Peaks overhang the Nile, at the most eight stades in height; but the eminence faces the mountains, namely a beetling brow of rocks mysteriously cut away, as if in a quarry, and the fountains of the Nile cling to the edge of the mountain, till they overbalance and fall on to the rocky eminence, from which they pour into the Nile as an expanse of whitening billows. But the effect produced upon the senses by this cataract, which is many times greater than the earlier ones, and the echo which leaps up therefrom against the mountains render it impossible to hear what your companion tells you about the river [18]. But the further road which leads up to the first springs of the river was impracticable, they tell us, and impossible to think of; for they tell many stories of the demons which haunt it, stories similar to those which Pindar in his wisdom puts into verse about the demon whom he sets over these springs to preserve the due proportions of the Nile.

CHAPTER XXVII

After passing the cataracts they halted in a village of the Ethiopians of no great size, and they were dining, towards the evening, mingling in their conversation the grave with the gay, when all on a sudden they heard the women of the village screaming and calling to one another to join in the pursuit and catch the thing; and they also summoned their husbands to help them in the matter. And the latter caught up sticks and stones and anything which came handy, and called upon one another to avenge the insult to their wives. And it appears that for ten months the ghost of a satyr had been haunting the village, who was mad after the women and was said to have killed two of them to whom he was supposed to be specially attached. The companions, then, of Apollonius were frightened out of their wits till Apollonius said: "You need not be afraid, for it's only a satyr that is running amuck here." "Yes, by Zeus," said Nilus, "it's the one that we naked sages have found insulting us for a long time past and we could never stop his jumps and leaps." "But," said Apollonius, "I have a remedy against these hell-hounds, which Midas is said once to have employed; for Midas himself had some of the blood of satyrs in his veins, as was clear from the shape of his ears; and a satyr once, trespassing on his kinship with Midas, made merry at the expense of his ears, not only singing about them, but piping about them. Well, Midas, I understand, had heard from his mother that when a satyr is overcome by wine he falls asleep, and at such times comes to his senses and will make friends with you; so he mixed wine which he had in his palace in a fountain and let

---

[18] *Or* "render investigation of the stream a trial to the ears."

the satyr get at it, and the latter drank it up and was overcome. And to show that the story is true, let us go to the head man of the village, and if the villagers have any wine, we will mix it with water for the satyr and he will share the fate of Midas' satyr." They thought it a good plan, so he poured four Egyptian jars of wine into the trough out of which the village cattle drank, and then called the satyr by means of some secret rebuke or threat; and though as yet the latter was not visible, the wine sensibly diminished as if it was being drunk up. And when it was quite finished, Apollonius said: "Let us make peace with the satyr, for he is fast asleep." And with these words he led the villagers to the cave of the nymphs, which was not quite a furlong away from the village; and he showed them a satyr lying fast asleep in it, but he told them not to hit him or abuse him, "For," he said, "his nonsense is stopped for ever." Such was this exploit of Apollonius, and, by heavens, we may call it not an incidental work in passing, but a masterwork of his passing by[19]; and if you read the sage's epistle, in which he wrote to an insolent young man that he had sobered even a satyr demon in Ethiopia, you will perforce call to mind the above story. But we must not disbelieve that satyrs both exist and are susceptible to the passion of love; for I knew a youth of my own age in Lemnos whose mother was said to be visited by a satyr, as he well might to judge by this story; for he was represented as wearing in his back a fawn-skin that exactly fitted him, the front paws of which were drawn around his neck and fastened over his chest. But I must not go further into this subject; but, anyhow, credit is due as much to experience of facts as it is to myself.

CHAPTER XXVIII

When he had come down from Ethiopia the breach with Euphrates grew wider and wider, especially on account of the daily disputes and discussions; though he left them to Menippus and Nilus to conduct, and seldom himself attacked Euphrates, being much too busy with the training of Nilus.

After Titus had taken Jerusalem, and when the country all round was filled with corpses, the neighboring races offered him a crown; but he disclaimed any such honor to himself, saying that it was not himself that had accomplished this exploit, but that he had merely lent his arms to God, who had so manifested his wrath; and Apollonius praised his

---

[19] I try to render the pun of the original.

action, for therein he displayed a great deal of judgment and understanding of things human and divine, and it showed great moderation on his part that he refused to be crowned because he had shed blood. Accordingly Apollonius indited to him a letter which he sent by the hands of Damis and of which the text was as follows:

"Apollonius sends greetings to Titus the Roman general. Whereas you have refused to be proclaimed for success in war and for shedding the blood of your enemies, I myself assign to you the crown of temperance and moderation, because you thoroughly understand what deeds really merit a crown. Farewell."

Now Titus was overjoyed with this epistle, and replied: "In my own behalf I thank you, no less then in behalf of my father, and I will not forget your kindness; for although I have captured Jerusalem, you have captured me."

CHAPTER XXX

And after Titus had been proclaimed autocrat in Rome and rewarded with the meed of his valor, he went away to become the colleague in empire of his father; but he did not forget Apollonius, and thinking that even a short interview with him would be precious to himself, he besought him to come to Tarsus; and when he arrived he embraced him, saying: "My father has told me by letter everything in respect of which he consulted you; and lo, here is his letter, in which you are described as his benefactor and the being to whom we owe all that we are. Now though I am only just thirty years of age, I am held worthy of the same privileges which my father only attained at the age of sixty. I am called to the throne and to rule, perhaps before I have learned myself to obey, and I therefore dread lest I am undertaking a task beyond my powers." Thereupon Apollonius, after stroking his neck, said (for had as stout a neck as any athlete in training): "And who will force so sturdy a bull-neck as yours under the yoke?" "He that from my youth up reared me as calf," answered Titus, meaning his own father, and implying that he could only be controlled by the latter, who had accustomed him from childhood to obey himself. "I am delighted then," said Apollonius, "in the first place to see you prepared to subordinate yourself to your father, whom without being his natural children so many are delighted to obey, and next to see you rendering to his court a homage in which others will associate yourself. When youth and age are paired in authority, is there any lyre or any flute that will produce so sweet a harmony and so nicely blended? For the qualities of old age will be associated with those of youth, with the result that old age will gain in strength and youth in discipline."

CHAPTER XXXI

"And for myself, O man of Tyana," answered Titus, "can you give me any precepts as to how to rule and exercise the authority of a sovereign?" "Only such rules," replied the other, "as you have laid upon yourself; for in so submitting yourself to your father's will, it is, I think, certain that you will grow like him. And I should like to repeat to you on this occasion a saying of Archytas, which is a noble one and worth committing to memory. Archytas was a man of Tarentum who was learned in the lore of Pythagoras, and he wrote a treatise on the education of children, in which he says: Let the father be an example of virtue to his children, for fathers also will the more resolutely walk in the path of virtue because their children are coming to resemble them. But for myself, I propose to associate with you my own companion Demetrius, who will attend you as much as you like and instruct you in the whole duty of a good ruler." "And what sort of wisdom, O Apollonius, does this person possess?" "Courage," he replied, "to speak the truth unabashed by anyone, for he possesses the constancy and strength of character of a cynic." And as Titus did not seem very pleased to hear the name of dog[20], he continued: "And yet in Homer, Telemachus, when he was young, required, it appears, two dogs, and the poet sends these to accompany the youth to the market place of Ithaca, in spite of their being irrational animals; but you will have a dog to accompany you who will bark in your behalf not only at other people, but at yourself in case you go wrong, and he will bark withal wisely, and never irrationally." "Well," said the other, "give me your dog to accompany me, and I will even let him bite me, in case he feels I am committing injustice." "I will write him a letter, for he teaches philosophy in Rome." "Pray do so," said Titus, "and I wish I could get someone to write to you in my behalf, and induce you to share with me my journey to Rome." "I will come there," said the other, "whenever it is best for both of us."

---

[20] A cynic means literally a canine philosopher.

CHAPTER XXXII

Then Titus dismissed the company, and said: "Now that we are alone, O man of Tyana, you will allow me perhaps to ask you a question upon matters of grave importance to myself." "Pray do so," said the other, "and do so all the more readily because the matter is so important." "It is about my own life," said the other, "and I would feign know whom I ought most to be on my guard against. That is my question, and I hope you will not think me cowardly for already being anxious about it." "Nay, you are only cautious," said the other, "and circumspect; for a man ought to be more careful about this than about anything else." And glancing at the Sun he swore by that god that he had himself intended to address Titus about this matter even if he had not asked him. "For," he said, "the gods have told me to warn you, so long as your father is alive, to be on your guard against his bitterest enemies, but after his death against your own kith and kin." "And," said Titus, "in what way am I to die?" "In the same way," said the other, "as Odysseus is said to have died, for they say that he too met with his death by the sea." Damis interprets the above utterance as follows: Namely, that he was to be on his guard against the cusp of the fish called the trygon, with which they say Odysseus was wounded. Anyhow, after he had occupied the throne for two years, in succession of his father, he died through eating the fish called the sea-hare; and this fish, according to Damis, causes secret humors in the body worse and more fatal than anything else either in the sea or on land. And Nero, he says, introduced this sea-hare in his dishes to poison his worst enemies; and so did Domitian in order to remove his brother Titus, not because he objected to sharing his throne with his brother, but to sharing it with one who was both gentle and good. Such was their conversation in private, after which they embraced one another in public, and as Titus departed Apollonius greeted him with these last words: "Pray you, my King, overcome your enemies by your arms, but your father by your virtues."

CHAPTER XXXIII

But the letter to Demetrius ran as follows: "Apollonius, the Philosopher, sends greeting to Demetrius the cynic.

"I have made a present of you to the Emperor Titus, that you may instruct him how to behave as a sovereign, and take care that you confirm the truth of my words to him, and make yourself, anger apart, everything to him. Farewell."

CHAPTER XXXIV

Now the inhabitants of Tarsus had previously detested Apollonius, because of the violent reproaches which he addressed to them, owing to the fact that through their languid indifference and sensual indolence they could not put up with the vigor of his remarks. But on this occasion they became such devoted admirers of our hero as to regard him as their second founder and the mainstay of their city. For on one occasion the Emperor was offering a sacrifice in public, when the whole body of citizens met and presented a petition to him asking for certain great favors; and he replied that he would mention the matter to his father, and be himself their ambassador to procure them what they wanted; whereupon Apollonius stepped forward and said: "Supposing I convicted some who are standing here of being your own and your father's enemies, and of having sent legates to Jerusalem to excite a rebellion, and of being the secret allies of your most open enemies, what would happen to them?" "Why, what else," said the Emperor, "than instant death?" "Then is it not disgraceful," replied Apollonius, "that you should be instant in demanding their punishment, and yet dilatory in conferring a boon; and be ready yourself to undertake the punishment, but reserve the benefaction until you can see and consult your father?" But the king, over-delighted with this remark, said: "I grant the favors they ask for, for my father will not be annoyed at my yielding to truth and to yourself."

CHAPTER XXXV

So many were the races which they say Apollonius had visited until then, eager and zealous for others as they for him. But his subsequent journeys abroad, though they were numerous, were yet not so many as before, nor did he go to fresh districts which he was not already acquainted with; for when he came down from Ethiopia he made a long stay on the sea-board of Egypt, and then he returned to Phoenicia and Cilicia, and to Ionia and Achaea, and Italy, never failing anywhere to show himself the same as ever. For, hard as it is to know oneself, I myself consider it still harder for the sage to remain always himself; for he cannot ever reform evil natures and improve them, unless he has first trained himself never to alter in his own person. Now about these matters I have discoursed at length in other treatises, and shown those of my readers who were careful and hard students, that a man who is really a man will never alter his nature nor become a slave. But lest I should unduly prolong this work by giving a minute account of the several teachings which he addressed to individuals, and lest on the other hand I should skip over any important chapter of a life, which I am taking so much pains to transmit to those who never knew Apollonius, I think it time to record more important incidents and matters which will repay the remembering; for we must consider that such episodes are comparable to the visits to mankind paid by the sons of Asclepius.

CHAPTER XXXVI

There was a youth who, without having any education of his own, undertook to educate birds, which he kept in his home to make them clever; and he taught them to talk like human beings and to whistle tunes like flute-players. Apollonius met him and asked: "How are you occupying yourself?" And when he replied, and told him all about his nightingales and his blackbirds, and how he trained the tongues of stone curlews—as he had himself a very uneducated accent—Apollonius said: "I think you are spoiling the accents of the birds, in the first place because you don't let them utter their own notes, which are so sweet that not even the best musical instruments could rival or imitate them, and in the second place because you yourself talk the vilest Greek dialects and are only teaching them to stutter like yourself. And what is more, my good youth, you are also wasting your own substance; for when I look at all your hangers-on, and at your get-up, I should say that you are a delicately bred and somewhat wealthy man; but sycophants steal honey from people like yourself, being ready with tongue poised against them for a sting. And what will be the use to you of all this bird-fancying when the time comes? For if you collected all the songbirds in the world, it would not help you to shake off the parasites that cling to you and oppress you; nay you are forced to shower your wealth upon them and cast your gold before them, and you scatter tidbits before dogs; and to stop their barking you must give again and again, until at last you will find yourself reduced to hunger and to poverty.

"What you want is some splendid diversion which will instantly make some alteration in your character, otherwise you will wake up one day and find that you have been plucked of your wealth as if it were plumage, and that you are a fitter subject to excite the birds to lament than to sing. The remedy you need to effect such a change is not a very great one; for there is in all cities a class of men, whose acquaintance you have never made, but who are called schoolmasters. You give them a little of your substance with the certainty of getting it back with interest; for they will teach you the rhetoric of the Forum, and it is not a difficult art to acquire. I may add that, if I had known you as a child, and come across you then, I should have advised you assiduously to attend at the doors of the philosophers and sophists, so as to be able to hedge round your habitation with a wider learning; but, since it is too late for you to manage that, at any rate learn to plead for yourself; for remember, if you had acquired a more complete training and education, you would have resembled a man who is heavy-armed and therefore formidable; yet, if you thoroughly learn this branch, you will at any rate be equipped like a light-armed soldier or a slinger, for you will be able to fling words at your sycophants, as you would stones at dogs." The young man took to heart this advice, and he gave up wasting his time over birds and betook himself to school, much to the improvement both of his judgment and oh his tongue.

CHAPTER XXXVII

Two stories are told in Sardes, one that the River Pactolus used to bring down gold dust to Croesus, and the other that trees are older than earth. The former story Apollonius said he accepted because it was probable, for that there had once been a sand of gold on mount Tmolus, and that the showers of rain had swept it down into the river Pactolus; although subsequently, as is generally the case in such matters, it had given out, being all washed away. But the second story he ridiculed and said: "You pretend that trees were created before the earth; well, I have been studying all this time, yet never heard of the stars being created before the heaven." The inference he wished to convey was that nothing could be created as long as that in which it grows does not exist.

CHAPTER XXXVIII

The ruler of Syria had plunged into a feud, by disseminating among the citizens suspicions such that when they met in assembly they all quarreled with one another. But a violent earthquake happening to occur, they were all cowering, and as is usual in the case of heavenly portents, praying for one another. Apollonius accordingly stepped forward and remarked: "It is God who is clearly anxious to reconcile you to one another, and you will not revive these feuds since you cherish the same fears." And so he implanted in them a sense of what was to happen to them, and made each faction entertain the same fears as the other.

CHAPTER XXXIX

Here is another incident worth recording. A certain man was sacrificing to mother Earth in hope of finding a treasure, and he did not hesitate to offer a prayer to Apollonius with that intent. He, perceiving what he was after, said: "I see that you are a formidable man in business." "Nay, but an unlucky one," remarked the other, "that have nothing except a few pence, and not enough to feed my family." "You seem," said the other, "to keep a large household of idle servants, for you yourself seem not to be wanting in wits." But the man shed a quiet tear and answered: "I have four daughters, who want four dowries, and, when my daughters have had their dowries assigned to them, my capital, which is now only 20,000 drachmas, will have vanished; and they will think that they have got all too little, while I shall perish because I shall have nothing at all." Therefore Apollonius took compassion on him and said: "We will provide for you, myself and mother Earth, for I hear that you are sacrificing to her." With these words he conducted the man into the suburbs, as if he were going to buy some fruit, and there he saw an estate planted with olive-trees; and being delighted with the trees, for they were very good ones and well grown, and there was a little garden in the place, in which he saw bee-hives and flowers, he went into the garden as if he had important business to examine into, and then, having put up a prayer to Pandora, he returned to the city. Then he proceeded to the owner of the field, who had amassed a fortune in the most unrighteous manner, by informing against the estates of Phoenicians, and said: "For how much did you purchase such and such an estate, and how much labor have you spent upon it?" The other replied that he had bought the estate a year before for the sum of 15,000 drachmas, but that as yet he had spent no labor upon it, whereupon Apollonius persuaded him to sell it to him for 20,000 drachmas, which he did, esteeming the 5,000 a great windfall. Now the man who wanted to find the treasure did not in the least understand the gift that was made him, indeed he hardly considered it a fair bargain, because, whereas he might have kept the 20,000 drachmas that he had in hand, he now reflected that the estate which he purchased for the sum might suffer from frost and hailstorms and from other influences ruinous to the crops. But when he found a jar almost at once in the field containing 3,000 darics, close by the beehive in the little garden, and when he got a very large yield from the olive-trees, when everywhere else the crops had failed, he began to hymn the praises of the sage, and his house was crowded with suitors for the hand of his daughters urging their suits upon him.

CHAPTER XL

Here is another story which I came upon about Apollonius, and which deserves to be put upon record: There was a man who was in love with a nude statue of Aphrodite which is erected in the island of Cnidus; and he was making offerings to it, and said that he would make yet others with a view to marrying the statue. But Apollonius, though on other grounds he thought his conduct absurd, yet as the islanders were not averse of the idea, but said that the fame of the goddess would be greatly enhanced if she had a lover, determined to purge the temple of all this nonsense; and when the Cnidians asked him if he would reform their system of sacrifice or their litanies in any way, he replied: "I will reform your eyes, but let the ancestral service of your temple as it is." Accordingly he called to him the languishing lover and asked him if he believed in the existence of the gods: and when he replied that he believed in their existence so firmly that he was actually in love with them, and mentioned a marriage with one of them which he hoped to celebrate shortly, Apollonius replied: "The poets have turned your poor head by their talk of unions of Anchises and Peleus and other heroes with goddess; but I know this much about loving and being loved: gods fall in love with gods, and human beings with human beings, and animals with animals, and in a word like with like, and they have true issue of their own kind; but when two beings of different kinds contract a union, there is no true marriage or love. And if only you would bear in mind the fate of Ixion, you would never have dreamed of falling in love with beings so much above you. For he, you remember, is portrayed across the heaven tortured upon a wheel; and you, unless you get out of this shrine, will perish wherever you are upon earth, nor will you be able to say that the gods have been unjust in their sentence upon you." Thus he put a stop to this mad freak, and the man went away who said he was in love, after sacrificing in order to gain forgiveness.

CHAPTER XLI

At one time the cities on the left side of the Hellespont were visited by earthquakes, and Egyptians and Chaldaeans went begging about through them to collect money, pretending that they wanted ten talents with which to offer sacrifices to earth and to Poseidon. And the cities began to contribute under the stress of fear, partly out of their common funds and partly out of private. But the imposters refused to offer the sacrifices in behalf of their dupes unless the money was deposited in the banks. Now the sage determined not to allow the peoples of the Hellespont to be imposed upon; so he visited their cities, and drove out the quacks who were making money out of the misfortunes of others, and when he divined the causes of the supernatural wrath, and by making such offerings as suited each case averted the visitation at small cost, and the land was at rest.

CHAPTER XLII

The emperor Domitian about the same time passed a law against making men eunuchs, and against planting fresh vineyards, and also in favor of cutting down vineyards already planted, whereon Apollonius, who was visiting the Ionians, remarked: "These rescripts do not concern me, for I, alone perhaps of mankind, require neither to beget my kind nor to drink wine; but our egregious sovereign seems not aware that he is sparing mankind, while he eunuchises the earth." This witticism emboldened the Ionians to send a deputation to the emperor in behalf of their vines, and ask for a repeal of the law which ordered the earth to be laid waste and not planted.

CHAPTER XLIII

Here too is a story which they tell of him in Tarsus. A mad dog had attacked a lad, and as a result of the bite the lad behaved exactly like a dog, for he barked and howled and went on all four feet using his hands as such, and ran about in that manner. And he had been ill in this way for thirty days, when Apollonius, who had recently come to Tarsus, met him and ordered a search to be made for the dog which had done the harm. But they said that the dog had not been found, because the youth had been attacked outside the wall when he was practicing with javelins, nor could they learn from the patient what the dog was like, for he did not even know himself any more. Then Apollonius reflected for a moment and said: "O Damis, the dog is a white shaggy sheep-dog, as big as an Amphilochian hound, and he is standing at a certain fountain trembling all over, for he is longing to drink the water, but at the same time is afraid of it. Bring him to me to the bank of the river, where there are the wrestling grounds, merely telling that it is I who call him." So Damis dragged the dog along, and it crouched at the feet of Apollonius, crying out as a suppliant might do before an altar. But he quite tamed it by stroking it with his hand, and then he stood the lad close by, holding him with his hand; and in order that the multitude might be cognizant of so great a mystery, he said: "The soul of Telephus of Mysia has been transferred into this boy, and the Fates impose the same things upon him as upon Telephus." And with these words he bade the dog lick the wound all round where he had bitten the boy, so that the agent of the wound might in turn be its physician and healer. After that the boy returned to his father and recognized his mother, and saluted his comrades as before, and drank of the waters of the Cydnus. Nor did the sage neglect the dog either, but after offering a prayer to the river he sent the dog across it; and when the dog had crossed the river, he took his stand on the opposite bank, and began to bark, a thing which mad dogs rarely do, and he folded back his ears and wagged his tail, because he knew that he was all right again, for a draught of water cures a mad dog, if he has only the courage to take it.

Such were the exploits of our sage in behalf of both temples and cities; such were the discourses he delivered to the public or in behalf of different communities, and in behalf of those who were dead or who were sick; and such were the harangues he delivered to wise and unwise alike, and to the sovereigns who consulted him about moral virtue.

BOOK VII

CHAPTER I

I am aware that the conduct of philosophers under despotism is the truest touchstone of their character, and am in favor of inquiring in what way any one man displays more courage than another. And my argument also considers me to consider the point; for during the reign of Domitian, Apollonius was beset by accusations and writs of information, the several origins, sources and counts of which I shall presently enlarge upon; and as I shall be under the necessity of specifying the language which he used and the role which he assumed, when he left the court after convicting the tyrant rather than being himself convicted, so I must first of all enumerate all the feats of wise men in the presence of tyrants which I have found worthy of commemoration, and contrast them with the conduct of Apollonius. For this I think is the best way of finding out the truth.

CHAPTER II

Zeno then of Elea, who was the father of dialectic, was convicted of an attempt to overthrow the tyranny of Nearchus the Mysian; and being put to the rack he refused to divulge the names of his accomplices, though he accused of disloyalty those who were loyal to the tyrant, with the result that, whereas they were put to death on the assumption that his accusations were true, he effected the liberation of the Mysians, by tripping despotism up over itself. And Plato declares that he took up the cause of the liberation of the people of Sicily, and associated himself in this enterprise with Dion. And Phyton, when he was banished from Rhegium, fled to Dionysius the tyrant of Sicily; but being treated with more honor than an exile might expect, he realized that the tyrant had designs also upon Rhegium; and he informed the people there of this by letter. But he was caught doing so by the tyrant, who forthwith fastened him to one of his siege engines alive, and then pushed it forward against the walls, imagining that the inhabitants of Rhegium would not shoot at the machine in order to spare Phyton. He, however, cried out to them to shoot, for, said he: "I am the target of your liberty." And Heraclides and Python who slew Cotys the Thracian were both of them young men, and they embraced the principles of the Academy and made themselves wise and so free men. And who does not know the story of Callisthenes of Olynthus? He on one and the same day delivered a panegyric and of an attack upon the Macedonians, just at the time when they were at the acme of their power; and they put him to death for exciting their displeasure. Then there were Diogenes of Sinope and Crates of Thebes, of whom the former went direct to Chaeronea, and rebuked Philip for his treatment of the Athenians, on the ground that, though asserting himself to be a descendant of Heracles he yet was destroying by force of arms those who had taken up arms in defense of the descendants of Heracles. The other Crates, when Alexander declared that he would rebuild Thebes for his sake, replied that he would never stand in need of a country or of a city, which anyone could raze to the ground by mere force of arms. Many more examples of this kind can be adduced, but my treatise does not allow me to prolong them. It is indeed incumbent upon me to criticize these examples, not in order to show that they were not as remarkable as they are universally famous, but only to show that they fell short of the exploits of Apollonius, in spite of their being the best of their kind.

CHAPTER III

About the conduct of Zeno of Elea then, and about the murder of Cotys there is nothing very remarkable; for as it is easy to enslave Thracians and Getae, so it is an act of folly to liberate them; for indeed they do not appreciate freedom, because, I imagine, they do not esteem slavery to be base. I will not say that Plato somewhat lacked wisdom when he set himself to reform the affairs of Sicily rather than those of Athens, or that he was sold in all fairness when, after deceiving others, he found himself deceived, for I fear to offend my readers. But the despotic sway of Dionysius over Sicily was not solidly based when Phyton of Rhegium made his attempt against him, and in any case he would have been put to death by him, even if the people of that city had not shot their bolts at him; his achievement, then, I think, was by no means wonderful: he only preferred to die in behalf of the liberty of others rather than to endure the death penalty to make himself a slave. And as for Callisthenes, even today he cannot acquit himself of baseness; for in first commending and then attacking one and the same set of people, he either attacked those whom he felt to be worthy of praise, or he praised those whom he ought to have been openly attacking. Moreover a person who sets himself to abuse good men cannot escape the charge of being envious, while he who flatters the wicked by his very praises of them draws down upon his own head the guilt of their misdeeds, for evil men are only rendered more evil when you praise them. And Diogenes, if he had addressed Philip in the way he did before the battle of Chaeronea instead of after it, might have preserved him from the guilt of taking up arms against Athens; but instead of doing so he waited till harm was done, when he could only reproach him, not reform him. As for Crates, he must needs incur the censure of every patriot for not seconding Alexander in his design of recolonizing Thebes. But Apollonius had not to fear for any country that was endangered, nor was he in despair of his own life, nor was he reduced to silly and idle speeches, nor was he championing the cause of Mysians or Getae, nor was he face to face with one who was only sovereign of a single island or of an inconsiderable country, but he confronted one who was master both of sea and land, at a time when his tyranny was harsh and bitter; and he took his stand against the tyrant in behalf of the welfare of the subjects, with the same spirit of purpose as he had taken his stand against Nero.

CHAPTER IV

Some may think that his attitude towards Nero was a mere bit of skirmishing, because he did not come to close quarters with him, but merely undermined his despotism by his enocouragement of Vindex, and the terror with which he inspired Tigellinus. And there are certain braggarts here who foster the tale that it required no great courage to assail a man like Nero who led the life of a female harpist or flautist. But what, I would ask, have they to say about Domitian? For he was vigorous in body, and he abjured all those pleasures of music and song which wear away and soften down ferocity; and he took pleasure in the sufferings of others and in any lamentations they uttered. And he was in the habit of saying that distrust is the best safeguard of the people against their tyrants and of the tyrant against the multitude; and though he thought that a sovereign ought to rest from all hard work during the night, yet he deemed it the right season to begin murdering people in. And the result was that while the Senate had all its most distinguished members cut off, philosophy was reduced to cowering in a corner, to such an extent that some of its votaries disguised themselves by changing their dress and ran away to take refuge among the western Celts, while others fled to the deserts of Libya and Scythia, and others again stooped to compose orations in which his crimes were palliated.

But Apollonius, like Tiresias, who is represented by Sophocles as addressing to Oedipus the word:

'For 'tis not in your slavery that I live, but in that of Loxias,' chose wisdom as his mistress, and escaped scot-free from paying tribute to Domitian. Applying to himself, as if it were an oracle, the verse of Tiresias and of Sophocles, and fearing nothing for himself, but only pitying the fate of others, he set himself to rally round him all the younger men of the Senate, and husband such intelligence as he saw discerned in many of them; and he visited the provinces and in the name of philosophy he appealed to the governors, pointing out to them that the strength of a tyrant is not immortal, and that the very fact of their being dreaded exposes them to defeat. And he also reminded them of the Panathenaic festival in Attica, at which hymns are sung in honor of Harmodius and Aristogeiton, and of the sally that was made from Phyle, when thirty tyrants at once were overthrown; and he also reminded them of the ancient history of the Romans, and of how they too had been a democracy, after driving out despotism, arms in hand.

CHAPTER V

And on occasion when a tragic actor visited Ephesus and came forward in the play called the Ino, and when the governor of Asia was one of the audience, a man who was though still young and of very distinguished rank among the consuls, was nevertheless very nervous about such matters, just as the actor finished the speech in which Euripides describes in his iambics how tyrants after long growth of their power are destroyed by little causes, Apollonius leapt up and said: ""But yonder coward understand neither Euripides nor myself!"

CHAPTER VI

When moreover the news was brought how notable a purification of the goddess Hestia of the Romans Domitian had carried out, by putting to death three of the Vestal virgins who had broken their vows and incurred the pollution of marriage, when it was their duty to minister in purity to the Athena of Ilion and to he fire which was worshipped in Rome, he exclaimed: "O Sun, would that thou couldst too be purified of the unjust murders with which the whole world is now filled." Nor did he do all this in private, as a coward might, but he proclaimed his sentiments and aspirations amidst the crowd and before all.

CHAPTER VII

On another occasion when after the murder of Sabinus, one of his own relations, Domitian was about to marry Julia, who was herself the wife of the murdered man, and Domitian's own niece, being one of the daughters of Titus, Ephesus was about to celebrate the marriage with sacrifice, Apollonius interrupted the rites, by exclaiming: "O thou night of the Danaids of yore, how unique thou wast!"

CHAPTER VIII

The following then is the history of his acts in Rome. Nerva was regarded as a proper candidate for the throne which after Domitian's death he occupied with so much wisdom, and the same opinion was entertained of Orfitus and of Rufus. Domitian accused the two latter of intriguing against himself, and they were confined in islands, while Nerva was commanded to live in Tarentum. Now Apollonius had been intimate with them all the time that Titus shared the throne with his father, and also reigned after his father's death; and he was in constant correspondence with them on the subject of self-control, being anxious to enlist them on the side of the sovereigns whose excellence of character he esteemed. But he did his best to alienate them from Domitian, on account of his cruelty, and encouraged them to espouse the cause of the freedom al all. Now it occurred to him that his epistles conveying advice to them were fraught with danger to them, for many of those who were in power were betrayed by their own slaves and friends and womankind, and there was not at the time any house that could keep a secret; accordingly he would take now one and now another of the discreetest of the companions, and say to them: "I have a brilliant secret to entrust to you; for you must betake yourself as my agent to Rome to so and so," mentioning the party, "and you must hold converse with him and do the utmost I could do to win him over." But when he heard that they were banished for having displayed a tendency to revolt against the tyrant, and yet had from timidity abandoned their plans, he delivered a discourse on the subject of the Fates and of Destiny in the grove of Smyrna in which stands the statue of the river Meles.

CHAPTER IX

And being aware that Nerva would before long become sovereign, he went on to explain in his oration that not even tyrants are able to force the hand of destiny, and directing the attention of his audience to the brazen statue of Domitian which had been erected close by that of Meles, he said: "Thou fool, how much art thou mistaken in thy views of Destiny and Fate. For even if thou shouldst slay the man who is fated to be despot after thyself, he shall come to life again." This saying was reported to Domitian by the malevolence of Euphrates, and though no one knew to which of the personages above mentioned this oracle applied, yet the despot in order to allay his fears determined to put them to death. But in order that he might seem to have an excuse for doing so, he summoned Apollonius before him to defend himself on the charge of holding secret relations with them. For he considered that if he came, he could get a sentence pronounced against him, and so avoid the imputation of having put people to death without trial, seeing that they would have been convicted through Apollonius, or in the alternative case, if the latter by some ruse avoided an open trial, then the fate of the others would all the more certainly be sealed, because sentence would have been passed on them by their own accomplice.

CHAPTER X

Moved by these considerations Domitian had already written to the governor of Asia, directing the man of Tyana to be arrested and brought to Rome, when the latter foreseeing in his usual way through a divine instinct what was coming, told his companions that he needed to depart on a mysterious voyage; and they were reminded of the opinion enunciated by Abaris of old, and felt that he was intent upon some such scheme. Apollonius however, without revealing his intention even to Damis, set sail in his company for Achaea, and having landed at Corinth and worshipped the Sun about midday, with his usual rites, embarked in the evening for Sicily and Italy. And falling in with a favorable wind and a good current that ran in his direction, he reached Dicaearchia on the fifth day. There he met Demetrius who passed for being the boldest of the philosophers, simply because he did not live far away from Rome, and knowing that he had moved to get out of the way of the tyrant, yet said by way of amusing himself: "I have caught you in your luxury, dwelling here in the most blessed part of happy Italy, if indeed she be happy, here where Odysseus is said to have forgotten in the company of Calypso the smoke of his Ithacan home." Thereupon Demetrius embraced him and after sundry pious ejaculations said: "O ye gods, what will come upon philosophy, if she risks the loss of such a man as yourself?" "And what risks does she run?" asked he. "Those, surely, a foreknowledge of which brought you here," said the other; "for if I do not know what is in your mind, then I do not know what is in my own. But let us not conduct our conversation here, but let us retire where we can talk together alone, and let only Damis be present whom, by Heracles, I am inclined to consider an Iolaus of your labors."

CHAPTER XI

With these words, Demetrius led them to the villa in which Cicero lived of old, and it is close by the city. There they sat down under a plane tree where the grasshoppers were chirping to the soft music of the summer's breeze, when Demetrius glancing up at them, remarked: "O ye blessed insects and unfeignedly wise, it would seem then that the Muses have taught you a song which is neither actionable, nor likely to be informed against; and they made you superior to all wants of the belly, and settled you far above all human envy to live in these trees, in which you sit and sing in your blessedness about your own and the Muses' prerogative of happiness." Now Apollonius understood the drift of this apostrophe, but it jarred upon him as inconsistent with the strenuous professions of his friend. "It seems then," he said, "that, though you only wanted to sing the praises of grasshoppers, you could not do it openly, but came cowering hither, as if there were a public law against anyone praising the grasshoppers." "I said what I did," he replied, "not by way of praising them, but of signifying that while they are left unmolested in their concert halls, we are not allowed even to mutter; for wisdom has been rendered a penal offense. And whereas the indictment of Anytus and Meletus ran: Socrates commits wrong in corrupting youth and introducing a new religion, we are indicted in such terms as these: So and so commits wrong by being wise and just and gifted with understanding of the gods no less than of men, and with a wide knowledge of the laws. And as for yourself, so far forth as you are cleverer and wiser than the rest of us, so much the more cleverly is the indictment against you drawn up; for

Domitian intends to implicate you in the charges for which Nerva and his associates were banished." "But for what crime," said Apollonius, "are they banished?" "For what is reckoned by the persecutor to be the greatest of latter-day crimes. He says that he has caught these persons in the act of trying to usurp his throne, and accuses you of instigating their attempt by mutilating, I think, a boy." "What, as if it were by an eunuch, that I want his empire overthrown?" "It is not that," he replied, "of which we are falsely accused; but they declare that you sacrificed a boy to divine the secrets of futurity which are to be learned from an inspection of youthful entrails; and in the indictment your dress and manner of life are also impugned, and the fact of your being an object of worship to some. This then is what I have heard from our Telesinus, no less your intimate than mine." "What luck," exclaimed Apollonius, "if we could meet Telesinus: for I suppose you mean the philosopher who held consular rank in the reign of Nero." "The same," he said, "but how are we to come across him? For despots are doubly suspicious of any man of rank, should they find him holding communication with people who lie under such an accusation as you do. And Telesinus, moreover, gave way quietly before the edict which has lately been issued against philosophers of every kind, because he preferred to be in exile as a philosopher, to remain in Rome as a consul." "I would not have him run any risks on my account anyhow," said Apollonius, "for the risks he runs in behalf of philosophy are serious enough.

CHAPTER XII

"But tell me this, Demetrius, what do you think I had better say or do in order to allay my own fears?" "You had better not trifle," said the other, "nor pretend to be afraid when you foresee danger; for if you really thought these accusations terrifying, you would have been away by now and evaded the necessity of defending yourself from them." "And would you run away," said Apollonius, "if you were placed in the same danger as myself?" "I would not," he replied, "I swear by Athena, if there were someone to judge me; but in fact there is no fair trial, and if I did offer a defense, no one would even listen to me; or if I were listened to, I should be slain all the more certainly because I was known to be innocent. You would not, I suppose, care to see me choose so cold-blooded and lavish a death as that, rather than one which befits a philosopher. And I imagine that it behoves a philosopher to die in the attempt to liberate his city or to protect his parents and children and brothers and other kinsfolk, or to die struggling for his friends, who in the eyes of the wise are more precious than mere kinsfolk, or for favorites that have been purchased by love. But to be put to death not for true reasons, but for fancy ones, and to furnish the tyrant with a pretext for being considered wise, is much worse and more grievous than to be bowed and bent high in the sky on a wheel, as they say Ixion was. But it seems to me the very fact of your coming here will be the beginning of your trial; for though you may attribute your journey hither to your quiet conscience, and to the fact that you would have never ventured upon it if you were guilty, Domitian will credit you with nothing of the kind; but will merely believe that you ventured on so hardy a course because you possess some mysterious power. For think, ten days, they say, have not elapsed since you were cited to appear, and you turn up at the court, without even having heard as yet that you were to undergo a trial. Will not that be tantamount to justifying the accusation, for everyone will think that you foreknew the event, and the story of the boy will gain credit therefrom? And take care that the discourse which the say you delivered about the Fates and Necessity in Ionia does not come true of yourself; and that, in case destiny has some cruelty in store, you are not marching straight to meet it with your hands tied, just because you won't see that discretion is the better part of valor. And if you have not forgotten the affairs of Nero's reign, you will remember my own case, and that I showed no coward's dread of death. But then one gained some respite: for although Nero's harp was ill attuned to the dignity that befits a king, and clashed therewith, yet in other ways its music harmonized not unpleasantly with ours, for he was induced thereby to grant a truce to his victims, and stay his murderous hand. At any rate he did not slay me, although I attracted his sword to myself as much by your discourses as by my own, which were delivered against the bath; and the reason why he did not slay me was that just then his voice improved, and he achieved, as he thought, a brilliant melody. But where's the royal nightingale, and where the harp to which we can today make our peace-offerings? For the outlook of today is unredeemed by music, and full of spleen, and this tyrant is as little likely to be charmed by himself, as by other people. It is true that Pindar says in praise of the lyre that it charms the savage beast of Ares and stays his hand from war; but this ruler, although he has established a musical contest in Rome, and offers a civic crown for those who win therein, nevertheless slew some of them, for whom it was the proverbial swan-sung that they piped or sang. And you should also consider our friends and their safety, for you will certainly ruin them as well as yourself, if you make a show of being brave, or use arguments which will not be listened to. But your life lies within your reach; for here are ships—you see how many there are—some about to sail for Libya, others for Egypt, others for Phoenicia and Cyprus, others direct to Sardinia, other still for places beyond Sardinia. It were best for you to embark on one of these provinces; for the hand of tyranny is less heavy upon these distinguished men, if it perceives that they only desire to live quietly and not put themselves forward."

CHAPTER XIII

Damis was so impressed by the arguments of Demetrius that he exclaimed: "Well, you anyhow are a friend and by your presence you can do a very great service to my master here. As for me, I am of little account, and if I advised him not to throw somersaults upon naked swords, nor expose himself to risks with tyrants, than whom none were ever yet deemed harsher, he would not listen to me. As a matter of fact I should never have known, if I had not met you, what he meant by his journey hither; for I follow him more readily, more blindly, than another man would follow himself; and if you asked me where I am bound or for what, I should merely excite your laughter by telling you that I was traversing the seas of Sicily and the bays of Etruria, without knowing in the least why I took ship. And if only I were courting these dangers after I had received open warning, I could then say to those who asked me the question, that Apollonius was courting death, and that I was accompanying him on board ship because I was his rival in his passion. But as I know nothing of this matter, it's time for me to speak of what I do know; and I will say it in the interests of my master. For if I were put to death, it would not do much harm to philosophy, for I am like the esquire of some distinguished soldier, and am only entitled to consideration because I am his suite. But if someone is going to be set on to slay him, and tyrants find it easy to contrive plots and to remove obstacles from their path, the I think a regular trophy will have been raised over the defeat of philosophy in the person of the noblest of her human representatives; and as there are many people lurking in our path, such as were Anytus and Meletus, writs of information will be scattered from all quarters at once against the companions of Apollonius; one will be accused of having laughed when his master attacked tyranny, another of having encouraged him to talk, a third of having suggested to him a topic to talk about, a fourth of having left his lecture-room with praise on his lips for what he had heard. I admit that one ought to die in the cause of philosophy in the sense of dying for one's temples, one's own walls, and one's sepulchers; for there are many famous heroes who have embraced death in order to save and protect such interests as those; but I pray that neither I myself may die in order to bring about the ruin of philosophy, and that no one else either may die for such an object who loves philosophy and loves Apollonius."

CHAPTER XIV

Apollonius answered thus: "We must make allowance for the very timid remarks which Damis has made about the situation; for he is a Syrian and lives on the border of Media, where tyrants are worshipped, and hence does not entertain a lofty idea of freedom; but as for yourself, I do not see how you can defend yourself at the bar of philosophy from the charge of trumping up fears, from which, even if there were really any reason for them, you ought to try to wean him; instead of doing so you try to plunge into terror a man who was not even afraid of such things as were likely to occur. I would indeed have a wise man sacrifice his life for the objects you have mentioned, but any man without being wise should equally die for them; for it is an obligation of law that we should die in behalf of our freedom, and an injunction of nature that we should die in behalf of our kinsfolk or of our friends or darlings. Now all men are the slaves of nature and of law; the willing slaves of nature, as the unwilling ones of law. But it is the duty of the wise in a still higher degree to lay down their lives for the tenets they have embraced. Here are interests which neither law has laid upon us, nor nature planted in us from birth, but to which we have devoted ourselves out of mere strength of character and courage. In behalf therefore of these, should anyone try to violate them, let the wise man pass through fire, let him bare his neck for the axe, for he will not be overcome by any such threats, nor driven to any sort of subterfuge; but he will cleave to all he knows as firmly as if it were a religion in which he had been initiated. As for myself, I am acquainted with more than other human beings, for I know all things, and what I know, I know partly for good men, partly for wise ones, partly for myself, partly for the gods, but for tyrants nothing. But that I am not come on any fool's errand, you can see if you will; for I run no risk of my life myself, nor shall I die at the hands of a despot, however much I might wish to do so; but I am aware that I am gambling with the lives of those whom I bear such relation as the tyrant chooses, whether he count me their leader or their supporter. But if I were to betray them by holding back or by cowardly refusal to face the accusation, what would good men think of me? Who would not justly slay me, for playing with the lives of men to whom was entrusted everything I had besought of heaven? And I would like to point out to you, that I could not possibly escape the reputation of being a traitor.

"For there are two kinds of tyrants; the one kind put their victims to death without trial, the other after they have been brought before a court of law. The former kind resemble the more passionate and prompt of wild beasts, the other kind resemble the gentle and more lethargic ones. That both kinds are cruel is clear to everybody who takes Nero as an example of the impetuous disposition which does not trouble about legal forms, Tiberius, on the other hand of the tardy and lurking nature; for the former destroyed his victims before they had any suspicion of what was coming, and the other after he had tortured them with long drawn-out terror. For myself I consider those crueler who make a pretense of legal trial, and of getting a verdict pronounced in accordance with the laws; for in reality they set them at defiance, and bring in the same verdict as they would have done without any real trial, giving the name of law to the mere postponement of their own spleen. The very fact of their being put to death in legal form does not deprive the wretches so condemned to death of that compassion on the part of the crowd, which should be tendered like a winding sheet to the victims of injustice. Well, I perceive that the present ruler cloaks his tyranny under legal forms. But it seems to me that he ends by condemnation without trial; for he really sentences men before they enter the court, and then brings them before it as if they had not yet been tried. Now one who is formally condemned by a verdict in court, can obviously say he perished owing to an illegal sentence, but how can he that evades his trial escape the implied verdict against himself? And supposing, now that the fate of such distinguished persons also rests on me, I do manage to run away from the crisis which equally impends over them and myself, what can save me from no matter where I go on all the earth from the brand of infamy? For let us suppose that you have delivered yourself of all these sentiments, and that I have admitted their correctness and acted on them, and that in consequence our friends have been murdered, what prayers could I offer in such a case for a favorable voyage? What haven could I cast anchor in? To whom could I set out on any voyage? For methinks I should have to steer clear of any land over which the Romans rule, and should have to seek men who are my friends, and yet do not live in sight of the tyrant, and that would be Phraotes, and the Babylonian, and the divine Iarchas, and the noble Thespesion. Now supposing I set out for Ethiopia, what, my excellent friend, could I tell Thespesion? For if I concealed this episode, I should prove myself a lover of falsehood, nay worse, a slave; while if I frankly confessed all to him, I could only use such words as these: O Thespesion, Euphrates slandered me to you and accused me of things that are not on my conscience; for he said that I was a boaster and a miracle-monger, and one that violated wisdom, especially that of the Indians; but while I am none of these things, I am nevertheless a betrayer of my own friends, and their murderer, and utterly unreliable and so forth; and if there is any wreath for virtue, I come to wear it, because I have ruined the greatest of the Roman houses so utterly, that henceforth they are left desolate. You blush, Demetrius, to hear such words; I see that you do so. What then, if you turn from Thespesion to Phraotes and imagine me fleeing to India to take refuge with such a man as he? How should I look him in the face? How should I explain the motive of my flight? Should I not have to say that when I visited him before, I was a gentleman not too faint-hearted to lay down my life for my friends; but that after enjoying his society, I had at your bidding thrown away with scorn this divinest of human privileges. And as for Iarchas, he surely would not ask me any questions at all when I arrived, but just as Aeolus once bade Odysseus quit his island with ignominy, because he had made a bad use of the gift of a good wind which he had bestowed on him, so Iarchas, I imagine, would drive me from his eminence, and tell me that I had disgraced the draught I there had from the cup of Tantalus. For they require a man who stoops and drinks of that goblet, to share the dangers of his friends. I know, Demetrius, how clever you are at chopping logic, and this, I believe, is why you will tender me some further advice, such as this: But you must not resort to those you have named, but to men with whom you have never had anything to do, and then your flight will be secure; for you will find it easier to lie hidden among people who do not know you. Well, let me examine this argument too, and see whether there is anything in it. For this is how I regard it: I consider that a wise man does nothing in private nor by himself alone; I hold that not even his inmost thoughts can be so devoid of witness, that he himself at least is not present with himself; and whether the Pythian inscription was suggested by Apollo himself, or by some man who had a healthy conscience, and was therefore minded to publish it as an aphorism for all, I hold that the sage who 'knows himself,' and has his own conscience as his perpetual companion, will never cower before things that scare the many, nor venture upon courses which others would engage upon without shame. For being the slaves of despots, they have been ready at times to betray to them even their dearest; because just as they trembled at imaginary terrors, so they felt no fear where they should have trembled.

"But Wisdom allows of none these things. For beside the Pythian epigram, she also praises Euripides who regarded 'conscience in the case of human beings as a disease which works their ruin, whenever they realize that they have done wrong.' For it was such conscience that brought up before Orestes and depicted in his imagination the shapes of the Eumenides, when he had gone mad with wrath against his mother; for whereas reason decides what should be done, conscience revises the resolutions taken by reason. If then reason chooses the better part, conscience forthwith escorts a man to all the temples, into all the by-streets, into all groves of the gods, and into all haunts of mankind, applauding him and singing his praises. She will even hymn his merits as he sleeps, and will weave around him a chorus of angels from the world of dreams; but if the determination of reason trip and fall into evil courses, conscience permits not the sinner to look others in the face, nor to address them freely and boldly with his lips; and she drives him away from temples and from prayer. For she suffers him not even to uplift his hands in prayer to the images, but strikes them down as he lifts them, as the law strikes down those who rebel against it; and she drives such men from every social meeting, and terrifies them in their sleep; and while she turns into dreams and windy forms all that they see by day, and any things they think they hear or say, she lends to their empty and fantastic flutterings of heart truth and substantial reality of well-found terror. I think then that I have clearly shown you, and that truth itself will convince you, that my conscience will convict me wherever I go, whether to people that know me, or to people that do not, supposing I were to betray my friends; but I will not betray even myself, but I will boldly wrestle with the tyrant, hailing him with the words of the noble Homer: Ares is as much my friend as thine."

CHAPTER XV

Damis was so impressed by this address, he tells us, that he took fresh resolution and courage, and Demetrius no longer despaired of Apollonius, but rather praising and agreeing with his appeal, wished godspeed to him in his perilous enterprise and to his mistress Philosophy for whose sake he braved so much. And he led them, Damis says, to where he was lodging; but Apollonius declined and said: "It is now eventide, and about the time of the lighting up of the lamps and I must set out for the port of Rome, for this is the usual hour at which these ships sail. However we will dine together another time, when my affairs are on a better footing; for just now some charge would be trumped up against yourself of having dined with an enemy of the Emperor. Nor must you come down to the harbor with us, lest you should be accused, merely for having conversed with me, of harboring criminal designs." Demetrius accordingly consented, and after embracing them he quitted them, though he often turned back to look towards them and wiped tears from his eyes. But Apollonius looked at Damis and said: "If you are firmly resolved, and as courageous as myself, let us both embark upon the ship; but if you are dispirited it is better for you to remain here, for you can live with Demetrius during the interval, since he is as much your friend as mine." But Damis took him up and said: "What could I think of myself, if after you have so nobly discoursed today about the duty of sharing the dangers of one's friends, when they fall upon them, I let your words fall on deaf ears, and abandoned you in the hour of danger, and this although until now I have never shown cowardice where you are concerned?" "You speak rightly," said Apollonius, "so let us depart; I will go as I am, but you must needs disguise yourself as a man of the people, nor must you wear your hair long as you do now, and you must exchange your philosopher's cloak for this linen garment, and you must put away the shoes you wear. But I must tell you what my intention is in this; for it were best to hold out as long as we can before the trial: then I do not wish that you should be a sharer of my fate through being detected by your dress, which will certainly betray you and lead to your arrest; but I would rather that you followed me in the guise of one not sworn to my philosophy, but just attached to me for other reasons, and so accompanying me in all I do." This is the reason why Damis put off his Pythagorean garb; for he says he did not do it through cowardice, nor through any regret at having worn it, but merely because he approved of a device to which he accommodated himself to suit the expedience of the moment.

CHAPTER XVI

They sailed from Dicaearchia, and on the third day they put in to the mouth of the Tiber from which it is a fairly short sail up to Rome. Now the Emperor's sword was at that time in the keeping of Aelianus, a person who long ago had been attached to Apollonius, because he once met him in Egypt. And although he said nothing openly in his favor to Domitian, for that his office did not allow of his doing—for how could he have praised to his sovereign's face one who was supposed to be an object of detestation any more than he could intercede in his behalf as for a friend of his own?—nevertheless whatever means there were of helping him in an unobtrusive way, he resorted to in his behalf; and accordingly at the time when, before he arrived, Apollonius was being calumniated to Domitian, he would say: "My sovereign, sophists ar all prattle and flippancy; and their art is all show, and they are so eager to die because they get no good out of life; and therefore they don't wait for death to come of itself, but try to anticipate and draw it on themselves by provoking those who hold the sword. This I think was the reason which weighed with Nero and prevented his being drawn on by Demetrius into slaying him. For as he saw that he was anxious for death, he let him off not because he wished to pardon him, but because he disdained to put him to death. Moreover in the case of Musonius the Tyrrhenian, who opposed his rule in many ways, he only kept him in the island called Gyara; and Hellenes are so fond of sophists, that at that time they were all making voyages by ship to visit him, as they now do to visit the spring; for until Musonius went there, there was no water in the island, but he discovered a spring, which the Greeks celebrate as loudly as they do the horse's spring at Helicon."

CHAPTER XVII

In this way Aelian tried to put off the king until Apollonius arrived, and then he began to use more address; for he ordered Apollonius to be arrested and brought into his presence. And when the counsel for the prosecution began to abuse him as a wizard and an adept at magic, Aelian remarked, "Keep yourself and your charges against him for the Royal Court." But Apollonius remarked: "If I am a wizard, how is it I am brought to trial? And if I am brought to trial, how can I be a wizard? Unless indeed the power of slander is so great that even wizards cannot get the better of it." Then when the accuser was about to say something still more foolish, Aelian cut him short and said: "Leave me the time that will elapse until his trial begins; for I intend to examine the sophist's character privately, and not before yourselves; and if he admits his guilt, then the pleadings in the court can be cut short, and you can depart in peace, but if he denies his guilt, the emperor will try him." He accordingly passed into his secret court where the most important accusations and causes were tried in strict privacy, and said to the company: "Do you depart hence, and let no one remain to listen, for such is the will of the Emperor."

CHAPTER XVIII

And when they were alone, he said: "I, O Apollonius, was a stripling at the time when the father of the present sovereign came to Egypt to sacrifice to the gods, and to consult you about his own affairs. I was a tribune only then, but the Emperor took me with him because I was already versed in war; while you were so friendly with myself, that when the Emperor was receiving deputations from the cities, you took me aside and told me of what country I was and what was my name and parentage; and you foretold to me that I should hold this office which is accounted by the multitude the highest of all, and superior to all human positions at once, although to myself it means much trouble and much unhappiness. For I am the sentinel of the harshest of tyrants, whom if I betray, I am afraid of the wrath of heaven. But I have shown you how friendly I am towards yourself, for in reminding you how our friendship began, I have surely made it clear to you that it can never cease, as long as we can remember those beginnings......If I have said I would question you in private about the charges which your accuser has drawn up against you, it was only a good-natured pretext on my part for obtaining an interview with you, in order to assure you of my own good will, and to warn you of the Emperor's designs. Now what his verdict will be in your case I do not know; but his temper is that of people who are anxious to condemn a person, but are ashamed to do so except upon some real evidence, and he wishes to make you an excuse for destroying these men of consular rank. So his wishes you see are criminal, but he observes a certain formality in his actions in order to preserve a semblance of justice. And I, too, in my turn, must pretend to be exasperated with you; for if he suspects me of any leniency, I do not know which of us will be the first to perish."

CHAPTER XIX

Apollonius replied: "Since we are talking without any restraint and you have told me all that is in your heart, I in turn am bound to tell you no less; and since you also take a philosopher's view of your own position, as one might do who has most thoroughly studied philosophy in my society, and, by Heaven, inasmuch as you are so kindly disposed towards us as to imagine you run a common risk with myself, I will tell you exactly what I think. It was in my power to run away from you to many parts of the earth, where your authority is not recognized, and where I should have found myself among wise men, men much wiser than myself, and where I might have worshipped the gods in accordance with the principles of sound reason. I had only to go to the haunts of men who are more beloved of the gods than are the people of this city, men among whom such things as informers and writs of accusation are unknown, because, since they neither wrong one another nor are wronged, they stand in no need of law-courts. But I am come to offer my defense, because I fear to be branded as a traitor; for, if I ran away instead of stating and defending myself, those who are running risks on my account would be brought to ruin. But I would have you tell me what are the accusations against which I have to defend myself."

CHAPTER XX

"The counts of the indictment," replied the other, "are as varied as they are numerous; for your style of dress is assailed in them and your way of living in general, and your having been worshipped by certain people, and the fact that in Ephesus once you delivered an oracle about the famine; and also that you have uttered certain sentiments to the detriment of the sovereign, some of them openly, some of them obscurely and privately, and some of them on the pretense that you learned them from heaven. But the charge which most appeals to the credulity of the Emperor, although I cannot credit it in the least, for I know that you are opposed even to shedding the blood of victims, is the following: they say that you visited Nerva in the country, and that you cut up an Arcadian boy for him when he was consulting the auspices against the Emperor; and that by such rites as these you roused his ambitions; and that all this was done by night when the moon was already on the wane. This is the accusation as compared with which we need not consider any other, because it far outweighs them all. For if the accuser attacks your dress and your mode of life and your gift of foreknowledge, it is only by way, I assure you, of leading up to this charge; and it was moreover these peculiarities which prompted you to commit the crime of conspiring against the Emperor, so he says, and emboldened you to offer such a sacrifice. You must then be prepared to defend yourself upon these counts, and I would only ask you in what you say to show great respect for the sovereign." And Apollonius replied: "That I shall show no disrespect, you may clearly gather from the fact that I am come here to justify myself; and even if my circumstances were such as to embolden me to treat a despot in a haughty manner, I should anyhow submit myself to a man like yourself who also loves me. For though it does not so much matter if you merely fall into the bad graces of an enemy—for your enemies will hate you not for reasons which make you an object of public suspicion, but for private causes of offense which you have given them—nothing is graver than to give a friend reason to think ill of you: this is worse than all your enemies put together can effect, for no man can avoid being disliked by the public too for his ill conduct."

CHAPTER XXI

These words impressed Aelian as very sensible; and he bade him be of good courage, while he himself formed the conviction that here was a man whom nothing could terrify or startle, and who would not flinch, even if the head of the Gorgon were brandished over him. He accordingly summoned the jailors who had charge of such cases and said: "My orders are to detain this man, until the Emperor be informed of his arrival and learn from his lips all he has said to me." And he said this with the air of a man very much enraged; and then he went into the palace and began to attend to the duties of his office.

At this point Damis records an incident which in a way resembles and in a way is unlike the episode related of Aristides long ago at Athens. For they were ostracizing Aristides because of his virtue, and he had no sooner passed the gates of the city than a rustic came up to him and begged him to fill up his voting sherd against Aristides. This rustic knew no more to whom he was speaking than he knew how to write; he only knew that Aristides was detested because he was so just. Now on this occasion a tribune who knew Apollonius perfectly well, addressed him and asked him in an insolent manner, what had brought him to such a pass. Apollonius replied that he did not know. "Well," said the other, "I can tell you: for it is allowing yourself to be worshipped by your fellow-men that has led you to be accused of setting yourself on a level with the gods." "And who is it," asked the other, "that has paid me this worship?" "I myself," said the other, "when I was still a boy in Ephesus, at a time when you stayed our epidemic." "Lucky it was both for you," and for the city of Ephesus that was saved." "Well this is a reason," said the other, "why I have prepared a method of defense for yourself, which will rid you of the charge against you. For let us go outside the gates, and if I cut of your head off with my sword, the accusation will have defeated itself and you will go scot free; but if you terrify me to such an extent that I drop my sword, you must needs be thought a divine being, and then it will be seen that there is a basis of truth in the charges made against you." So much coarser and ruder was this fellow than the man who wished to banish Aristides, and he uttered his words with grimace and mocking laughter, but Apollonius affected not to have heard him, and went on with his conversation with Damis about the delta, about which they say the Nile is divided into two branches.

CHAPTER XXII

Aelian next summoned him and ordered him into prison, where the captives were not bound, "until," he said, "the Emperor shall have leisure, for he desires to talk with you privately before taking any further steps." Apollonius accordingly left the law-court and passed into the prison, where he said: "Let us talk, Damis, with the people here. For what else is there for us to do until the time comes when the despot will give me such audience as he desires?" "Will they not think us babblers," said Damis, "and bores, if we interrupt them in the preparation of their defense, and moreover, it is a mistake to talk philosophy with men so broken in spirit as they." "Nay," said Apollonius, "they are just the people who most want someone to talk to them and comfort them. For you may remember the verses of Homer in which he relates how Helen mingled in the bowl of wine certain drugs from Egypt to drown the heartache of the heroes; well, I think that Helen must have picked up the lore of the Egyptians, and have sung spells over the dejected heroes through their bowl of wine, so healing them by a blending of words and wine." "And that is likely enough," said Damis, "seeing that she came to Egypt and was escorted by Proteus; or, if we prefer Homer's account, was well acquainted with Polydamna, the daughter of Thon. However let us dismiss these topics for the moment, for I want to ask you something." "I know," said Apollonius, "what you are going to ask me, for I am sure you wish me to tell you what my conversation was about with the consul, and what he said, and whether he was formidable and severe or gentle to me." And forthwith he told Damis all that had passed. Thereupon Damis prostrated himself before him and said: "Now I am ready to believe that Leucothea did really once give her veil to Odysseus, after he had fallen out of his ship and was paddling himself over the sea with his hands. For we are reduced to just as awful and impossible a plight, when some god, as it seems to me, stretches out his hand over us, that we fall not away from all hope of salvation." But Apollonius disapproved of the way he spoke, and said: "How long will you continue to cherish these fears, as if you could never understand that wisdom amazes all that is sensible of her, but is herself not amazed by anything." "But we," said Damis, "are brought here before one who is quite insensible, and who not only cannot be amazed by us, but would not allow anything in the world to amaze him." "Seest thou not," said Apollonius, "O Damis, that he is maddened with pride and vanity?" "I see it, how can I not?" said the other. "Well," said Apollonius, "you have just got do despise the despot just in proportion as you get to know him."

CHAPTER XXIII

They were talking like this, when someone, a Cilician I think, came up and said: "I, gentlemen, am brought to this pass by my wealth." And Apollonius replied: "If your wealth was acquired by other than holy methods, for example by piracy and administration of deadly drugs, or by disturbing the tombs of ancient kings which are full of gold and treasure, you deserve not only to be put on your trial, but also to forfeit your life; for these things are wealth no doubt, but of an infamous and inhuman kind. But if you acquired your wealth by inheritance or by commerce such as befits free men and not by petty traffic, who could be so cruel as to deprive you under color of law of what you have acquired with its venerable sanction?" "My property," said the other, has accrued to me from several of my relations, and has centered itself in my single household; and I use it, not as if it belonged to other people, for it is my own; yet not as my own, for I share it freely with all good men. But the informers accused me of having acquired my wealth to the prejudice of the despot; for they say that, if I attached myself to another as his accomplice, my wealth would weigh heavily in his favor. And there is actually an oracular air about the charges made against us, such as that all excess of wealth engenders insolence, or that more than ordinary wealth makes its owner carry his head too high and rouses in him a spirit of pride; and that it prevents him from being a good subject and obeying the laws and rulers who are sent to the provinces; they say indeed that it is very nearly tantamount to giving them a box on the ears, because they grovel to wealthy men or connive at their crime, on account of the influence which wealth gives.

"Now when I was a stripling, before I had as much as a hundred talent to call my own, I used to think such apprehensions as ridiculous and I had small anxiety on the score of my property; but when my paternal uncle died and in a single day I came in for a reversion of five hundred talents, my mind underwent such a change as those who break horses effect, when they cure them of being unruly and intractable. And as my riches increased and flowed in to me by land and by sea, I became so much the slave of anxiety about them, that I poured out my substance, partly upon sycophants whom I had to flatter in order to stop their mouths by means of such blackmail, and partly upon governors whose influence I wished to enlist on my side against those who plotted against me, and partly on my kinsmen, to prevent them being jealous of my wealth, and partly on my slaves for fear they should become worse than they were and complain of being neglected. And I also had to support a magnificent flock of friends, for the latter were full of solicitude for me; and some insisted on helping me with their own hands, and others with their warnings and advice. But although I thus fenced my wealth about, and surrounded myself so securely with fortifications, I now am imperiled by it, and I am not yet sure that I shall escape with my life." And Apollonius answered: "Take heart, for you have your wealth to go surety for your life; for if it is your wealth which has led to your being confined in bonds, it is your wealth also which, when it is dissipated, will not only release you from this prison, but from the necessity of cherishing and flattering those sycophants and slaves whose yoke it has imposed upon your neck."

CHAPTER XXIV

Another man came and said that he was being prosecuted, because at a public sacrifice in Tarentum, where he held office, he had omitted to mention in the public prayers that Domitian was the son of Athena. Said Apollonius: "You imagined that Athena could not possibly have a son, because she is a virgin for ever and ever; but you forgot, methinks, that this goddess once on a time bore a dragon to the Athenians."

CHAPTER XXV

Another man was confined in the prison on the following charge: He had a property in Acarnania near the mouth of the Achelous; and he had been in the habit of sailing about the islands called the Echinades in a small boat, and he noticed that one of them was already joined to the mainland; and he planted it all over with fruitful trees and vines producing sweet wine. So he made it a convenient habitation for himself, for he also brought in water in sufficient quantities for the island from the mainland. In consequence, an accusation was trumped up against him, that he had a guilty conscience, and that it was because he was conscious of having committed crimes beyond description, that he transported himself and quitted all other land, feeling that he polluted it, and at the same time had chosen for himself the same form of release as Alcmaeon the son of Amphiareus had done, when after his mother's murder he went and lived on the delta of the Achelous. Even if he had not committed the same crime as Alcmaeon, he must yet, they said, have on his conscience horrible deeds, not falling short of his. Although he denied these insinuations, and declared that he only went to live there for the sake of peace and quiet, he had nevertheless, they said, been accused and brought to justice, and for this reason he was cast into prison.

CHAPTER XXVI

Several prisoners, for there were about fifty of them in this prison, approaches Apollonius inside it, and uttered such lamentations as the above. Some of them were sick, some of them had given way to dejection, some of them expected death with certainty and with resignation, some of them bewailed and called upon their children and their parents and their wives. Whereupon, "O Damis," said Apollonius, affected by the spectacle, "it seems to me that these people need the drug which I alluded to when I first entered. Whether it be an Egyptian remedy, or whether it grows in every land and only needs wisdom enough to cut it from its root out of her own gardens, let us administer some of it to these poor people, lest their own feelings destroy them before Domitian can do it." "Let us do so," said Damis, "for they seem in need of it." Accordingly Apollonius called them all together and said: "Gentlemen, who are sharing with me the hospitality of this poor roof, I am wrung with pity for you, because I feel that you are undoing yourselves, before you know in the least whether the accuser will undo you. For it seems to me that you are ready to put yourselves to death and anticipate the death sentence which you expect will be pronounced against you; and so you show actual courage where you should feel fear, and fear where you should be courageous. This should not be; but you should bear in mind the words of Archilochus of Paros who says that the patience under adversity which he called endurance was a veritable discovery of the gods; for it will bear you up in your misery, just as a skillful pilot carries the bow of his ship above the wash of the sea, whenever the billows are raised higher than his bark. Nor should you consider as desperate this situation into which you have been brought against your wills, but I myself of my own accord.

"For if you admit the charges brought against you, you ought rather to deplore the day when your judgment and impulses betrayed you into unjust and cruel courses of action. But if you, my friend yonder, deny that you took up your residence in the island of Achelous for the reason which your accuser alleges; and you there, that you ever raised your wealth to the peril and endangering of the sovereignty; and you again that you of set purpose deprived the sovereign of his pretension to be called the son of Athena,—if, I say, you can prove that the several reasons alleged for your being, each of you, here in such parlous plights, are unfounded, what then is the meaning of all this lamentation about things which have no existence or reality? For instead of crying after your friends and relatives, you ought rather to feel just as much courage as you now feel despair; for such I imagine are the rewards of the endurance I have described. But perhaps you would argue that confinement here and life in a prison are hard to bear in themselves? Or do you look upon them as the mere beginning of what you expect to suffer? Or do you think that they are punishment sufficient in themselves, even if you are exposed to nothing else in the way of penalty? Well, I understand human nature, and I will preach you a sermon which is very unlike the prescriptions of physicians, for I shall implant strength in you and will avert death from you. We men are in a prison all that time which we choose to call life. For this soul of ours, being bound and fettered in a perishable body, has to endure many things, and be the slave of all the affections which visit humanity; and the men who first invented a dwelling seem to me not to have known that they were only surrounding their kind in a fresh prison; for, to tell you the truth, all those who inhabit palaces and have established themselves securely in them, are, I consider, in closer bonds in them than any whom they may throw into bonds "And when I think of cities and walls, it seems to me that these are common prisons, so that the merchants are in chains, in chains no less than the members of the Assembly, and the frequenters also of spectacles, as well as those who organize public processions. Then there are the Scythians who go about upon wagons; they are just as much in chains as ourselves; for rivers like the Ister and the Thermodon and the Tanais hem them in, and they are very difficult to cross, except when they are hard frozen; and they fix up their houses on their wagons, and they imagine they are driving about, when they are merely cowering in them. And if you don't think it too silly a thing to say, there are those who teach that the ocean also encompasses the earth in order to chain it in. Come, O ye poets, for this is your domain. Recite your rhapsodies to this despondent crowd, and tell them how Kronos was once put in bonds by the wiles of Zeus; and Ares, the most warlike of gods, was first enchained in heaven by Hephaestus, and later upon earth by the sons of Aloeus. When we think of these things, and reflect on the many wise and blessed men who have been thrown into prison by wanton mobs, or insulted by despots, let us accept our fate with resignation, that we may not be found inferior to those who have accepted the same before us." Such were the words which he addressed to his companions in the prison, and they had such an effect upon them that most of them took their food and wiped away their tears, and walked in hope, believing that they could never come to harm as long as they were in his company.

CHAPTER XXVII

On the next day he was haranguing them in a discourse of the same tenor, when a man was sent into the prison privately by Domitian to listen to what he said. In his deportment this person had a downcast air and, as he himself admitted, looked as if he ran a great risk. He had great volubility of speech, as is usually the case with sycophants who have been chosen to draw up eight or ten informations. Apollonius saw through the trick and talked about themes which could in no way serve his purpose; for he told his audience about rivers and mountains, and he described wild animals and trees to them, so that they were amused, while the informer gained nothing to his purpose. And when he tried to draw him away from these subjects, and get him to abuse the tyrant, "My good friend," said Apollonius, "you say what you like, for I am the last man in the world to inform against you; but if I find anything to blame in the Emperor, I'll say it to his face."

CHAPTER XXVIII

There followed other episodes in this prison, some of them insidiously contrived, and others of mere chance, and not of sufficient importance to merit my notice. But Damis, I believe, has recorded them in his anxiety to omit nothing; I only give what is to the point. It was evening, and it was already the fifth day of his imprisonment, when a certain person entered the prison, who spoke the Hellenic tongue, and said: "Where is the man of Tyana?" And taking Apollonius aside he said: "It is tomorrow that the Emperor will give you an audience." And this he appeared to have heard direct from Aelian. "I will keep your secret," said Apollonius, "for it is only Aelian, I think, who can know so much." "Moreover," said the other, "word has been given to the chief jailer to supply you with everything which you may want." "You are very kind," said Apollonius, "but I lead exactly the same life here as I would outside; for I converse about casual topics, and I do not need anything." "And do you not, O Apollonius, need someone to advise you how to converse with the Emperor?" "Yes by heaven," he replied, "if only he will not try to get me to flatter him." "And what if he merely advised you not to slight him nor flout him?" "He could give no better advice," said Apollonius, "and it is what I have made up my own mind to do." "Well, it was about this that I am come," said the other, "and I am delighted to find you so sensibly disposed; but you ought to be prepared for the way in which the Emperor speaks, and also for the disagreeable quality of his face; for he talks in a deep voice, even if he is merely engaged in a gentle conversation, and his eyebrows overhang the sockets of his eyes and his cheeks are so bloated with bile, that this distinguishes him more than anything else. We must not be frightened, O man of Tyana, by these characteristics, for they rather belong to nature than to anything else, and they always are the same." And Apollonius replied:

"If Odysseus could go into the cave of Polyphemus, without having been informed beforehand either of the giant's size, or what he ate, or of how he thundered with his voice, and yet did not lose his presence of mind, though he was in some trepidation to begin with; and if he left his cave after acquitting himself like a man, I too shall be quite satisfied if I get off with my own life and with that of my companions, in whose behalf I incur this risk." Such were the words that passed between him and his visitor, and after reporting them to Damis he went to sleep.

CHAPTER XXIX

And about dawn a notary came from the Royal court, and said: "It is the Emperor's orders, O Apollonius, that you should repair to his court at the time when the market-place is full; not indeed as yet to make your defense, for he wants to see you and find out who you are, and to talk with you alone." "And why," said Apollonius, "do you trouble me with these details?" "Are you not then Apollonius?" said the other. "Yes, by Heaven," he said, "and of Tyana too." "To whom then," said the other, "should I give this message?" "To those who will take me thither," he replied, "for I suppose that I shall have to get out of this prison somehow." "Orders have already been given," replied the other, "to them, and I will come here in good time, and I only came to give you the message now, because the orders were issued late last night."

CHAPTER XXX

He accordingly went away: but Apollonius after resting himself a little while on his bed said, "Damis, I need sleep, for I have had a bad night trying to remember what Phraotes once told me." "Well," said the other, "if you had to keep awake, you had much better have occupied yourself in preparing for so great an occasion as now is announced to you." "And how could I prepare myself," said Apollonius, "when I do not even know what questions he will ask of me?" "Then are you going to defend your life extempore?" said Damis. "Yes, by Heaven," he replied, "for it is an extempore life that I have always led. But I want to tell you what I could remember of the conversation with Phraotes, for I think you will find it very profitable under the circumstances. Phraotes enjoined the tamers of lions not to strike them, for he said that they bear you a grudge if they are struck; but also not to flatter them, because that tends to make them proud and fierce; but he advised them rather to stroke them with the hand at the same time that they threatened them, as the best way of reducing them to obedience and docility. Well, he made these remarks not really about lions—for we were not interested about how to keep lions and wild beasts—but he was really supplying a curb and rein for tyrants of such a kind as he thought would in practice keep them within the lines of good sense and moderation." "This story," said Damis, "is indeed most apposite to the manners of tyrants; but there is also a story in Aesop about a certain lion who lived in a cave, and Aesop says that he was not sick, but only pretended to be so, and that he seized on other wild animals who went to visit him; and accordingly the fox made the remark: 'What are we to do with him, for no one ever quits his residence, nor are any tracks to be seen of his visitors going out again?'" And Apollonius remarked: "Well, as for myself I should have regarded your fox as a cleverer animal, if he had gone in to see the lion, and instead of being caught had issued from the cave safely and left clear tracks behind him."

CHAPTER XXXI

After making this remark, he took a short nap, just enough to close his eyes, and when day came he offered his prayers to the Sun, as best as he could in prison, and then he conversed with all who came up and asked him questions; and so about the time when the market fills a notary came and ordered him to repair at once to court, adding: "Lest we should not get there in time for the summons in his presence." And Apollonius said: "Let us go," and eagerly went forth. And on the way four bodyguards followed him, keeping at a greater distance from him than would an escort merely to guard him. And Damis also followed in his train, in some trepidation indeed, but apparently plunged in thought. Now the eyes were all turned upon Apollonius, for not only were they attracted by his dress and bearing, but there was a godlike look in his eyes, which struck them with astonishment; and moreover the fact that he had come to Rome to risk his life for his friends conciliated the good wishes even of those who were evilly disposed to him before. When he halted at the Palace and beheld the throng of those who were either being courted or were courting their superiors, and heard the din of those who were passing in and out, he remarked: "It seems to me, O Damis, that this place resembles a bath; for I see people outside hastening in, and those within, hastening out; and some of them resemble people who have been thoroughly washed, and others those who have not been washed at all." This saying is the inviolable property of Apollonius, and I wish it to be reserved to him and not ascribed to this man and that, for it is so thoroughly and genuinely his, that he has repeated it in one of his letters. There he saw a very old man who was trying to get an appointment, and in order to do so was groveling before the Emperor and fawning upon him. "Here is one," he said, "O Damis, whom not even Sophocles so far has been able to run away from a master who is raging mad." "Yes, a master," said Damis, "that we ourselves, Apollonius, have chosen for our own; for that is why we are standing here at such gates as these." "It seems to me, O Damis," said the other, "that you imagine Aeacus to be warden of these gates, as he is said to be of the gates of Hades; for verily you look like a dead man." "Not dead yet," said Damis, "but shortly to be so." And Apollonius answered: "O Damis, you do not seem to me to take very kindly to death, although you have been with me some time, and have studied philosophy from your first youth. But I had imagined that you were prepared for it, and had also acquainted yourself with all the strategy and tactical resources that I have at my command; for just as men in battle, no matter how heavily armed they are, require not merely pluck, but also a knowledge of tactics to interpret to them the right opportunities of battle, so also philosophers must wait for the right opportunities when to die; so that they be not taken off their guard, nor like suicides rush into death, but may greet their enemies upon ground of their own good choosing. But that I made my choice well of a moment to die in and found an occasion worthy of a philosopher, supposing anyone wants to kill him, I have both proved to others before whom I defended myself in your presence, and am tired of teaching yourself the same."

CHAPTER XXXII

So far these matters then; but when the Emperor had leisure, having got rid of all his urgent affairs, to give an audience to our sage, the attendants whose office it was conducted him into the palace, without allowing Damis to follow him. And the Emperor was wearing a wreath of olive leaves, for he had just been offering a sacrifice to Athena in the hall of Adonis and this hall was bright with baskets of flowers, such as the Syrians at the time of the festival of Adonis make up in his honor, growing them under their very roofs. Though the Emperor was engaged with his religious rites, he turned round, and was so much struck by Apollonius' appearance, that he said: "O Aelian, it is a demon that you have introduced to me." But Apollonius, without losing his composure, made free to comment upon the Emperor's words, and said: "As for myself, I imagined that Athena was your tutelary goddess, O sovereign, in the same way as she was Diomede's long ago in Troy; for she removed the mist which dulls the eyes of men from those of Diomede, and endowed him with the faculty of distinguishing gods from men. But the goddess has not yet purged your eyes as she did his, my sovereign; yet it were well, if Athena did so, that you might behold her more clearly and not confuse mere men with the forms of demons." "And you," said the Emperor, "O philosopher, when did you have this mist cleared away from your eyes?" "Long ago," said he, "and ever since I have been a philosopher." "How comes it then," said the Emperor, "that you have come to regard as gods persons who are most hostile to myself?" "And what hostility," said Apollonius, "is there between yourself and Iarchas or Phraotes, both of them Indians and the only human beings that I regard as gods and meriting such a title?" "Don't try to put me off with Indians," said the Emperor, "but just tell me about your darling Nerva and his accomplices." "Am I to plead his cause," said Apollonius, "or—?" "No, you shall not plead it," said the Emperor, "for he has been taken red-handed in guilt; but just prove to me, if you can, that you are not yourself equally guilty as being privy to his designs." "If," said Apollonius, "you would hear how far I am in his counsel, and privy to his designs, please hear me, for why should I conceal the truth?" Now the Emperor imagined that he was going to hear Apollonius confess very important secrets, and that whatever transpired would conduce to the destruction of the persons in question.

CHAPTER XXX

But Apollonius seeing him on tip-toe with expectation, merely said: "For myself, I know Nerva to be the most moderate of men and the gentlest and the most devoted to yourself, as well as a good ruler; though he is so averse to meddling in high matters of State, that he shrinks from office. And as for his friends, for I suppose you refer to

Rufus and Orphitus—these men also are discreet, so far as I know, and averse from wealth, somewhat sluggish to do all they lawfully may; while as for revolution, they are the last people in the world either to plan it or to take part with another who should do so." But the Emperor was inflamed with anger at what he heard and said: "Then you mean to say that I am guilty of slander in their cases, since you assert that they are good men, only sluggish, whom I have ascertained to be the vilest of man kind and usurpers of my throne. For I can imagine that they too, if I put the question to them about you, would in their turn deny that you were a wizard and a hot-head and a braggart and a miser, and that you looked down on the laws. And so it is, you accursed rascals, that you all hold together like thieves. But the accusation shall unmask everything; for I know, as well as if I had been present and taken part in everything, all the oaths which you took, and the objects for which you took them, and when you did it, and what was, your preliminary sacrifice." At all this Apollonius did not even blench, but merely remarked: "It is not creditable to you, O sovereign, nor is it congruous with the law, that you should either pretend to try a case affecting persons about whom you have already made up your mind, or should have made it up before ever you have tried them. But if you will have it so, permit me at once to begin and plead my defense. You are prejudiced against me, my sovereign, and you do me a greater wrong than could any false informer, for you take for granted, before you hear them, accusations which he only offers to prove." "Begin your defense," said the Emperor, "at any point you like, but I know very well where to draw the line, and with what it is best to begin."

CHAPTER XXXIV

From that moment he began to insult the sage, by cutting off his beard, and hair, and confining him among the vilest felons; and as regards his hair being shaved, Apollonius remarked: "It had not occurred to me, O sovereign, that I risked losing my hair." And as regards his imprisonment in bonds, he remarked: "If you think me a wizard, how will you ever fetter me? And if you fetter me, how can you say that I am a wizard?" "Yes," replied the Emperor, "for I will not release you until you have turned into water, or into some wild animal, or into a tree." "I will not turn into these things," said Apollonius, "even if I could, for I will not ever betray men who, in violation of all justice, stand in peril and what Iam, that I will remain; but I am ready to endure all you can inflict upon my vile body, until I have finished pleading the cause of these persons." "And who," asked the Emperor, "is going to plead your cause?" "Time," replied Apollonius, "and the spirit of the gods, and the passion for wisdom which animates me."

CHAPTER XXXV

Such was the prelude of his defense, which he made in private to Domitian, as Damis outlines it. But some have, out of malignity, perverted the facts, and say that he first made his defense, and only then was imprisoned, at the same time that he was also shorn; and they have forged a certain letter in the Ionic dialect, of tedious prolixity, in which they pretend that Apollonius went down on his knees to Domitian and besought him to release him of his bonds. Now Apollonius, it is true, wrote his testament in the Ionian style of language; but I never met with any letter of his composed in that dialect, although I have come across a great many of them; nor did I ever find any verbosity in any letter of the sage's, for they are laconically brief as if they had been unwound from the ferule of a herald. Moreover, he won his cause and quitted the court, so how could he ever have been imprisoned after the verdict was given? But I must defer to relate what happened in the law court. I had best narrate first what ensued after he was shaved and what he said in his discourses, for it is worthy of notice.

CHAPTER XXXVI

For after the sage had been confined for two days in prison, some one came to the prison, and said that he had purchased the right to visit him, and that he was come to advise him how to save his life. This person then was a native of Syracuse, and was mind and mouthpiece of Domitian; and he had been suborned, like the earlier one, by him. But he had a more plausible mission; for whereas the first one beat about the bush, this one took up his parable straight from what he saw before him, and said: "Heavens, who would ever have thought of Apollonius being thrown into chains?" "The person who threw him," said Apollonius, "for surely he would not have done so, if he had not thought of it." "And who ever thought that his ambrosial locks could be cut off?" "I myself," said Apollonius, "who wore them." "And how can you endure it?" said the other. "As a man well may bear it who is brought to this pass neither with nor without his will." "And how can your leg endure the weight of the fetters?" "I don't know," said Apollonius, "for my mind is intent upon other matters." "And yet the mind," said the other, "must attend to what causes pain." "Not necessarily," said Apollonius, "for if you are a man like myself, your mind, will either not feel the pain or will order it to cease." "And what is it that occupies your mind?" "The necessity," answered Apollonius, "of not noticing such things." Then the other reverted to the matter of his locks and led the conversation round to them again, whereupon Apollonius remarked,

"It is lucky for you, young man, that you were not one of the Achaeans long ago in Troy; for it seems to me that you would have raised a terrible hullabaloo over the locks of Achilles, when he cut them off in honor of Patroclus, supposing he really did so, and you would at least have swooned at such a spectacle. For if as you say, you are full of pity for my locks which were all grey and frowzy, what would you not have felt over those of Achilles which were nicely curled and auburn?"

The other of course had only made his remarks out of malice, in order to see what would make Apollonius wince, and, by Heaven, to see whether he would reproach his sovereign on account of his sufferings. But he was so shut up by the answers he got that he said: "You have incurred the royal displeasure on several grounds, but in particular on those for which Nerva and his friends are being prosecuted, namely of injuring the government. For certain informations have been conveyed to him about your words in Ionia, when you spoke of him in hostile and embittered tones. But they say that he attaches little importance to that matter, because his anger is whetted by the graver charges, and this although the informer from whom he learnt those first charges is a very distinguished person of great reputation." "A new sort of Olympic winner is this you tell me of," said Apollonius, "that pretends to win distinction by the weightiness of his slanders. But I quite realize that he is Euphrates, who, I know, does everything against me which he can; and these are far from being the worst injuries which he has done me. For hearing once on a time that I was about to visit the naked sages of Ethiopia, he set himself to poison their minds against me and if I had not seen through his malignant designs, I should probably have gone away without even seeing their company." The Syracusan then, much astonished at this remark, said: "Then you think it a much lesser thing to be traduced to the Emperor than to forfeit your good repute in the eyes of the naked sages owing to the insinuations dropped against you by Euphrates?" "Yes, by Heaven," he said, "for I was going there as a learner, whereas I am come here with a mission to teach." "And what are you going to teach?" said the other. "That I am," said Apollonius, "a good and honorable man, a circumstance this of which the Emperor is not yet aware." "But you can," said the other, "get out of your scrape if you only will teach him things, which if you had told him before you came here, you would never have been cast into prison." Now Apollonius understood that the Syracusan was trying to drive him into some such admission as the Emperor had tried to get out of him, and that he imagined that out of sheer weariness of his imprisonment he would tell some falsehood to the detriment of his friends, and, accordingly he answered: "My excellent friend, if I have been cast into prison for telling Domitian the truth, what would happen to me if I refrained from telling it? For he apparently regards truth as something to be punished with imprisonment, just as I regard falsehood."

CHAPTER XXXVII

The Syracusan was so much struck with the superiority of his philosophical talent (for after saying this he went away), that he promptly left the prison; but Apollonius glancing at Damis said: "Do you understand this Python?" "I understand," said he, "that he has been suborned to trip you up; but what you mean by Python, and what is the sense of such a name, I do nor know." "Python," replied Apollonius, "of Byzantium, was, they say, a rhetor skillful to persuade men to evil courses. He was sent in the interests of Philip, son of Amyntas, on an embassy to the Hellenes to urge their enslavement, and though he passed by other states, he was careful to go to Athens, just at a time when rhetoric most flourished there. And he told them that they did a great injury to Philip, and made a great mistake trying to liberate the Hellenic nation. Python delivered these sentiments, as they say, with a flood of words, but no one save Demosthenes of the Paeanian deme spoke to the contrary and checked his presumption; and he reckons it amongst his achievements that he bore the brunt of his attack unaided. Now I would never call it an achievement that I refused to be drawn into the avowals which he wanted. Nevertheless I said that he was employed on the same job as Python, because he has come here as a despot's hireling to tender me monstrous advice."

CHAPTER XXXVIII

Damis says that though Apollonius uttered many more discourses of the same kind, he was himself in despair of the situation, because he saw no way out of it except such as the gods have vouchsafed to some in answer to prayer, when they were in even worse straits. But a little before midday, he tells us that he said: "O man of Tyana,"—for he took a special pleasure, it appears, in being called by that name,—"what is to become of us?" "Why what has become of us already," said Apollonius, "and nothing more, for no one is going to kill us." "And who," said Damis, "is so invulnerable as that? But will you ever be liberated?" "So far as it rests with the verdict of the court," said Apollonius, "I shall be set at liberty this day, but so far as depend upon my own will, now and here." And with these words he took his leg out of the fetters and remarked to Damis: "Here is proof positive to you of my freedom, to cheer you up." Damis says that it was then for the first time that he really and truly understood the nature of Apollonius, to wit that it was divine and superhuman, for without sacrifice—and how in prison could he have offered any?—and without a single prayer, without even a word, he quietly laughed at the fetters, and then inserted his leg in them afresh, and behaved like a prisoner once more.

CHAPTER XXXIX

Now simple-minded people attribute such acts as this to wizardry, and they make the same mistake in respect of many purely human actions. For athletes resort to this art, just as do all who have to undergo a contest in their eagerness to win; and although it contributes nothing to their success, nevertheless these unfortunate people, after winning by mere chance as they generally do, rob themselves of the credit and attribute it to this art of wizardry. Nor does any amount of failure in their enterprises shake their faith in it, they merely say such things as this: "If I had only offered this sacrifice or that, if I had only burnt that perfume in place of another, I should not have failed to win." And they really believe what they say. Magic also besieges the doors of merchants no less, for we shall find them too attributing their successes in trade to the wizard or magician, no less than they ascribe their losses to their own parsimony and to their failure to sacrifice as often as they should have done. But is especially lovers who are addicted to this art; for as the disease which they suffer from in any case renders them liable to be deluded, so much so that they go to old hags to talk about it, it is no wonder, I think, that they resort to these impostors and give ear to their quackeries. They will accept from them a magic girdle to wear, as well as precious stones, some of the bits of stone having come from the depths of the earth and others from the moon and stars; and then they are given all the spices which the gardens of India yield; and the cheats exact vast sums of money from them for all this, and yet do nothing to help them at all. For let their favorites only give them the least encouragement, or let the attractions of the lover's presents advance his suit in the very least, and he at once sets out to laud the art as able to achieve anything; while if the experiment does not come off, he is as ready as ever to lay the blame on some omission, for he will say that he forgot to burn the spice, or to sacrifice or melt up that, and that everything turned upon that and it was impossible to do without it. Now the various devices and artifices by which they work signs from heaven and all other miracles on a wide scale, have been actually recorded by certain authors, who laugh outright at the art in question. But for myself I would gladly denounce such arts in order to prevent young men from resorting to its professors, lest they become accustomed to such things even in fun. This digression has led me far enough from my subject; for why should I attack any further a thing which is equally condemned by nature and by law?

CHAPTER XL

After Apollonius had thus revealed himself to Damis, and held some further conversation, about midday someone presented himself to them and made the following intimation verbally: "The Emperor, Apollonius, releases you from these fetters by the advice of Aelian; and he permits you to take up your quarters in the prison where criminals are not bound, until the time comes for you to make your defense, but you will probably be called upon to plead your cause five days from now." "Who then," said Apollonius, "is to get me out of this place?" "I," said the messenger, "so follow me." And when the prisoners in the free prison saw him again, they all flocked round him, as around one restored to them against all expectations; for they entertained the same affectionate longing for Apollonius as children do for a parent who devotes himself to giving them good advice in an agreeable and modest manner, or who tells them stories of his own youth; nor did they try to hide their feelings; and Apollonius continued incessantly to give them advice.

CHAPTER XLI

And on the next day he called Damis and said: "My defense has to be pleaded by me on the day appointed, so do you betake yourself in the direction of Dicaearchia, for it is better to go by land; and when you have saluted Demetrius, turn aside to the sea-shore where the island of Calypso lies; for there you shall see me appear to you." "Alive," asked Damis, "or how?" Apollonius with a smile replied: "As I myself believe, alive, but as you will believe, risen from the dead." Accordingly he says that he went away with much regret, for although he did not quite despair of his master's life, yet he hardly expected him to escape death. And on the third day he arrived at Dicaearchia, where he at once heard news of the great storm which had raged during those days; for a gale with rain had burst over the sea, sinking some of the ships that were sailing thither, and driving out of their course those which were tending to Sicily and the straits of Messina. And then he understood why it was that Apollonius had bidden him to go by land.

CHAPTER XLII

The events which followed are related by Damis, he says, from accounts given by Apollonius, both to himself and Demetrius. For he relates that there came to Rome from Messene in Arcadia a youth remarkable for his beauty, and found there many admirers, and above all Domitian, whose rivals even the former did not scruple to declare themselves, so strong was their attachment. The youth however was too high-principled and respected his honor. Now had it been gold that he scorned or possessions or horses, or such other attractions and lures as sundry persons seek to corrupt young people with, we had no call to praise him, for the seducer can hardly dispense with such preparations. But he was tempted with larger honors than all those put together who ever attracted the glances of sovereigns, yet he disdained them all for himself. In consequence, he was cast into prison by his own admirer's orders. He came up to Apollonius, and made as if he would speak to him, but, being counseled by his modesty to keep silent, did not venture to. Apollonius noticed this and said: "You are confined here, and yet are not of an age to be a malefactor, like ourselves who are hardened sinners." "Yes, and I shall be put to death," said the other; "for by our latter-day laws self-respect is honored with capital punishment." "So it was in the time of Theseus," answered Apollonius, "for Hippolytus was murdered by his own sire for the same reason." "And I too," said the other, " am my own father's victim. For though I am an Arcadian from Messene, he did not give me an Hellenic education, but sent me here to study law; and when I had come here for that purpose the Emperor cast an evil eye on me." But Apollonius feigned not to understand what he meant and said: "Tell me, my boy, surely the Emperor does not imagine you have blue eyes, when you have, as I see, black ones? Or that you have a crooked nose, whereas it is square and regular, like that of a well executed Hermes? or has he not made some mistake about your hair? For, methinks, it is sunny and gleaming, and your mouth too is so regular, that whether you are silent or talking, it is equally comely, and you carry your head freely and proudly. Surely the Emperor must be mistaking all these traits for others, or you would not tell me he has cast an evil eye on you." "That is just what ruined me," said the other, "for he has condescended to favor me and instead of sparing what he praises is prepared to insult me as a woman's lovers might." Apollonius admired the Arcadian too much to ply him with such question as what he thought of sleeping together, as whether it was disgraceful or not, and others of the sort, as he noticed that he blushed and was not decorous in his language; so he only put to him the question: "Have you any slaves in Arcadia?" "Why yes, many," replied the lad. "What conversation to them," said Apollonius, "do you consider yourself as holding?" "That," he replied, "which the laws assign to me, for I am their master." "And must slaves obey their masters or disdain the wishes of those who are masters of their persons?" The other discerned the drift of his question and answered: "I know indeed how irresistible and harsh is the power of tyrants, for they are inclined to use it to overpower even free men, but I am master of my person and shall guard it inviolate." "How can you do that," said Apollonius, "for you have to do with an admirer who is prepared to run amuck of your youth, sword in hand?" "I shall simply hold out my neck, which is all his sword requires." Whereupon Apollonius commended him, and said: "I perceive you are an Arcadian." Moreover, he mentions this youth in one of his letters, and gives a much more attractive account of him than I have done in the above, and while praising him for his high principles to his correspondent, adds that he was not put to death by the tyrant. On the contrary, after exciting admiration by his firmness, he returned by ship to Malea, and was held in more honor by the inhabitants of Arcadia than the youths who among the Lacedaemonians surpass their fellows in their endurance of the scourge.

BOOK VIII

CHAPTER I

Let us now repair to the law court to listen to the sage pleading his cause; for it is already sunrise and the doors are thrown open to admit the celebrities. And the companions of the Emperor say that he had taken no food today, because, I imagine, he was so absorbed in examining the documents of the case. For they say he was holding in his hands a roll of writing of some sort, sometimes reading it with anger, and sometimes more calmly. And we must needs figure him as one who was angry with the law for having invented such things as courts of justice.

CHAPTER II

But Apollonius, as we meet him in this conjuncture seems to regard the trial as a dialectical discussion, rather than as a race to be run for his life; and this we may infer from the way he behaved before he entered the court. For on his way thither he asked the secretary who was conducting him, where they were going; and when the latter answered that he was leading him to the court, he said: "Whom am I going to plead against?" "Why," said the other, "against the accuser of course, and the Emperor will be judge." "And," said Apollonius, "who is going to judge between myself and the Emperor? For I shall prove that he is wronging philosophy." "And what concern," said the other, "has the Emperor for philosophy, even if he does happen to be wrong?" "Nay, but philosophy," said Apollonius, "is much concerned about the Emperor, that he should govern as he should." The secretary commanded this sentiment, for indeed he was already favorably disposed to Apollonius, as he proved from the very beginning. "And how long will your pleading last by the water-clock's reckoning? For I must know this before the trial begins." "If," said Apollonius, "I am allowed to plead as long as the necessities of the suit require me to, the whole of the Tiber might run through the meter before I should have done; but if I am only to answer the questions put to me, then it depends on the cross-examiner how long I shall be making my answers." "You have cultivated," remarked the other, "contrary talents when you thus engage to talk about one and the same matter both with brevity and with prolixity." "They are not contrary talents," said Apollonius, "but resemble each other. And moreover there is a mean composed between the two, which I should not myself allege to be a third, but a first requisite for a pleader; and for my own part I am sure that silence constitutes a fourth excellence much required in a law-court." "Anyhow," said the other, "it will do you no good nor anyone who stands in great peril." "And yet," said Apollonius, "it was of great service to Socrates of Athens, when he was prosecuted." "And what good did it do him," said the other, "seeing that he died just because he would say nothing?" "He did not die," said Apollonius, "though the Athenians thought he did."

CHAPTER III

This was how he prepared himself to confront the despot's maneuvers; and as he waited before the court another secretary came up and said: "Man of Tyana, you must enter the court with nothing on you." "Are we then to take a bath," said Apollonius, "or to plead?" "The rule," said the other, "does not apply to dress, but the Emperor only forbids you to bring in here either amulet, or book, or any papers of any kind." "And not even a cane," said Apollonius, "for the back of the idiots who gave him such advice as this?" Whereat the accuser burst into shouts: "O my Emperor," he said, "this wizard threatens to beat me, for it was I who gave you this advice." "Then," said Apollonius, "it is you who are a wizard rather than myself; for you say that you have persuaded the Emperor of my being that which so far I have failed to persuade him that I am not." While the accuser was indulging in this abuse, one of the freedmen of Euphrates was at his side, whom the latter was said to have sent from Ionia with news of what Apollonius had there said in his conversations, and also with a sum of money which was presented to the accuser.

CHAPTER IV

Such were the preliminary skirmishes which preceded the trial, but the conduct of the trial itself was as follows: The court was fitted up as if for an audience listening to a panegyrical discourse; and all the illustrious men of the city were present at the trial, because the Emperor was intent upon proving before as many people as possible that Apollonius was an accomplice of Nerva and his friends. Apollonius, however, ignored the Emperor's presence so completely as not even to glance at him; and when his accuser upbraided him for want of respect, and bade him turn his eyes upon the god of all mankind, Apollonius raised his eyes to the ceiling, by way of giving a hint that he was looking up to Zeus, and that he regarded the recipient of such profane flattery as worse than he who administered it. Whereupon the accuser began to bellow and spoke somewhat as follows: "'tis time, my sovereign, to apportion the water, for if you allow him to talk as long as he chooses, he will choke us. Moreover I have a roll here which contains the heads of the charges against him, and to these he must answer, so let him defend himself against them one by one."

CHAPTER V

The Emperor approved of this plan of procedure and ordered Apollonius to make his defense according to the informer's advice; however, he dropped out other accusations, as not worth discussion, and confined himself to four questions which he thought were embarrassing and difficult to answer. "What induces you, he said, "Apollonius, to dress yourself differently from everybody else, and to wear this peculiar and singular garb?" "Because," said Apollonius, "the earth which feeds me also clothes me, and I do not like to bother the poor animals." The emperor next asked the question: "Why is it that men call you a god?" "Because," answered Apollonius, "every man that is thought to be good, is honored by the title of god." I have shown in my narrative of India how this tenet passed into our hero's philosophy. The third question related to the plague in Ephesus: "What motived," he said, "or suggested your prediction to the Ephesians that they would suffer from a plague?" "I used," he said, "O my sovereign, a lighter diet than others, and so I was the first to be sensible of the danger; and if you like, I will enumerate the causes of pestilences." But the Emperor, fearful, I imagine, lest Apollonius should reckon among the causes of such epidemics his own wrong-doing, and his incestuous marriage, and his other misdemeanors, replied: "Oh, I do not want any such answers as that." And when he came to the fourth question which related to Nerva and his friends, instead of hurrying straight on to it, he allowed a certain interval to elapse, and after long reflection, and with the air of one who felt dizzy, he put his question in a way which surprised them all; for they expected him to throw off all disguise and blurt out the names of the persons in question without any reserve, complaining loudly and bitterly of the sacrifice; but instead of putting the question in this way, he beat about the bush, and said: "Tell me, you went out of your house on a certain day, and you traveled into the country, and sacrificed the boy—I would like to know for whom?" And Apollonius as if he were rebuking a child replied: "Good words, I beseech you; for I did leave my house, I was in the country; and if this was so, then I offered sacrifice: and if I offered it, then I ate of it. But let these assertions be proved by trustworthy witnesses." Such a reply on the part of the sage aroused louder applause than beseemed the court of an Emperor; and the latter deeming the audience to have borne witness in favor of the accused, and also not a little impressed himself by the answers he had received, for they were both firm and sensible, said: "I acquit you of the charges; but you must remain here until we have had a private interview." Thereat Apollonius was much encouraged and said: "I thank you indeed, my sovereign, but I would fain tell you that by reason of these miscreants your cities are in ruin, and the islands full of exiles, and the mainland of lamentations, and your armies of cowardice, and the Senate of suspicion. Accord me also, if you will, opportunity to speak; but if not, then send someone to take my body, for my soul you cannot take. Nay, you cannot take even my body,

"For thou shalt not slay me, since—I tell thee—I am not mortal."

And with these words he vanished from the court, which was the best thing he could do under the circumstances, for the Emperor clearly intended not to question him sincerely about the case, but about all sorts of irrelevant matters. For he took great credit to himself for not having put Apollonius to death, nor was the latter anxious to be drawn into such discussions. And he thought that he would best effect his end if he left no one in ignorance of his true nature, but allowed it to be known to all to be such that he had it in him never to be taken prisoner against his own will. Moreover he had no longer any cause for anxiety about his friends; for as the despot had not the courage to ask any questions about them, how could he possibly put them to death with any color of justice upon charges for which no evidence had been presented in court? Such was the account of the proceedings of the trial which I found.

CHAPTER VI

But inasmuch as he had composed an oration which he would have delivered by the clock in defense of himself, only the tyrant confined him to the questions which I have enumerated, I have determined to publish this oration also. For I am well aware, indeed, that those who highly esteem the style of buffoons will find fault in it, as being less chaste and severe in its style than they consider it should be, and as too bombastic in language and tone. However, when I consider that Apollonius was a sage, it seems to me that he would have unworthily concealed his true character if he had merely studied symmetry of endings, and antithesis, clicking his tongue as if it had been a castanet. For these tricks suit the genius of rhetoricians, though they are not necessary even to them. For forensic art, if it be too obvious, is apt to betray him who resorts to it as anxious to impose upon the judges; whereas if it is well concealed, it is likely to carry off a favorable verdict; for true cleverness consists in concealing from the judges the very cleverness of the pleader. But when a wise man is defending his cause—and I need not say that a wise man will not arraign another for faults which he has the will and strength to rebuke—he requires quite another style than that of the hacks of the law-court; and though his oration must be well-prepared, it must not seem to be so, and it should possess a certain elevation almost amounting to scorn, and he must take care in speaking not to throw himself on the pity of the judges. For how can he appeal to the pity of others who would not condescend to solicit anything? Such an oration will my hero's seem to those who shall diligently study both myself and him; for it was composed by him in the following manner:

CHAPTER VII (i)

(i) "My prince, we are at issue with one another concerning matters of grave moment; for you run such a risk as never autocrat did before you, that namely of being thought to be animated by a wholly unjust hatred of philosophy; while I am exposed to a worse peril than was ever Socrates at Athens, for though the accusers taxed him in their indictment with introducing new beliefs about demons, they never went so far as to call him or think him a demon. Since, however, so grave a peril besets us both, I will not hesitate to tender you the advice of whose excellence I am myself convinced. For since the accuser has plunged us into this struggle, the many have been led to form a false opinion of both myself and of you. They have come to imagine that you will listen only to the counsels of anger, with the result that you will even put me to death, whatever death means, and that I in turn shall try to evade this tribunal in some of the ways there are—and they were, my prince, myriad—of escaping from it. Though rumors have reached my ears, I have not contracted any prejudice against you, nor have I done you the injury of supposing you will hear my cause otherwise than in accordance with the strictest principles of equity; for in conformity with the laws I submit myself to their pronouncement. And I would advise you also to do the same; for justice demands that you should neither prejudge the case, nor take your seat on the bench with your mind made up to the belief that I have done you any wrong. If you were told that the Armenian, the Babylonian and other foreign potentates were about to inflict some disaster on you, which must lead to the loss of your empire, you would, I am sure, laugh outright; although they have hosts of cavalry, all kinds of archers, a gold bearing soil and, as I know full well, a teeming population. And yet you distrust a philosopher, naked of means of offense, and are ready to believe he is a menace to the autocrat of the Romans—all this on the mere word of an Egyptian sycophant. Never did you here such tales from Athena, whom you allege to be your guardian spirit, unless indeed, great Heavens!, their flattering and falsely accusing others has so increased the influence of these miscreants, that you would pretend that whereas in insignificant matters, such as sore eyes, and avoidance of fevers and inflammation of the bowels, the Gods are your apt advisers, manipulating and healing you after the manner of physicians of anyone of these maladies you may be suffering from, they, nevertheless, in matters which imperil your throne and your life, give you no counsel either as to the persons you should guard against or as to the weapons you should employ against them, but, instead of coming to your aid, leave you to the tender mercies of false accusers, whom you regard as the Aegis of Athena or the hand of Zeus, just because they assert that they understand your welfare better even than do the gods, and that they watch over you in the hours of their waking and sleeping, if indeed these wretches can sleep after pouring out such wicked lies and compiling ever and anon whole Iliads such as this one.

That they should keep horses and roll theatrically into the forum in chariots drawn by snowy teams, that they should gorge themselves off dishes of silver and gold, parade favorites that cost them two or three myriad sesterces, that they should go on committing adultery as long as they are not found out and then and not before, marry the victims of their lusts when they are caught red-handed, that their splendid successes should be hailed with applause, as often as some philosopher or consul, absolutely innocent, falls into their toils and is put to death by yourself—all this I am willing to concede to the license of these accursed wretches and to their brazen indifference to the public eye and to law; but that they should give themselves the airs of superhuman beings and presume to know better than the gods, I cannot approve or allow; and the mere rumor of it fills me with horror. And if you allow such things to be, they will perhaps accuse even yourself of offending against established religion. I know that my tone is rather that of a censor than that of a defendant; if so, you must pardon me for thus speaking up in behalf of the laws, with the recognition of whose authority by yourself stands and falls that of your own.

CHAPTER VII (ii)

(ii) Who then will be my advocate while I am defending myself? For if I called upon Zeus to help me, under whom I am conscious of having passed my life, they will accuse me of being a wizard and of bringing heaven down to earth. Let us then appeal in this matter to one whom I deny to be dead, although the many assert it, I mean your own father, who held me in the same esteem in which you behold him; for he made you, and was in turn made by me. He, my prince, shall assist my defense, because he knows my character much better than yourself; for he came to Egypt before he was raised to the throne, as much to converse with me about the Empire as to sacrifice to the gods of Egypt. And when he found me with my long hair and dressed as I am at this moment, he did not ask me a single question about my costume, because he considered that everything about me was well; but he admitted that he had come thither on my account, and after commending me and saying to me things which he would have said to no one else, and having heard from me what he would have heard from no one else, he departed. I most confirmed him in his aspirations for the throne, when others had already sought to dissuade him,—in no unfriendly spirit, I admit, though you anyhow can not agree with them; for those who tried to persuade him not to assume the reins of Empire were assuredly on their way to deprive you of the succession to him by which you now hold. But by my advice he did not hold himself unworthy, he said, of the kingdom which lay within his grasp and of making you the heirs thereto; and he fully acknowledged the entire wisdom of my advice, and he was raised himself to the pinnacle of greatness, as in turn he raised yourselves. Now if he had looked upon me as a wizard, he would never have taken me into his confidence, for he did not come and say such things as this to me: Compel the Fates or compel Zeus to appoint me tyrant, or to work miracles and portents in my behalf, and show me the sun rising in the west and setting at the point where he rises. For I should not have thought him a fit person for empire in he had either considered me as an adept in such art, or resorted to such tricks in pursuit of a crown which it behoved him to win by his virtues alone. More than this my conversation with him was held publicly in a temple, and wizards do not affect temples of the gods as their places of reunion; for such places are inimical to those who deal in magic, and they cloak their art under the cover of night and every sort of darkness, so as to preclude their dupes from the use of their eyes and ears. It is true that he also had a private conversation with me, but there were present at it beside myself Euphrates and Dion, one of them my bitter enemy, but the other my firmest friend; for may never come a time when I shall not reckon Dion among my friends. Now I ask you, who would begin to talk wizardry in the presence of wise men or of men anyhow laying claim to wisdom? And who would not be equally on his guard both among friends and among enemies of betraying his villainy? And moreover our conversation on that occasion was directed against wizards; for you surely will not suppose that your own father when he was aspiring to the throne set more confidence in wizards than in himself, or that he got me to put pressure upon heaven, that he might obtain his object, when, on the contrary, he was confident of winning the crown before ever he came to Egypt; and subsequently he had more important matters to talk over with me, namely the laws and the just acquisition of wealth, and how the gods ought to be worshipped, and what blessings they have in store for those monarchs who govern their people in accordance with the laws. These are the subjects which he desired to learn about, and they are all the direct opposite of wizardry; for if they count for anything at all, there will be an end of the black art.

CHAPTER VII (iii)

(iii) And there is another point, my prince, which merits your attention. The various arts known to mankind, in spite of the differences of their functions and achievements, are yet all concerned to make money, some earning less, some earning more, and some just enough to live upon; and not only the base mechanic arts, but of the rest those which are esteemed liberal [21] arts as well as those which only border upon being liberal, and true philosophy is the only exception. And by liberal arts I mean poetry, music, astronomy, the art of the sophist and of the orator, the merely forensic kinds excepted; and by the arts which border upon liberal I mean those of the painter, modeller, sculptor, navigator, agriculturist, in case the latter waits upon the seasons; for these arts are not very inferior to the liberal professions. And on the other hand, my prince, there are the pseudo-liberal arts of jugglers, which I would not have you confuse with divination, for this is highly esteemed, if it be genuine and tell the truth, though whether it is an art, I am not sure. But I anyhow affirm wizards to be professors of a pseudo-liberal art, for they have get men to believe that the unreal is real, and to distrust the real as unreal, and I attribute all such efforts to the imaginative fancy of the dupes; for the cleverness of this art is relative to the folly of the persons who are deceived by them, and who offer the sacrifices they prescribe; and its professors are given up wholly to filthy lucre, for all their parade of skill is devised by them in hope of gain, and they try to persuade people who are passionately attached to something or another that they are capable of getting everything for them. Do you then find me so opulent as to warrant me in supposing that I cultivate the sort of false and illiberal wisdom, the more so as your own father considered me to be above all pecuniary considerations? And to show you that I speak the truth, here is a letter to me from that noble and divine man, who in it praises me more especially for my poverty. It runs thus:

"The autocrat Vespasian to Apollonius the philosopher sends greetings.

"If all men, Apollonius, were disposed to be philosophers in the same spirit as yourself, then the lot no less of philosophy than poverty would be an extremely happy one; for your philosophy is pure and disinterested, and your poverty is voluntary. Farewell."

Let this be your sire's pleading in my behalf, when he thus lays stress upon the disinterestedness of my philosophy, and the voluntariness of my poverty. For I have no doubt he had in mind the episode in Egypt, when Euphrates and several of those who pretended to be philosophers approached him, and in no obscure language begged for money; whereas I myself not only did not solicit him for money, but

---

[21] I translate the same word σοφός in this passage by *liberal*, *wise*, and *clever* according to the context.

repudiated them as impostors for doing so. And I also showed an aversion from money from my first youth; for realizing that my patrimony, and it was a considerable property, was at best but a transitory toy, I gave it up to my brothers and to my friends and to the poorer of my relatives, so disciplining myself from my very home and hearth to want nothing. I will not dwell upon Babylon and the parts of India beyond the Causasus and the river Hyphasis, through which I journeyed ever true to myself. But in favor of my life here and no less of the fact that I have never coveted money, I will invoke the testimony of the Egyptian here; for he accuses me of every sort of evil deed and design, yet we hear nothing from him of how much money I made by these villainies, nor of how much gain I had in view; indeed he thinks me such a simpleton as to practice my wizardry for nothing, and whereas others only commit its crimes for much money, he thinks that I commit them for none at all. It is as if I cried my wares to the public in such terms as the following: Come, O ye Dupes, for I am a wizard; and I practice my art not for money, but free, gratis, and for nothing; and so you shall earn a great reward, for each of you will go off with nothing but dangers and writs of accusation.

CHAPTER VII (iv)

(iv) But without descending to such silly arguments, I would like to ask the accuser which of his counts I ought to take first. And yet why need I ask him? for at the beginning of his speech he dwelt upon my dress, and by Zeus, upon what I eat and what I do not eat. O divine Pythagoras, do thou defend me upon these counts; for we are put upon our trial for a rule of life of which thou wast the discoverer, and of which I am the humble partisan. For the earth, my prince, grows everything for mankind; and those who are pleased to live at peace with the brute creation want nothing, for some fruits they can cull from earth, others they win from her furrows, for she is the nurse of men, as suits the seasons; but these men, as it were deaf to the cries of mother earth, whet their knife against her children in order to get themselves dress and food. Here then is something which the Brahmans of India themselves condemned, and which they taught the naked sages of Egypt also to condemn; and from them Pythagoras took his rule of life, and he was the first of Hellenes who had intercourse with the Egyptians. And it was his rule to give up and leave her animals to the earth; but all things which she grows, he declared, were pure and undefiled, and ate of them accordingly, because they were best adapted to nourish both body and soul. But the garments which most men wear made of the hides of dead animals, he declared to be impure; and accordingly clad himself in linen, and on the same principles had his shoes woven of byblus. And what were the advantages which he derived from such purity? Many, and before all the privilege of recognizing his own soul. For he had existed in the age when Troy was fighting about Helen, and he had been the fairest of the sons of Panthus, and the best equipped of them all, yet he died at so young an age as to excite the lamentations even of Homer. Well after that he passed into several bodies according to the decree of Adrastea, which transfers the soul from body to body, and then he again resumed the form of man, and was born to Mnesarchides of Samos, this time a sage instead of a barbarian, and an Ionian instead of a Trojan, and so immune from death that he did not even forget that he was Euphorbus. I have then told you who was the begetter of my own wisdom, and I have shown that it is no discovery of my own, but an inheritance come to me from another. And as for myself though I do not condemn or judge those who make it part of their luxury to consume the red-plumaged bird, or the fowls from Phasis or the land of the Paeones, which are fattened up for their banquets by those who can deny nothing to their bellies, and though I have never yet brought an accusation against anyone, because they buy fish for their tables at greater prices than grand seigneurs ever gave for their Corinthian chargers, and though I have never grudged anyone his purple garment nor his soft raiment and Pamphylian tissues—yet I am accused and put upon my trial, O ye gods, because I indulge in asphodel and dessert of dried fruits and pure delicacies of that kind.

CHAPTER VII (v)

(v) Nor even is my mode of dress protected from their calumnies, for the accuser is ready to steal even that off my back, because it has such vast value for wizards. And yet apart from my contention about the use of living animals and lifeless things, according as he uses one or the other of which I regard a man as impure or pure, in what way is linen better than wool? Was not the latter taken from the back of the gentlest of animals, of a creature beloved of the gods, who do not disdain themselves to be shepherds, and, by Zeus, once held the fleece to be worthy of a golden form, if it was really a god that did so, and if it be not a mere story? On the other hand linen is grown and sown anywhere, and there is no talk of gold in connection with it. Nevertheless, because it is not plucked from the back of a living animal, the Indians regard it as pure, and so do the Egyptians, and I myself and Pythagoras on this account have adopted it as our garb when we are discoursing or praying or offering sacrifice. And it is a pure substance under which to sleep of a night, for to those who live as I do dreams bring the truest of their revelations.

CHAPTER VII (vi)

(vi) Let us next defend ourselves from the attack occasioned by the hair which we formerly wore, for one of the counts of the accusation turns upon the squalor thereof. But surely the Egyptian is not entitled to judge me for this, but rather the dandies with their yellow and well-combed locks; and let them bring dangling along the company of their lovers and the mistresses of their revels. Let them congratulate and compliment themselves upon their locks and on the myrrh which drips from them; but think me everything that is unattractive, and if a lover of anything, of abstention from love. For I am inclined to address them thus: O ye poor wretches, do not falsely accuse an institution of the Dorians; for the wearing of your hair long has come down from the Lacaedemonians who affected it in the period when they reached the height of their military fame; and a king of Sparta, Leonidas, wore his hair long in token of his bravery, and in order to appear dignified to his friends, yet terrible to his enemies. For these reasons Sparta wears her hair long no less in his honor than in that of Lycurgus and of Iphitus. And let every sage be careful that the iron knife does not touch his hair, for it is impious to apply it thereto; inasmuch as in his head are all the springs of his senses, and all his intuitions, and it is the source from which his prayers issue forth and also his speech, the interpreter of his wisdom. And whereas Empedocles fastened a fillet of deep purple around his hair, and walked proudly about the streets of the Hellenes, composing hymns to prove that he would pass from humanity and become a god, I only wear my hair disheveled, and I have never needed to sing such hymns about it, yet am hailed before the law courts as a criminal. And what shall I say of Empedocles? Which had he most reason to praise, the man himself or his contemporaries for their happiness, seeing that they never leveled false accusation against him for such a reason?

CHAPTER VII (vii)

(vii) But let us say no more about my hair, for it has been cut off, and the accusation has been forestalled by the same hatred which inspires the next count, a much more serious one from which I must now defend myself. For it is one calculated to fill not only you, my prince, but Zeus himself with apprehension. For he declares that men regard me as a god, and that those who have been thunderstruck and rendered stark-mad by myself proclaim this tenet in public. And yet before accusing me there are things which they should have informed us of, to wit, by what discourses, or by what miracles of word or deed I induced men to pray to me; for I never talked among Hellenes of the goal and origin of my soul's past and future transformations, although I knew full well what they were; nor did I ever disseminate such opinions about myself; nor came forth with presages and oracular strains, which are the harvest of candidates for divine honors. Nor do I know of a single city in which a decree was passed that the citizens should assemble and sacrifice in honor of Apollonius. And yet I have been much esteemed in the several cities which asked for my aid, whatever the objects were for which they asked it, and they were such as these: that their sick might be healed of their diseases, that both their initiations and their sacrifices might be rendered more holy, that insolence and pride might be extirpated, and the laws strengthened. And whereas the only reward which I obtained in all this was that men were made much better than they were before, they were all so many boons bestowed upon yourself by me. For as cow-herds, if they get the cows into good order earn the gratitude of their owners, and as shepherds fatten the sheep for the owner's profit, and as bee-keepers remove diseases from the hive, so that the owner may not lose his swarm, so also I myself, I think, by correcting the defects of their polities, improved the cities for your benefit. Consequently if they did regard me as a god, the deception brought profit to yourself; for I am sure they were the more ready to listen to me, because they feared to do that which a god disapproved of. But in fact they entertained no such illusion, though they were aware that there is between man and God a certain kinship ,which enables him alone of the animal creation to recognize the Gods, and to speculate both about his own nature and the manner in which it participates in the divine substance. Accordingly man declares that his very form resembles God, as it is interpreted by sculptors and painters; and he is persuaded that his virtues come to him from God, and that those who are endowed with such virtues are near to God and divine.

But we need not hail the Athenians as the teachers of this opinion, because they were the first to apply to men the titles of just and Olympic beings and the like, though they are too divine, in all probability, to be applicable to man, but we must mention the Apollo in the Pythian temple as their author. For when Lycurgus from Sparta came to his temple, having just penned his code for the regulation of the affairs of Lacedaemon, Apollo addressed him, and weighed and examined the reputation he enjoyed; and at the commencement of his oracle the god declares that he is puzzled whether to call him a god or a man, but as he advances he decides in favor of the former appellation and assigns it to him as being a good man. And yet the Lacedaemonians never forced a lawsuit on this account upon Lycurgus, nor threatened him on the ground that he claimed to be immortal; for he never rebuked the Pythian god for so addressing him, but on the contrary the citizens agreed with the oracle, for I believe they were already persuaded of the fact before ever it was delivered.

And the truth about the Indians and the Egyptians is the following: The Egyptians falsely accuse the Indians of several things and in particular find fault with their ideas of conduct; but though they do so, they yet approve of the account which they have given of the creator of the Universe, and even have taught it to others, though originally it belonged to the Indians. Now this account recognizes God as the creator of all things, who brought them into being and sustains them; and it declares further that his motive in designing was his goodness. Since then these notions are kindred to one another, I carry the argument further and declare that good men have in their composition something of God. And by the universe which depends upon God the creator we must understand things in heaven and all things in the sea and on earth, which are equally open to all men to partake of, though their fortunes are not equal. But there is also a universe dependent on the good man which does not transcend the limits of wisdom, which I imagine you yourself, my prince, will allow stands in need of a man fashioned in the image of God. And what is the fashion of this universe? There are undisciplined souls which in their madness clutch at every fashion, and in their eyes laws are out of date and vain; and there is no good sense among them, but the honors which they pay to the gods really dishonor them; and they are in love with idle chatter and luxury which breed idleness and sloth, the worst of all practical advisers.

And there are other souls which are drunken and rush in all directions at once, and nothing will repress their antics, nor could do so, even if they drank all the drugs accounted, as the Mandragoras is, to be soporific. Now you need a man to administer and care for the universe of such souls, a god sent down by wisdom. For he is able to wean them from the lusts and passions, which they rush to satisfy with instincts too fierce for ordinary society, and from their avarice, which is such that they deny they have anything at all unless they can hold their mouths open and have the stream of wealth flow into it. For perhaps such a man as I speak of could even restrain them from committing murder; however, neither I myself nor even the God who created all things, can wash off them the guilt of that.

CHAPTER VII (viii)

(viii) Let me now, my prince, take the accusation which concerns Ephesus, since the salvation of that city was gained; and let the Egyptian be my judge, according as it best suits his accusation. For this is the sort of thing the accusation is. Let us suppose that among the Scythians or Celts, who live along the river Ister and Rhine, a city has been founded every whit as important as Ephesus in Ionia. Here you have a sally-port of barbarians, who refuse to be subject to yourself; let us then suppose that it was about to be destroyed by a pestilence, and that Apollonius found a remedy and averted it. I imagine that a wise man would be able to defend himself even against such a charge as that, unless indeed the sovereign desires to get rid of his adversaries, not by use of arms, but by plague; for I pray, my prince, that no city may ever be wholly wiped out, either to please yourself or to please me, nor may I ever behold in temples a disease to which those who lie sick should succumb in them. But granted that we are not interested in the affairs of barbarians, and need not restore them to health, since they are our bitter enemies, and not at peace with our race; yet who would desire to deprive Ephesus of her salvation, a city which took the basis of its race from the purest Attic source, and which grew in size beyond all other cities of Ionia and Lydia, and stretched herself out to the sea outgrowing the land on which she is built, and is filled with studious people, both philosophers and rhetoricians, thanks to whom the city owes her strength, not to her cavalry, but to the tens of thousands of her inhabitants in whom she encourages wisdom? And do you think that there is any wise man who would decline to do his best in behalf of such a city, when he reflects that Democritus once liberated the people of Abdera from pestilence, and when he bears in mind the story of Sophocles of Athens, who is said to have charmed the winds when they were blowing unseasonably, and who has heard how Empedocles stayed a cloud in its course when it would have burst over the heads of the people of Acragas?

CHAPTER VII (ix)

(ix) The accuser here interrupts me, you hear him yourself do so, my prince, and he remarks that I am not accused for having brought about the salvation of the Ephesians, but for having foretold that the plague would befall them; for this, he says, transcends the power of wisdom and is miraculous, so that I could never have reached such a pitch of truth if I were not a wizard and an unspeakable wretch. What then will Socrates say here of the lore which he declared he learned from his demonic genius? Or what would Thales and Anaxagoras, both Ionians, say, of whom one foretold a plenteous crop of olives, and the other not a few meteorological disturbances? Why, is it not a fact that they were brought before the law-courts upon other charges, but that no one ever heard among their accusations that of their being wizards, because they had the gift of foreknowledge? For that would have been thought ridiculous, and it would not have been a plausible charge to bring against men of wisdom even in Thessaly, where the women had a bad reputation for drawing the moon down to earth.

How then did I get my sense of the coming disaster at Ephesus? You have listened to the statement made even by my accuser, that instead of living like other people, I keep to a light diet of my own, and prefer it to the luxury of others, and I began by saying so myself. This diet, my king, guards my senses in a kind of indescribable ether or clear air, and forbids them to contract any foul or turbid matter, and allows me to discern, as in the sheen of a looking glass, everything that is happening or is to be. For the sage will not wait for the earth to send up its exhalations, or for the atmosphere to be corrupted, in case the evil is shed from above; but he will notice these things when they are impending, not so soon indeed as the gods, yet sooner than the many. For the gods perceive what lies in the future, and men what is going on before them, and wise men what is approaching. But I would have you, my prince, ask of me in private about the causes of pestilence; for they are secrets of a wisdom which should not be divulged to the many. Was it then my mode of living which alone develops such a subtlety and keenness of perception as can apprehend the most important and wonderful phenomena? You can ascertain the point in question, not only from other considerations, but in particular from what took place in Ephesus in connection with that plague. For the genius of the pestilence—and it took the form of a poor old man—I both detected, and having detected took it captive: and I did not so much stay the disease as pluck it out. And who the god was to whom I had offered my prayers is shown in the statue which I set up in Ephesus to commemorate the event; and it is a temple of the Heracles who averts disease, for I chose him to help me, because he is the wise and courageous god, who once purged of the plague the city of Elis, by washing away with the river-tide the foul exhalations which the land sent up under the tyranny of Augeas.

Who then do you think, my prince, being ambitious to be considered a wizard, would dedicate his personal achievement to a god? And whom would he get to admire his art, if he gave the credit of the miracle to God? And who offer his prayers to Heracles, if he were a wizard? For in fact these wretches attribute such feats to the trenches they dig and to the gods of the under-earth, among whom we must not class Heracles, for he is a pure deity and kindly to men. I offered my prayer to him once on a time also in the Peloponnese, for there was an apparition of a lamia there too; and it infested the neighborhood of Corinth and devoured good-looking young men. And Heracles lent me his aid in my contest with her, without asking of me any wonderful gifts—nothing more than honey-cake and frankincense, and the chance to do a salutary turn to mankind; for in the case of Eurystheus also this was the only guerdon which he thought of for his labors. I would ask you, my prince, not to be displeased at my mention of Heracles; for Athena had him under her care because he was good and kind and a Savior of man.

CHAPTER VII (x)

(x) But inasmuch as you bid me vindicate myself in the matter of the sacrifice, for I observe you beckoning with your hand for me to do so, hear my defense. It shall set the truth before you. In all my actions I have at heart the salvation of mankind, yet I have never offered a sacrifice in their behalf, nor will I ever sacrifice anything, nor touch sacrifices in which there is blood, nor offer any prayer with my eyes fixed upon a knife or the kind of sacrifice that he means. It is no

Scythian, my prince, that you have got before you, nor a native of some savage and inhospitable land; nor did I ever mingle with Massagetae or Taurians, for in that case I should have reformed even them and altered their sacrificial custom. But to what depth of folly and inconsequence should I have descended if, after talking so much about divination and about the conditions under which it flourishes or does not flourish, I, who understand better than anyone that the gods reveal their intentions to holy and wise men even without their possessing prophetic gifts, made myself guilty of bloodshed, by meddling with the entrails of victims, as unacceptable to myself as they are ill-omened? In that case the revelation of heaven would surely have abandoned me as impure.

However, if we drop the fact that I have a horror of any such sacrifice, and just examine the accuser in respect to the statements which he made a little earlier, he himself acquits me of this charge. For if, as he says, I could foretell the Ephesians the impending pestilence without use of any sacrifice whatever, what need had I of slaying victims in order to discover what lay within my cognizance without offering any sacrifice at all? And what need had I of divination in order to find out things of which I myself was already assured as well as another? For if I am to be put upon my trial on account of Nerva and his companions, I shall repeat what I said to you the day before yesterday when you accused me of such matters. For I regard Nerva as a man worthy of the highest office and of all the consideration that belongs to a good name and fame, but as one ill-calculated to carry through any difficult plan; for his frame is undermined by a disease which fills his soul with bitterness, and incapacitates him even for his home affairs. As to yourself, certainly he admires your vigor of body no less than he admires your judgment; and in doing so I think he is not singular, because men are by nature more prone to admire what they themselves lack the strength to do. But Nerva is also animated towards myself by feelings of respect; and I never saw him in my presence laughing or joking as he is accustomed to do among his friends; but like young men towards their fathers and teachers, he observes a reverence in every thing that he says in my presence, nay he even blushes; and because he knows that I appreciate and set so high a value upon modesty, he therefore so sedulously cultivates that quality, as sometimes to appear even to me humbler than beseems him. Who then can regard it as probable that Nerva is ambitious of Empire, when he is only too glad if he can govern his own household; or that a man who has not the nerve to discuss with me the greatest of all, or would concert with me plans which, if he thought like myself, he would not even concert with others? How again could I retain my reputation for wisdom and interpreting a man's judgment, if I believed overmuch in divination, yet wholly distrusted wisdom? As for Orphitus and Rufus, who are just and sensible men though somewhat sluggish, as I well know to be the case, if they that they are under suspicion of aspiring to become despots, I hardly know over which they make the greater mistake, over them or over Nerva; if however they are accused of being his accomplices, then I ask, which you would most readily believe, that Nerva was usurping the throne, or that they had conspired with him.

CHAPTER VII (xi)

(xi) I must confess that there are also other points which the accuser who brings me to the bar on these accounts should have entertained and considered: What sense was there in my aiding these revolutionists? For he does not say that I received any money from them, nor that I was tempted by presents to commit these crimes. But let us consider the point whether I might not have advanced great claims, but have deferred their recognition of them until the time came at which they expected to win the throne, when I might have demanded much and have obtained still more as my due. But how can you prove all this? Call to mind, my prince, your own reign and the reigns of your predecessors, I mean of your own brother, and of your father, and of Nero under whom they held office; for it was under these princes chiefly that I passed my life before the eyes of all, the rest of my time being spent on my visit to India. Well, of these thirty-eight years, for such is the period which has elapsed since then up to your own day, I have never come near the court of princes, except that once in Egypt, and then it was your father's, though he was not at that time actually Emperor; and he admitted that he came there on my account. Nor have I ever uttered anything base or humiliating either to emperors, or in behalf of emperors to peoples; nor have I made a parade of letters either when princes wrote them to me or otherwise by pretending that they wrote; nor have I ever demeaned myself by flattery of princes in order to win their largess. If then after long consideration of rich and poor, you should ask me in which class I register myself, I should say among the very rich, for the fact that I want nothing is worth to me all the wealth of Lydia and of Pactolus. Is it likely then that I who never would take presents from yourself whose throne I regarded as perfectly secure, should either have gone cadging to mere pretenders, and have deferred the receipt of my recompense from them until such time as I thought would find them emperors; or that I should plan a change of dynasty, who never once, for purposes of my advancement, resorted to that which was already established? And yet if you want to know how much a philosopher may obtain by flattery of the mighty, you have only got to look at the case of Euphrates. For why do I speak of his having got mere money out of them? Why, he has perfect fountains of wealth, and already at the banks he discusses prices as a merchant might, or a huckster, a tax-gatherer, a low money-changer, for all these roles are his if there is anything to buy or sell; and he clings like a limpet to the doors of the mighty, and you see him standing at them more regularly than any doorkeeper, indeed he has often been shut away by the doorkeepers as greedy dogs are; but he never yet bestowed a farthing upon any philosopher, but he walls up all his wealth within his own house, only supporting this Egyptian out of the money of others, and whetting against me a tongue which ought to have been cut out.

CHAPTER VII (xii)

(xii) However I will leave Euphrates to yourself; for unless you approve of flatterers you will find the fellow worse than I depict him; and I only ask you to listen to the rest of my apology. What then is it to be, and from what counts is to defend me? In the act of the accusation, my prince, a regular dirge is chanted over an Arcadian boy, whom I am accused of having cut up by night, perhaps in a dream, for I am sure I do not know. This child is said to be of respectable parentage and to have possessed all the good looks which Arcadians wear even in the midst of squalor. They pretend that I massacred him in spite of his entreaties and lamentations, and that after thus imbruing my hands in the blood of this child I prayed the gods to reveal the truth to me. So far they only attack myself in their charges, but what follows is a direct assault upon the gods; for they assert that the gods heard my prayers under such circumstances, and vouchsafed to me victims of good omen, instead of slaying me for my impiety. Need I say, O my prince, it is defiling even to listen to such stuff?

But to confine my pleadings to the counts which affect myself, I would ask who is this Arcadian? For since he was not of nameless parentage, and by no means slave-like in appearance, it is time for you to ask what was the name of those who begot him and of what family he was, and what city in Arcadia had the honor of rearing him, and from what alters he was dragged away in order to be sacrificed here. My accuser does not supply this information, in spite of his ingenuity in the art of lying. Let us then suppose it was only a slave in whose behalf he accuses me. For by heaven, we surely must class among slaves one who had neither name of his own, nor parentage, nor city, nor inheritance, must we not? For not a name is supplied anywhere. In that case who was the slave merchant who sold him? Who was it that bought him from the Arcadians? For if this breed is specially suitable for the butchering kind of diviners, he must surely have purchased the boy for much money. And some messenger must have sailed straight to the Peloponnese in order to fetch this Arcadian and conduct him to us. For though one can buy here on the spot slaves from Pontus or Lydia or Phrygia—for indeed you can meet whole droves of them being conducted hither, since these like other barbarous races have always been subject to foreign masters, and as yet see nothing disgraceful in servitude; anyhow with the Phrygians it is a fashion even to sell their children, and once they are enslaved, they never think any more about them—yet the Hellenes retain their love of liberty, and no man of Hellas will ever sell a slave out of his country; for which reason kidnappers and slave-dealers never resort thither, least of all Arcadia; for in addition to the fact that they are beyond all other Hellenes jealous of liberty, they also require a great number of slaves themselves. For Arcadia contains a vast expanse of grass land and of timber, which covers not only the highlands, but all the plains as well. Consequently they require a great many laborers, many goat-herds and swineherds, and shepherds and drivers either for the oxen or for the horses; and there is much need in the land of woodcutters, a craft to which they are trained from boyhood. And even if the land of Arcadia were not such as I have described, so that they could in addition afford like other nations to sell their own slaves abroad, what advantage could the wisdom the accuser babbles of derive by getting a child from Arcadia to murder and cut up? For the Arcadians are not so much wiser than other Hellenes, that their entrails should convey more bowel-lore than those of other people. On the contrary they are the most boorish of men, and resemble hogs in other ways and especially that they can stomach acorns.

It is possible that I have conducted my defense on more rhetorical lines than is my custom, in thus characterizing the habits of the Arcadians and digressing into the Peloponnese. What however is my right line of defense? This I think: I never sacrificed blood, I do not sacrifice it now, I never touch it, not even if it be shed upon an altar; for this was the rule of Pythagoras and likewise of his disciples, and in Egypt also of the Naked sages, and of the sages of India, from whom these principles of wisdom were derived by Pythagoras and his school. In adhering to this way of sacrifice they do not seem to the gods to be criminal; for the latter suffer them to grow old, sound in body and free from disease, and to increase in wisdom daily, to be free from tyranny of others, to be wanting in nothing. Nor do I think that it is absurd to ask the gods for benefits in exchange for pure sacrifices. For I believe that the gods have the same mind as myself in the matter of sacrifice, and that they therefore place those parts of the earth which grow frankincense in the purest region of the world, in order that we may use their resources for purposes of sacrifice without drawing the knife in their temples or shedding blood upon altars. And yet, it appears, I so far forgot myself and the gods as to sacrifice with rites which are not only unusual with myself, but which no human being would employ.

CHAPTER VII (xiii)

(xiii) Let me add that the very hour which my accuser alleges acquits me of this charge. For on that day, the day on which he says I committed this crime, I allow that, if I was in the country, I offered sacrifice, and that if I sacrificed, I ate of the victim. And yet, my prince, you repeatedly ask me if I was not staying in Rome at that time? And you too, O best of princes, were staying there; and yet you would not on that account admit you offered such a sacrifice; and my false accuser was there likewise, but he will not own on that account that he committed murder, just because he was living in Rome. And the same is the case of thousands of people, whom you would do better to expel as strangers, than expose to acts of accusation, if in these the mere fact of their having been in Rome is to be held to be a proof of their guilt. On the hand, the fact of my coming to Rome is in itself a disproof of the charge of revolutionary plotting; for to live in a city, where there are so many eyes to see and so many ears to hear things which are and which are not, is a serious handicap for anyone who desires to play at revolution, unless he be wholly intent upon his own death. On the contrary it prompts prudent and sensible people to walk slowly even when engaged in wholly permissible pursuits.

CHAPTER VII (xiv)

(xiv) What then, O sycophant, was I really doing on that night? Suppose I were yourself and was being asked this question, inasmuch as you are come to ask questions, why then the answer would be this: I was trumping up actions against decent and respectable people, and I was trying to ruin the innocent, and to persuade the Emperor by dint of hard lying, in order that while I myself climbed to fame, I might soil him with the blood of my victims. If again you ask me as a philosopher, I was praising the laughter with which Democritus laughed at all human affairs. But if you asked me as being myself, here is my answer: Philiscus of Melos, who was my fellow-pupil in philosophy for four years, was ill at the time; and I was sleeping out at his house, because he was suffering so terribly that he died of his disease. Ah, many are the charms I would have prayed to obtain, if they could have saved his life. Fain would I have known of any melodies of Orpheus, if any there are, to bring back the dead to us. Nay I verily think I would have made a pilgrimage even to the nether world for his sake, if such things were feasible; so deeply attached was I to him by all his conduct, so worthy of a philosopher and so much in accord with my own ideals. Here are facts, my prince, which you may learn also from Telesinus the consul; for he too was at the bedside of the man of Melos, and nursed him by night like myself. But if you do not believe Telesinus, because he is of the number of philosophers, I call upon the physicians to bear me witness, and they were the following: Seleucus of Cyzicus and Stratocles of Sidon. Ask them whether I tell the truth. And what is more, they had with them over thirty of their disciples, who are ready, I believe, to witness to the same fact; for if I were to summon hither the relatives of Philiscus, you might probably think that I was trying to interpose delays in the case; for they have lately sailed from Rome to the Melian country in order to pay their last sad respects to the dead. Come forward, O ye witnesses, for you have been expressly summoned to give your testimony upon this point."

(The witnesses give their evidence.)

"With how little regard then for the truth this accusation has been drawn up, is clearly proved by the testimony of these gentlemen; for it appears that it was not in the suburbs, but in the city, not outside the wall, but inside a house, not with Nerva, but with Philiscus, not slaying another, but praying for a man's life, not thinking of matters of State, but of philosophy, not choosing a revolutionist to supplant yourself, but trying to save a man like myself.

CHAPTER VII (xv)

(xv) What then is the Arcadian doing in this case? What becomes of the absurd stories of victims slain? What is the use of urging you to believe such lies? For what never took place will be real, if you decide that it did take place. And how, my prince, are you to rate the improbability of the sacrifice? For of course there have been long ago soothsayers skilled in the art of examining slain victims, for example I can name Megistias of Acarnania, Aristandrus of Lycia, and Silanus who was a native of Ambracia, and of these the Acarnanian was sacrificer to Leonidas the king of Sparta, and the Lycian to Alexander of Macedonia, and Silanus to Cyrus the Pretender; and supposing there had been found stored in the entrails of a human being some information truer or more profound or surer than usual, such a sacrifice was not difficult to effect; inasmuch as there were kings to preside over it, who had plenty of cup-bearers at their disposal, besides plenty of prisoners of war as victims; and moreover these monarchs could violate the law with impunity, and they had no fear of being accused, in case they committed so small a murder. But I believe, these persons had the same conviction which I also entertain, who am now in risk of my life of such accusation, namely that the entrails of animals which we slay while they are ignorant of death, are for that reason, and just because the animals lack all understanding of what they are about to suffer, free from disturbance. A human being however has constantly in his soul the apprehension of death, even when it does not as yet impend; how therefore is it likely that when death is already present and stares him in the face, he should be able to give any intimation of the future through his entrails, or be a proper subject for sacrifice at all?

In proof that my conjecture is right and consonant with nature, I would ask you, my prince, to consider the following points. The liver, in which adepts at this art declare the tripod of their divination to reside, is on the one hand not composed of pure blood, for all unmixed blood is retained by the heart which through the blood-vessels sends it flowing as if through canals over the entire body; the bile on the other hand lies over the liver, and whereas it is excited by anger, it is on the other hand driven back by fear into the cavities of the liver. Accordingly if, on the one hand, it is caused to effervesce by irritants, and ceases to be able to contain itself in its own receptacle, it overflows the liver which underlies it, in which case the mass of bile occupies the smooth and prophetic parts of the bowels; on the other hand, under the influence of fear and panic it subsides, and draws together into itself all the light which resides in the smooth parts; for in such cases even that pure element in the blood recedes to which the liver owes its spleen-like look and distension, because the blood in question by its nature drains away under the membrane which encloses the entrails and floats upon the muddy surface. Of what use then, my prince, is it to slay a human victim, if the sacrifice is going to furnish no presage? And human nature does render such rites useless for purposes of divination, because it has a sense of impending death; and dying men themselves meet their end, if with courage, then also with anger, and, if with despondency, then also with fear. And for this reason the art of divination, except in the case of the most ignorant savages, while recommending the slaying of kids and lambs, because these animals are silly and not far removed from being insensible, does not consider cocks an pigs and bulls worthy vehicles of its mysteries, because these creatures have too much spirit. I realize, my prince, that my accuser chafes at my discourse, because I find so intelligent a listener in yourself, for indeed you seem to me to give your attention to my discourse; and if I have not clearly enough explained any point in it, I will allow you to ask me any questions about it.

CHAPTER VII (xvi)

(xvi) I have then answered this Egyptian's act of accusation; but since I do not think I ought altogether to pass by the slanders of Euphrates, I would ask you, my prince, to judge between us, and decide which of us is more of a philosopher. Well then, whereas he strains every nerve to tell lies about myself, I disdain to do the like about him; and whereas he looks upon you as a despot, I regard you as a constitutional ruler; and while he puts the sword into your hand for use against me, I merely supply you with argument.

But he makes the basis of his accusation the discourses which I delivered in Ionia, and he says that they contain matter much to your disadvantage. And yet what I said concerned the topic of the Fates and of Necessity, and I only used as an example of my arguments the affairs of kings, because of your rank is thought to be the highest of human ranks; and I dwelt upon the influence of the Fates, and argued that the threads which they spin are so unchangeable, that, even if they decreed to someone a kingdom which at the moment belonged to another, and even it that other slew the man of destiny, to save himself from ever being deprived by him of his throne, nevertheless the dead man would come to life again in order to fulfill the decree of the Fates. For we employ hyperbole in our arguments in order to convince those who will not believe in what is probable, and it is just as if I had used such an example as this: He who is destined to become a carpenter, will become one even if his hands have been cut off: and he who has been destined to carry off the prize for running in the Olympic games, will not fail to win even if he broke his leg: and a man to whom the Fates have decreed that he shall be an eminent archer, will not miss the mark, even though he has lost his eyesight. And in drawing examples from Royalty I had reference I believe to the Acrisii and the house of Laïus, and to Astyages the Mede, and to many other monarchs who thought that they were well-established in their kingdoms, and of whom some slew their own children as they imagined and others their descendants, and yet were subsequently deprived by them of their thrones when they issued forth from obscurity in accordance with the decrees of fate. Well, if I were inclined to flattery, I should have said that I had your own history in my mind, when you were blockaded in this city by Vitellius, and the temple of Jupiter was burnt on the brow of the hill overlooking the city, and Vitellius declared that his own fortune was assured, so long as you did not escape him, this although you were at the time quite a stripling and not the man you are now; and yet, because the Fates had decreed otherwise, he was undone with all this counsels, while you are now in possession of his throne. However, since I abhor the concords of flattery, for it seems to me that they are everything that is out of time and out of tune, let me cut the string out of my lyre, and request you to consider that on that occasion I had not your fortunes in my mind, but was talking exclusively of questions of the Fates and of Necessity for it was in speaking of them that they accused me of having assailed yourself. And yet such an argument as mine is tolerated by most of the gods; and even Zeus himself is not angry when he hears from the poet in "the story of Lycia" this language:—

'Alas for myself, when Sarpedon...'

And there are other such strains referring to himself, such as those in which he declares that he yields the cause of his son to the Fates; and in the weighing of souls again the poets tell you that, although after his death he presented Minos the brother of Sarpedon with a golden scepter, and appointed him judge in the court of Aidoneus, yet he could not exempt him from the decree of the Fates. And you, my prince, why should you resent my argument when the gods put up with it, whose fortunes are forever fixed and assured, and who never slew poets on that account? For it is our duty to follow the Fates and obey them, and not take offense with the changes of fortune, and to believe in Sophocles when he says:—

'For the gods alone there comes no old age, nay, nor even death; but all other things are confounded by all-mastering time...'

No man ever put the truth so well. For the prosperity of men runs in a circle, and the span of happiness, my prince, lasts for a single day. My prosperity belongs to another and his to another, and his again to a third; and each in having hath not. Think of this, my prince, and put a stop to your decrees of exile, stay the shedding of blood, and have recourse to philosophy in your wishes and plans; for true philosophy feels no pangs. And in doing so wipe away men's tears; for at present echoes reach us from the sea of a thousand sighs, and they are redoubled from the continents, where each laments over his peculiar sorrows. Thence is bred an incalculable crop of evils, all of them due directly to slanderous tongues of informers, who render all men objects of hatred to yourself, and yourself, O prince, to all."

CHAPTER VIII

Such then was the oration which the sage had prepared beforehand, at the end whereof I found the last words of the earlier speech, namely:

"For thou shalt not kill me, since I tell thee I am not mortal," together with the words which preceded and led up to this quotation. But the effect upon the despot of his quitting the court in a matter so godlike and inexplicable was quite other than that which the many expected; for they expected him to make a terrific uproar and institute a hunt for the man, and to send forth proclamations over his empire to arrest him wherever they should find him. But he did nothing of the kind, as if he set himself to defeat man's expectations; or because he now at last realized that as against the sage he had no resources of his own. But whether he acted from contempt, let us conjecture from what ensued, for he will be seen confounded with astonishment rather than filled with contempt.

CHAPTER IX

For he had to hear another case after that of Apollonius, an action brought, I think, in connexion with a will by some city against a private individual; and he had forgotten not only the names of the parties, but also the matter at issue in the suit; for his questions were without meaning and his answers were not relevant to the case—all which argued the degree of astonishment and perplexity under which the despot labored, the more so because his flatterers had persuaded him that nothing could escape his memory.

CHAPTER X

Such was the condition to which Apollonius reduced the despot, making him a plaything of his philosophy who had been the terror of the Hellenes and the barbarians; and before midday he left the court, and at dusk appeared to Demetrius and Damis at Dicaearchia. And this accounts for his having instructed Damis to go by land to Dicaearchia, without waiting to hear his defense. For he had given no previous notice of his intentions, but had merely told the man who was mostly in his intimacy to do what best accorded with his plans.

CHAPTER XI

Now Damis had arrived the day before and had talked with Demetrius about the preliminaries of the trial; and the account filled the latter, when he listened to it, with more apprehension than you might expect of a listener when Apollonius was in question. The next day also he asked him afresh about the same particulars, as he wandered with him along the edge of the sea, which figures in the fables told about Calypso; for they were almost in despair of their master coming to them, because the tyrant's hand was hard upon all; yet out of respect for Apollonius' character they obeyed his instructions. Discouraged, then, they sat down in the chamber of the nymphs, where there is the cistern of white marble, which contains a spring of water which neither overflows its edges, nor recedes, even if water be drawn for it. They were talking about the quality of the water in no very serious manner; and presently, owing to the anxiety they felt about the sage, brought back their conversation to the circumstances which preceded the trial.

CHAPTER XII

Damis' grief had just broken out afresh, and he had made some such exclamation as the following: "Shall we ever behold, O ye gods, our noble and good companion?" when Apollonius, who had heard him—for as a matter of fact he was already present in the chamber of the nymphs—answered: "Ye shall see him, nay, ye have already seen him." "Alive?" said Demetrius, "For if you are dead, we have anyhow never ceased to lament you." Hereupon Apollonius stretched out his hand and said: "Take hold of me, and if I evade you, then I am indeed a ghost come to you from the realm of Persephone, such as the gods of the underworld reveal to those who are dejected with much mourning. But if I resist your touch, then you shall persuade Damis also that I am both alive and that I have not abandoned my body." They were no longer able to disbelieve, but rose up and threw themselves on his neck and kissed him, and asked him about his defense. For while Demetrius was of opinion that he had not even made his defense—for he expected him to be destroyed without any wrong being proved against him— Damis thought that he had made his defense, but perhaps more quickly than was expected; for he never dreamed that he had made it only that day. But Apollonius said: "I have made my defense, gentlemen, and have gained my cause; and my defense took place this very day not so long ago, for it lasted on even to midday." "How then," said Demetrius, "have you accomplished so long a journey in so small a fraction of the day?" And Apollonius replied: "Imagine what you will, flying ram or wings of wax excepted, so long as you ascribe it to the intervention of a divine escort."

"Well," said Demetrius, "I have always thought that your actions and words were providently cared for by some god, to whom you owe your present preservation, nevertheless pray tell us about the defense you made, what it consisted of and what the accusation had to say against you, and about the temper of the judge, and what questions he put, and what he allowed to pass of your pleas and what not—tell us at once in order that I may tell everything in turn to Telesinus, for he will never leave off asking me about your affairs; for about fifteen days back he was drinking with me in Antium, when he fell asleep at table, and just as the middle cup in honor of the good genius was being passed round he dreamed a dream; and he saw a fire spreading like a sea over the land, and it enveloped some men, and caught up others as they fled; for it flowed along, he said, exactly like water, but you alone suffered not the fate of the rest, but swam clean through it as it divided to let you through. And in honor of the gods who inspire such happy presages he poured out a libation in consequence of this dream, and he bade me be of good cheer on your account." And Apollonius said: "I am not surprised at Telesinus dreaming about me, for in his vigils, I assure he, he long ago occupied his mind about me; but as regards the trial, you shall learn everything, but not in this place; for it is already evening and it is time for us to proceed to the town; and it is pleasant too to talk as you go along the road, for conversation assists you on your way like an escort. Let us then start and discuss your questions as we go along, and I will certainly tell you of today's events in the court. For both of you known the circumstances which preceded the trial, the one of you because he was present, and the other because I am sure, by Zeus, he has not heard it once only, but again and again, if I know you well, my Demetrius. But I will relate to you what you do not know yet, beginning with my being summoned into the Emperor's presence, into which I was ushered naked." And he proceeded to detail to them his own words, and above all at the end of them the citation: "For thou shalt not kill me," and he told them exactly how he vanished from the seat of judgment.

CHAPTER XIII

Whereupon Demetrius cried out: "I thought you had come hither because you were saved; but this is only the beginning of your dangers, for he will proscribe you, seize your person, and cut off all means of escape." Apollonius, however, told Demetrius not to be afraid and encouraged him by saying; "I only wish that you were both no more easy for him to catch than I am. But I know exactly in what condition of mind the tyrant is at this moment; hitherto he has never heard anything except the utterances of flatterers, and now he had had to listen to the language of rebuke; such language breaks despotic natures down and enrages them. But I require some rest, for I have not bent the knee since I had this struggle." And Damis said: "Demetrius, my own attitude towards our friend's affairs was such that I tried to dissuade him from taking the journey which he has taken, and I believe you too gave him the same advice, namely that he should not rush of his own accord into dangers and difficulties; but when he was thrown into fetters, as I saw with my own eyes, and I was perplexed and in despair of his case, he told me that it rested with himself to release himself and he freed his leg from the fetters and showed it to me. Well, it was then for the first time that I understood our master to be a divine being, transcending all our poor wisdom and knowledge. Consequently, even if I were called upon to expose myself to still greater risks than these, I should not fear anything, as long as I was under his protection. But since the evening is at hand, let us go into the inn and minister to and take care of him." And Apollonius said: "Sleep is all I want, and everything else is a matter of indifference to me, whether I get it or whether I do not." And after that, having offered a prayer to Apollo and also to the Sun, he passed into the house in which Demetrius lived, and having washed his feet, and instructed Damis and his friend to take their supper, for he saw that they were fasting, he threw himself upon the bed, and having intoned some verses of Homer as a hymn to sleep, he took his repose, as if his circumstances gave him no just cause whatever for anxiety.

CHAPTER XIV

About dawn Demetrius asked him where on earth he would turn his steps, for there resounded in his ears the clatter of imaginary horsemen who he thought were already in hot pursuit of Apollonius on account of the rage of the tyrant, but Apollonius merely replied: "Neither he nor anyone else is going to pursue me, but as for myself I shall take sail for Hellas." "That is anyhow a dangerous voyage," said the other, "for the region is most exposed and open; and how are you going to be hid out in the open from one whom you cannot escape in the dark?" "I do need to lie hid," said Apollonius; "for if, as you imagine, the entire earth belongs to the tyrant, it is better to die out in the open than to live in the dark and in hiding." And turning to Damis he said: "Do you know of a ship that is starting for Sicily?" "I do," he replied, "for we are staying on the edge of the sea, and the crier is at our doors, and a ship is just being got ready to start, as I gather from the shouts of the crew, and from the exertions they are making over weighing anchor." "Let us embark," said Apollonius, "upon this ship, O Damis, for we will now sail to Sicily, and thence on to the Peloponnese." "I am agreeable," said the other; "so let is sail."

CHAPTER XV

They then said farewell to Demetrius, who was despondent about them, but they bade him hope for the best, as one brave man should for others as brave as himself, and then they sailed for Sicily with a favorable wind, and having passed Messina they reached Tauromenium on the third day. After that they arrived at Syracuse and put out for the Peloponnese about the beginning of the autumn; and having traversed the gulf they arrived after six days at the mouth of the Alpheus, where that river pours its waters, still sweet, into the Adriatic and Sicilian Sea. Here then they disembarked, and thinking it well worth their while to go to Olympia, they went and stayed there in the temple of Zeus, though without ever going further away than Scillus. A rumor as sudden as insistent now ran through the Hellenic world that the sage was alive and had arrived at Olympia. At first the rumor seemed unreliable; for besides that they were humanly speaking unable to entertain any hope for him inasmuch as they heard that he was cast into prison, they had also heard such rumors as that he had been burnt alive, or dragged about alive with grapnels fixed in his neck, or cast into a deep pit, or into a well. But when the rumor of his arrival was confirmed, they all flocked to see him from the whole of Greece, and never did any such crowd flock to any Olympic festival as then, all full of enthusiasm and expectation. People came straight from Elis and Sparta, and from Corinth away at the limits of the Isthmus; and the Athenians too, although they are outside the Peloponnese; nor were they behind the cities which are at the gates of Pisa, for it was especially the most celebrated of the Athenians that hurried to the temple, together with the young men who flocked to Athens from all over the earth. Moreover there were people from Megara just then staying at Olympia, as well as many from Boeotia, and from Argos, and all the leading people of Phocis and Thessaly. Some of them had already made Apollonius' acquaintance anxious to pick up his wisdom afresh, for they were convinced that there remained much to learn, more striking than what they had so far heard; but those who were not acquainted with him thought it a shame that they should seem never to have heard so great a man discourse. In answer to their questions then, of how he had escaped the clutches of the tyrant, he did not deem it right to say anything boastful; but he merely told them that he had made his defense and got away safely. However when several people arrived from Italy, who bruited abroad the episode of the lawcourt, the attitude of

Hellas came near to that of actual worship; the main reason why they thought him divine was this, that he never made the least parade about the matter.

CHAPTER XVI

Among the arrivals from Athens there was a youth who asserted that the goddess Athena was very well disposed to the Emperor, whereupon Apollonius said to him: "In Olympia please to stop your chatter of such things, for you will prejudice the goddess in the eyes of her father." But as the youth increased their annoyance by declaring that the goddess was quite right, because the Emperor was Archon Eponym of the city of Athens, he said: "Would that he also presided the Panathenaic festival." By the first of his answers he silenced him, for he showed that he held a poor opinion of the gods, if he considered them to be well disposed to tyrants: by his second he showed that the Athenians would stultify the decree which they passed in honor of Harmodius and Aristogeiton, if after seeing fit to honor these two citizens with statues in the market place for the deed they committed at the Panathenaic festival, they ended by conferring on tyrants the privilege of being elected to govern them.

CHAPTER XVII

Damis approached him at this time to ask him about money, because they had so very little left to defray the expense of their journey. "Tomorrow," said Apollonius, "I will attend to this." And on the next day he went into the temple and said to the priest: "Give me a thousand drachmas out of the treasury of Zeus, if you think he will not be too much annoyed." And the priest answered: "Not at that; what will annoy him will be if you do not take more."

CHAPTER XVIII

There was a man of Thessaly, named Isagoras, whom he met in Olympia and said: "Tell me, Isagoras, is there such a thing as a religious fair or festival?" "Why yes," he replied, "and by heaven there is nothing in the world of men, so agreeable and so dear to the gods." "And what is the material of which it is composed?" asked Apollonius; "It is as if I asked you about the material of which this image is made, and you answered me that it was composed of gold and ivory." "But," said the other, "what material, Apollonius, can a thing which is incorporeal be composed of?" "A most important material," replied Apollonius, "and most varied in character; for there are sacred groves in it, and race-courses and, of course, a theater, and tribes of men, some of them from neighboring countries, and others from over the borders, and even from across the sea. Moreover," he added, "many arts go to make up such a festival, and many designs, and much true genius, both of poets, and of civil counselors, and of those who deliver harangues on philosophic topics, and contests between naked athletes, and contests of musicians, as is the custom in the Pythian festival." "It seems to me," said the other, "O Apollonius, that the festival is not only something corporeal, but is made up of more wonderful material than are cities; for there is summoned together into one community on such occasions the best of the best, and the most celebrated of the celebrated."

"Then," said Apollonius, "O Isagoras, are we to consider the people we meet there in the same light as some people regard walls and ships, or do you need some other opinion of the festival?" "The opinion," answered the other, "which we have formulated, is quite adequate and complete, O man of Tyana, and we had better adhere to it." "And yet," said the other, "it is neither adequate nor complete to one who considers about is as I do; for it appears to me that ships are in need of men and men of ships, and that men would never have thought about the sea at all if they had not had a ship; and men are kept safe by walls and walls by men; and in the same way I consider a festival to be not only the meeting of human beings, but also the place itself in which they have to meet, and the more so, because walls and ships would never have come into being, unless there had been men's hands to build them, while these places, so far forth as they are deprived of their natural and original characteristics, are by the hands of men spoiled; for it was owing to their natural advantages that they were held worthy of being made their meeting-places; for though the gymnasiums and porticoes and fountains and houses have been all created by human art, just like the walls and the ships, yet this river Alpheus with the hippodrome and the stadium and the groves, existed, I suppose, before men came here, the one providing water for drinking and for the bath, and the second a broad plain for the horses to race in, and the third provided just the space required fro the athletes to raise the dust in as they run along in their races, namely a valley a stadium in length, and the groves supplied wreaths for the winners and served the athletes who were runners as a place to practice in. For I imagine that Heracles considered these facts, and because he admired the natural advantages of Olympia, he found the place worthy of the festival and games which are still held here."

CHAPTER XIX

After forty days, given up to discussions in Olympia, in which many topics were handled, Apollonius said: "I will also, O men of Hellas, discourse to you in your several cities, at your festivals, at your religious processions, at your mysteries, your sacrifices, at your public libations, and they require the services of a clever man; but for the present I must go down to Lebadea, for I have never yet had an interview with Trophonius, although I once visited his shrine." And with these words he at once started for Boeotia attended by every one of his admirers. Now the cavern in Lebadea is dedicated to Trophonius, the son of Apollo, and it can only be entered by those who resort thither in order to get an oracle, and it is not visible in the temple, but lies a little above it on a mound; and it is shut in by iron spits which surround it, and you descend into it as it were sitting down and being drawn down. Those who enter it are clad in white raiment, and are escorted thither with honey-cakes in their hands to appease the reptiles which assail them as they descend. But the earth brings them to the surface again, in some cases close by, but in other cases a long way off; for they are sent up to the surface beyond Locri and beyond Phocis, but most of them about the borders of Boeotia. Accordingly Apollonius entered the shrine and said: "I wish to descend into the cave in the interests of philosophy."

But the priests opposed him and though they told the multitude that they would never allow a wizard like him to examine and test the shrine, they pretended to the sage himself that there were forbidden days and days unclean for consulting. So on that day he delivered a discourse at the springs of Hercyne, about the origin and conduct of the shrine; for it is the only oracle which gives responses through the person himself who consults it. And when the evening approached, he went to the mouth of the cave with his train of youthful followers, and having pulled up four of the obelisks, which constitute a bar to the passage, he went down below ground wearing his philosopher's mantle, having dressed himself as if he were going to deliver an address upon philosophy—a step which the god Trophonius so thoroughly approved of, that he appeared to the priests and not only rebuked them for the reception they had given Apollonius, but enjoined them all to follow him to Aulis, for he said it was there that he would come to surface in such a marvelous fashion as no man before. And in fact he emerged after seven days, a longer period than it had taken anyone of those who until then had entered the oracle, and he had with him a volume thoroughly in keeping with the questions he had asked: for had gone down saying: "What, O Trophonius, do you consider the most complete and purest philosophy?" And the volume contained the tenets of Pythagoras, a good proof this, that the oracle was in agreement with this form of wisdom.

CHAPTER XX

This book is preserved in Antium, and the village in question, which is on the Italian seaboard, is much visited for the purpose of seeing it. I must acknowledge that I only heard these details from the inhabitants of Lebadea; but in regard to the volume in question I must set on record my conviction, that it was subsequently conveyed to the Emperor Hadrian at the same time as certain letters of Apollonius, though by no means all of them; and it remained in the palace at Antium, which was that one of his Italian palaces in which this Emperor took most pleasure.

CHAPTER XXI

From Ionia also there came to see him the band of companions who were named in Hellas the company of Apollonius; and mixing with the people of the place they formed a band of youths, remarkable for their number and for their philosophical enthusiasm. For the science of rhetoric had been left neglected and little attention was paid to the professors of the art, on the ground that their tongue was their only teacher; but now they were all impelled to study his philosophy. But he, like Gyges and Croesus, who they left the door of their treasures unlocked, in order that all who needed might fill their pockets from them, threw open the treasures of his wisdom to those who loved it, and allowed them to ask him questions upon every subject.

CHAPTER XXII

But certain persons accused him of avoiding attendance on governors at their visits, and of influencing his hearers rather to live in retirement instead; and one of them uttered the jest that he drove away his sheep as soon as he found any forensic orator approaching. "Yes, by Zeus," said Apollonius, "lest these wolves should fall upon my flock." What was the meaning of this sally? He saw these forensic orators looked up to by the multitude as they made their way up from poverty to great riches; and he saw that they so welcomed the feuds of others, that they actually conducted a traffic in hatred and feud; accordingly he tried to dissuade these young men from associating with them, and those that did so associate with them he sharply reproved, as if to wash off them a monstrous stain. For he had been long before on bad terms with them; and his experience of the prisons in Rome, and of the persons who were confined and perishing in them, so prejudiced him against the forensic art, as that he believed all these evils were due to sycophants and lawyers puffed up by their own cleverness, rather than to the despot himself.

CHAPTER XXIII

Just at the time when he was holding these conversations with the people of Hellas, the following remarkable portent overspread the heavens. The orb of the sun was surrounded by a wreath which resembled a rainbow, but dimmed the sunlight. That the heavenly sign portended a revolution was of course clear to all. However, when the governor of Hellas summoned Apollonius from Athens to Boeotia, and said: "I hear that you have a talent for understanding things divine," he replied: "Yes, and perhaps you have heard that I have some understanding of human affairs." "I have heard it," he replied, "and quite agree." "Since then," said Apollonius, "you are of one opinion with me, I would advise you not to pry into the intentions of the gods; for this is what human wisdom recommends you to do." And when he besought Apollonius to tell him what he thought, for he said he was afraid lest night should ensue and swallow up everything. "Be of good cheer," said Apollonius, "for there will be some light following such a night as this."

CHAPTER XXIV

After this, seeing that he had enough of the people of Hellas, after living for two years among them, he set sail for Ionia, accompanied by his society; and the greater part of his time he spent teaching philosophy at Smyrna and Ephesus, though he also visited the rest of the cities; and in none of them was he found to be an unwelcome guest, indeed they all considered him to be worth their regret when he left them, and to the better class of people he was a great boon.

CHAPTER XXV

And now the gods were about to cast down Domitian from his presidency of mankind. For it happened that he had just slain Clemens, a man of consular rank, to whom he had lately given his own sister in marriage; and he issued a command about the third or fourth day after the murder, that she also should follow her husband and join him. Thereupon Stephanus, a freed man of the lady, he who was signified by the form of the late portent, whether because the latest victim's fate rankled in his mind, or the fate of all others, made an attempt upon the tyrant's life worthy of comparison with the feats of the champions of Athenian liberty. For he concealed a dagger against his left fore-arm, and carrying his hand in a bandage, as if it were broken, he approached the Emperor as he left the law-court, and said: "I would have a private interview with you, my prince, for I have important news to communicate to you." The latter did not refuse him the audience, but took him apart into the men's apartment where he transacted business of state. Whereupon the assassin said; "Your bitter enemy, Clemens, is not dead, as you imagine, but he lives and I know where he is; and he is making ready to attack you." When the emperor uttered a loud cry over this information, before he could recover his composure, Stephanus threw himself upon him and drawing the dagger from the hand which he had trussed up, he stabbed him in the thigh, inflicting a wound which was not immediately mortal, though it was well-timed in view of the struggle that followed. The Emperor was still strong and full of bodily vigor, although he was about five and forty years of age; and in spite of the wound he closed with his assailant, and throwing him down, kneeled upon him and dug out his eyes and crushed his cheeks with the stand of a gold cup which lay thereby for use in sacred ceremonies, at the same time calling upon Athena to assist him.

Thereupon his bodyguard, realizing that he was in distress, rushed into the room pell-mell, and dispatched the tyrant, who had already swooned.

CHAPTER XXVI

Although this deed was done in Rome, Apollonius was a spectator of it in Ephesus. For about midday he was delivering an address in the groves of the colonnade, just at the moment when it all happened in the palace at Rome; and first he dropped his voice, as if he were terrified, and then, though with less vigor than was usual with him, he continued his exposition, like one who between his words caught glimpses of something foreign to his subject, and at last he lapsed into silence, like one who has been interrupted in his discourse. And with an awful glance at the ground, and stepping forward three or four paces from his pulpit, he cried: "Smite the tyrant, smite him"—not like one who derives from some looking glass a faint image of the truth, but as one who sees things with his own eyes, and is taking part in a tragedy. All Ephesus—for all Ephesus was at his lecture—was struck dumb with astonishment; but he, pausing like those who are trying to see and wait until their doubts are ended, said: "Take heart, gentlemen, for the tyrant has been slain this day; and why do I say today? Now it is, by Athena, even now at the moment I uttered my words, and then lapsed into silence." The inhabitants of Ephesus thought that this was a fit of madness on his part; and although they were anxious that it should be true, yet they were anxious about the risk they ran in giving ear to his words, whereupon he added: "I am not surprised at those who do not yet accept my story, for not even all Rome as yet is cognizant of it. But behold, Rome begins to know it: for the rumor runs this way and that, and thousands now are convinced of it; and they begin to leap for joy, twice as many as before, and twice as many as they, and four times as many, yea the whole of the populace there. And this news will travel hither also; and although I would have you defer your sacrifices in honor thereof to the fitting season, when you will receive this news, I shall proceed at once to pray to the gods for what I have seen."

CHAPTER XXVII

They were still skeptical, when swift runners arrived with the good news, and bore testimony to the sage's wisdom; for the tyrant's murder, and the day which brought the event to birth, the hour of midday and the murderers to whom he addressed his exhortation, everything agreed with the revelation which the gods had made to Apollonius in the midst of his harangue.

And thirty days later Nerva sent a letter to him to say that he was already in possession of the Empire of the Romans, thanks to the goodwill of the gods and to his good counsels; and he added that he would more easily retain it, if Apollonius would come to advise him. Whereupon at the moment the latter wrote to him the following enigmatically sentence: "We will, my prince, enjoy one another's company for a very long time during which neither shall we govern others, nor others us." Perhaps he realized, when he wrote thus, that it was not to be long before he himself should quit this human world, and that Nerva was only to retain the throne for a short time; for his reign lasted but one year and four months, when he left behind him the reputation of having been a sober and serious ruler.

CHAPTER XXVIII

But as he did not wish to seem to neglect so good a friend and ruler, he composed later on for him a letter giving him advice about matters of state; and calling Damis to him, he said: "You are wanted here, for this letter which I have written to the king contains secrets, and though it is written, they are of such a kind that they must be communicated orally either by myself or through you." And Damis declares that he only understood his master's device much later; for that the letter was composed in admirable style, and though it treated of important subjects, yet it might equally well have been sent through anyone else. What then was the sage's device? All though his life, he is said often to have exclaimed: "Live unobserved, and if that cannot be, slip unobserved from life." His letter then, and Damis' visit to Rome were of the nature of an excuse for getting the latter out of the way, in order that he might have not witness of his dissolution. Damis accordingly says that, though he was much affected at leaving him, in spite of his having no knowledge of what was coming, yet Apollonius, who knew full well, said nothing of it to him, and far from addressing him after the manner of those who are never to see one another again, so abundant was his conviction that he would exist forever, merely pledged him in these words: "O Damis, even if you have to philosophize by yourself, keep your eyes upon me."

CHAPTER XXIX

The memoirs then of Apollonius of Tyana which Damis the Assyrian composed, end with the above story; for with regard to the manner in which he died, if he did actually die, there are many stories, though, Damis has repeated none. But as for myself I ought not to omit even this, for my story should, I think, have its natural ending. Neither has Damis told us anything about the age of our hero; but there are some who say that he was eighty, others that he was over ninety, others again who say that his age far exceeded a hundred. He was fresh in all his body and upright, when he died, and more agreeable to look at than in his youth. For there is a certain beauty even in wrinkles, which was especially conspicuous in his case, as is clear from the likenesses of him which are preserved in the temple at Tyana, and from accounts which praise the old age of Apollonius more than was once praised the youth of Alcibiades.

CHAPTER XXX

Now there are some who relate that he died in Ephesus, tended by two maid servants; for the freedmen of whom I spoke at the beginning of my story were already dead. One of these maids he emancipated, and was blamed by the other one for not conferring the same privilege upon her, but Apollonius told her that it was better for her to remain the other's slave, for that would be the beginning of her well-being. Accordingly after his death this one continued to be the slave of the other, who for some insignificant reason sold her to a merchant, from whom she was purchased. Her new master, although she was not good-looking, nevertheless fell in love with her; and being a fairly rich man, made her his legal wife and had legitimate children with her. Others again say that he died in Lindus, where he entered the temple of Athena and disappeared within it. Others again say that he died in Crete in a much more remarkable manner than the people of Lindus relate. For they say that he continued to live in Crete, where he became a greater center of admiration than ever before, and that he came to the temple of Dictynna late at night. Now this temple is guarded by dogs, whose duty it is to watch over the wealth deposited in it, and the Cretans claim that they are as good as bears or any other animals equally fierce. None the less, when he came, instead of barking, they approached him and fawned upon him, as they would not have done even with people they knew familiarly. The guardians of the shrine arrested him in consequence, and threw him in bonds as a wizard and a robber, accusing him of having thrown to the dogs some charmed morsel. But about midnight he loosened his bonds, and after calling those who had bound him, in order that they might witness the spectacle, he ran to the doors of the temple, which opened wide to receive him; and when he had passed within, they closed afresh, as they had been shut, and there was heard a chorus of maidens singing from within the temple, and their song was this. "Hasten thou from earth, hasten thou to Heaven, hasten." In other words: "Do thou go upwards from earth."

CHAPTER XXXI

And even after his death, he continued to preach that the soul is immortal; but although he taught this account of it to be correct, he discouraged men from meddling in such high subjects. For there came to Tyana a youth who did not shrink from acrimonious discussions, and would not accept truth in argument. Now Apollonius had already passed away from among men, but people still wondered at his passing, and no one ventured to dispute that he was immortal. This being so, the discussions were mainly about the soul, for a band of youth were there passionately addicted to wisdom. The young man in question, however, would on no account allow the tenet of immortality of the soul, and said: "I myself, gentlemen, have done nothing now for over nine months but pray to Apollonius that he would reveal to me the truth about the soul; but he is so utterly dead that he will not appear to me in response to my entreaties, nor give me any reason to consider him immortal." Such were the young man's words on that occasion, but on the fifth day following, after discussing the same subject, he fell asleep where he was talking with them, and of the young men who were studying with him, some were reading books, and others were industriously drawing geometrical figures on the ground, when on a sudden, like one possessed, he leapt up still in a half sleep, streaming with perspiration, and cried out: "I believe thee." And, when those who were present asked him what was the matter; "Do you not see," said he, "Apollonius the sage, how that he is present with us and is listening to our discussion, and is reciting wondrous verses about the soul?" "But where is he?" the others asked, "For we cannot see him anywhere, although we would rather do so than possess all the blessings of mankind." And the youth replied: "It would seem that he is come to converse with myself alone concerning the tenets which I would not believe. Listen therefore to the inspired argument which he is delivering:

"The soul is immortal, and 'tis no possession of thine own, but of Providence,
"And after the body is wasted away, like a swift horse freed from its traces,
"It lightly leaps forward and mingles itself with the light air,
"Loathing the spell of harsh and painful servitude which it has endured.
"But for thee, what use is there in this? Some day, when thou art no more, thou shalt believe it.
"So why, as long as thou art among living beings, dost thou explore these mysteries?"

Here we have a clear utterance of Apollonius, established like an oracular tripod, to convince us of the mysteries of the soul, to the end that cheerfully, and with due knowledge of our own true nature, we may pursue our way to the goal appointed by the Fates. With any tomb, however, or cenotaph of the sage I never met, that I know of, although I have traversed most of the earth, and have listened everywhere to stories of his divine quality. And his shrine in Tyana is singled out and honored with royal officers: for neither have the Emperors denied to him the honors of which they themselves were held worthy.

www.ingramcontent.com/pod-product-compliance
Lightning Source LLC
Chambersburg PA
CBHW071656160426
43195CB00012B/1482